T0330160

Economic Growth, Transition and Globalization in China

ADVANCES IN CHINESE ECONOMIC STUDIES

Series Editor: Yanrui Wu, *Associate Professor in Economics, University of Western Australia, Australia*

The Chinese economy has been transformed dramatically in recent years. With its rapid economic growth and accession to the World Trade Organisation, China is emerging as an economic superpower. China's development experience provides valuable lessons to many countries in transition.

Advances in Chinese Economic Studies aims, as a series, to publish the best work on the Chinese economy by economists and other researchers throughout the world. It is intended to serve a wide readership including academics, students, business economists and other practitioners.

Titles in the series include:

The Evolution of the Stock Market in China's Transitional Economy
Chien-Hsun Chen and Hui-Tzu Shih

Financial Reform and Economic Development in China
James Laurenceson and Joseph C.H. Chai

China's Telecommunications Market
Entering a New Competitive Age
Ding Lu and Chee Kong Wong

Banking and Insurance in the New China
Competition and the Challenge of Accession to the WTO
Chien-Hsun Chen and Hui-Tzu Shih

The Chinese Stock Market
Efficiency, Predictability and Profitability
Nicolaas Groenewold, Yanrui Wu, Sam Hak Kan Tang and Xiang Mei Fan

High-Tech Industries in China
Chien-Hsun Chen and Hui-Tzu Shih

Economic Growth, Transition and Globalization in China
Yanrui Wu

Economic Growth, Transition and Globalization in China

Edited by

Yanrui Wu

University of Western Australia

ADVANCES IN CHINESE ECONOMIC STUDIES

Edward Elgar
Cheltenham, UK • Northampton, MA, USA

Published by
Edward Elgar Publishing Limited
Glensanda House
Montpellier Parade
Cheltenham
Glos GL50 1UA
UK

Edward Elgar Publishing, Inc.
136 West Street
Suite 202
Northampton
Massachusetts 01060
USA

A catalogue record for this book
is available from the British Library

Library of Congress Cataloguing in Publication Data

International Conference on "Transition, Growth, and Globalization in China" (2005 : Perth, W.A.)
    Ecomomic growth, transition, and globalization in China / edited by Yanrui Wu.
        p. cm. — (Advances in Chinese economic studies series)
    Selected papers from the International Conference on "Transition, Growth, and Globalization in China," held July 7-8, 2005, in Perth, W.A
Includes bibliographical references and index.
    1. China—Economic conditions—1976-2000—Congresses. 2. China—Economic conditions—2000—Congresses. 3. Globalization—Economic aspects—China—Congresses. I. Wu, Yanrui. II. Title. III. Series.
    HC427.92.1578 2005
    338.951—dc22   2006041791

ISBN-13: 978 1 84542 768 9
ISBN-10: 1 84542 768 8

Printed and bound in Great Britain by MPG Books Ltd, Bodmin, Cornwall.

Contents

Contents

Contributors

Anping Chen, School of Economics and Finance, Xi'an Jiaotong University, Xi'an, Shaanxi Province, P. R. China.

Yuk-shing Cheng, Department of Economics, Hong Kong Baptist University, Renfrew Road, Kowloon Tong, Hong Kong.

Erbiao Dai, the International Centre for the Study of East Asian Development (ICSEAD), 11-4 Otemachi, Kokurakita, Kitakyushu, 803-0814, Japan

Nicolaas Groenewold, School of Economics and Commerce, University of Western Australia, Australia.

Jianwu He, Development Research Center, the State Council, P. R. China.

Yongzhi Hou, Development Research Center, the State Council, P. R. China.

Nazrul Islam, the International Centre for the Study of East Asian Development (ICSEAD), 11-4 Otemachi, Kokurakita, Kitakyushu, 803-0814 Japan.

James Laurenceson, School of Economics, University of Queensland, Brisbane, Queensland 4072, Australia.

Guoping Lee, School of Economics and Finance, Xi'an Jiaotong University, Xi'an, Shaanxi Province, P. R. China.

Shantong Li, Development Research Center, the State Council, P. R. China.

Sung-ko Li, Department of Economics, Hong Kong Baptist University, Renfrew Road, Kowloon Tong, Hong Kong.

Yunzhong Liu, Development Research Center, the State Council, P. R. China.

Ingrid Nielsen, Department of Management, Monash University, Victoria, Australia.

Fengming Qin, School of Economics, Shandong University, P. R. China.

Hiroshi Sakamoto, the International Centre for the Study of East Asian Development (ICSEAD), 11-4 Otemachi, Kokurakita, Kitakyushu, 803-0814, Japan.

Abu Siddique, School of Economics and Commerce, University of Western Australia, Australia.

Russell Smyth, Department of Management, Monash University, Victoria, Australia.

Michael Thorpe, Curtin Business School, Curtin University of Technology, Australia.

Yanrui Wu, School of Economics and Commerce, University of Western Australia, Australia.

Sheng Yu, Asia Pacific School of Economics and Government, Australian National University, Australia.

Preface

This edited volume contains selected papers presented at the International Conference on "Transition, Growth and Globalization in China" held in Perth on 7-8 July 2005. The papers were chosen through a double-blind refereeing process and subsequently revised following the referees' comments. The conference was organised jointly by the School of Economics and Commerce, University of Western Australia (UWA) and the Chinese Economic Studies Association of Australia (CESAA). It was generously supported by UWA (the Vice-Chancellor's office, Business School and the School of Economics and Commerce), AusAID (Canberra), Australia-China Council (DFAT, Canberra), Australia-China Business Council (WA Branch) and Edward Elgar Publishing.

I thank all contributors for their participation in this project and for their cooperation in finalising the chapters in time. I also thank Will Millsteed who read through the final draft of the chapters. Work on this volume was partly completed while I was visiting the East Asian Institute, National University of Singapore in the second half of 2005. I am grateful for the support provided by the Institute's staff, in particular the director (Professor Wang Gunwu) and research director (Professor John Wong). I would also like to thank Clare Yu for her excellent research assistance throughout this project.

Finally, I am indebted to my colleagues in the economics group of UWA for their support and encouragement. Many of them kindly acted as either a chairperson or a discussant at the conference. Paul Miller (Ex-Head of the School of Economics and Commerce), Iain Watson (Head, School of Economics and Commerce) and Tracey Thorton (Dean, Business School) have been very supportive of earlier fund-raising activities for the conference. Their support is greatly appreciated.

Yanrui Wu
University of Western Australia
Perth

1. Introduction

Yanrui Wu

Dramatic changes have taken place in the Chinese economy and society since the initiative of economic reforms in 1978. The literature documenting these changes has mushroomed.[1] This book adds to the literature by exclusively focusing on issues associated with China's economic growth, transition and globalization. In this introductory chapter, I will first present a brief review of China's recent economic performance. Then I will discuss economic transition since 1978. Subsequently, I shed some light on globalization in the Chinese economy and society. This is followed by an outline of the chapters in this volume.

CHINA'S RECENT GROWTH

China's growth since 1978 has been impressive by all measures. During 1978-2004, the average annual rates of growth in GDP and GDP per capita were 9.5 and 8.2 per cent, respectively, though these rates fluctuated over time (see Figure 1.1). Many developments were responsible for China's recent economic rise. In particular, two factors have played important roles in promoting China's growth. The first factor is investment which has been growing at the real rate of 12 per cent annually during 1979-2004.[2] This high rate of growth has been supported by a high rate of savings and a massive inflow of foreign direct investment (FDI). The ratio of domestic savings over GDP increased from 10.1 per cent in 1979 to 74.8 per cent in 2004, for instance.[3] During the same period, FDI increased from non-existence in 1977 to US$60.6 billion in 2004 (National Bureau of Statistics 2005). The second factor is external demand. China's economic policies in the past decades have been very pro-trade. As a result, the value of China's exports has grown at the average rate of 18 per cent during 1979-2004.[4]

Furthermore, China's high economic performance is linked with rapid growth in total factor productivity (TFP). The latter measures the component of economic growth which is not explained by the changes in factor inputs such as labour and capital. The rate of TFP growth gives an indication of economic growth sustainability in the long run. Though economists are still

debating the role of TFP in economic growth, most empirical studies show
that TFP growth has played an important role in China's recent growth. For
example, several studies show that on average the contribution of TFP to
China's economic growth ranges from 30 to 50 per cent in the 1980s and
1990s.[5] These estimates imply that China's economic growth is sustainable
in the long run.

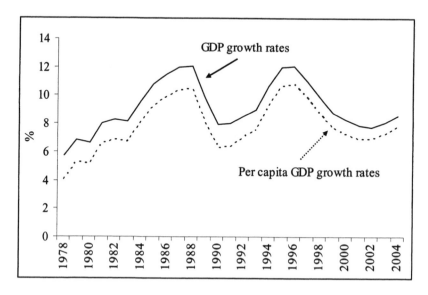

Notes: The growth rates are five-year moving averages. Raw data are drawn from the National
Bureau of Statistics (2000, 2005).

Figure 1.1 Growth rates of GDP and per capita GDP in China, 1978-2004

There is another important source of growth which is yet to be exploited in
China. That is domestic consumption which has lagged behind the growth in
investment and exports, especially in recent years. During 2000-2004, for
example, the annual real rate of growth in domestic consumption was 6.76
per cent while those of investment and exports were 13.45 and 25.40 per
cent, respectively.[6] However, recent developments in the real estate and
automobile sectors may signal the beginning of a consumption boom. For
instance, during 2001-2004, the number of private motor vehicles increased
annually by 24.1 per cent and the area of housing under construction rose
annually by 16.2 per cent according to the National Bureau of Statistics
(2005). These changes will further boost China's growth. Although sustained
growth has substantially strengthened and will continue to raise China's
economic power, there is still a long way to go for the country to restore its
17th-century ranking when China was the richest nation in the world.

According to the forecasts in Figure 1.2, it will take two more decades for China to catch up with the US even if GDP is measured in purchasing power parity dollars. On a per capita basis, the process of catch-up will be much longer as China's per capita income of $1100 in 2003 was only a tiny fraction of the US income per capita of $37,870 according to the World Bank (2005).

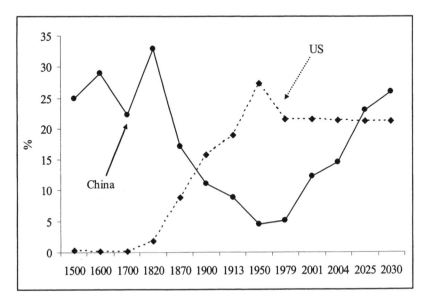

Notes: Data for 1500-2001 are based on Maddison (2003) who derived historical GDP figures in international dollars for the world economies. GDP shares for 2004, 2025 and 2030 are author's own estimates using China's real growth rates during 2001-2004 and an assumed annual rate of growth of 5.6 per cent for China, 3.0 per cent for the world and 2.95 per cent for the US during 2001-2030.

Figure 1.2 GDP share over the world total: China vs US

ECONOMIC TRANSITION

Rapid growth has transformed the Chinese economy from a centrally planned regime to a market-oriented economic entity, and from an agrarian economy to an industrial power. This transition can be evaluated in several ways.

First, dramatic changes in the economic structure have taken place. Since 1978 China has become more industrialized with the manufacturing sector accounting for 46.2 per cent of GDP in 2004.[7] In the meantime, the role of the primary or agricultural sector has declined. Its output share over the national total fell from 28.1 per cent in 1978 to 13.1 per cent in 2004.[8]

Agricultural employment share also decreased from 70.5 per cent in 1978 to 46.9 per cent in 2004 though this reduction is not as dramatic as the fall of agricultural output share (National Bureau of Statistics 2005).

Second, the role of the private sector has expanded substantially. At the beginning of economic reforms in 1978, the state sector was almost the only player in the economy. For example, statistics compiled by the National Bureau of Statistics (2000) show that in 1980 the state and collectively owned sectors accounted for 99.5 per cent of gross industrial output, 86.9 per cent of total investment in fixed assets and 99.2 per cent of urban employment. Since the economic reform was initiated, the private sector has been accepted gradually and permitted to expand over time. In March 2004 China's Constitution was formally revised. Protection of private property is for the first time included in the Constitution. The private sector has already changed from a trivial player to the dominant force in the Chinese economy. For example, the non-state sector was responsible for 91.1 per cent of total employment and created more than 58 per cent of total industrial value-added in 2004.[9] In 2004, just about 23 per cent of total investment was funded by budgetary allocation and domestic loans (Figure 1.3). Thus, private capital was the main source of funding in 2004.

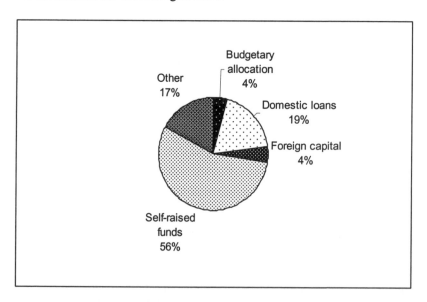

Source: China Statistical Abstract 2005 compiled by the National Bureau of Statistics and published by China Statistics Press, Beijing.

Figure 1.3 Sources of funding for China's total investment in 2004

Third, urbanization has been slow due to the implementation of stringent internal migration policies for decades. It has however accelerated in recent years due to a policy shift since the 1990s. In 2004, urban population accounted for 41.8 per cent of China's total population, an increase of about 24 percentage points over the 17.9 per cent in 1978 (National Bureau of Statistics 2000, 2005). It can be anticipated that urbanization will increase dramatically in the coming years as new policies and regulations at both the national and local levels have been implemented to encourage rural out-migration.

GLOBALIZATION

Associated with growth and transition is the increasing integration of the Chinese economy with the international community. International integration or globalization can be measured in several ways though the concept itself is controversial.[10]

The most popular indicator of globalization is the role of international trade in an economy. As mentioned in the preceding section, external trade has been one of the main drivers of economic growth in China in the past decades. Trade has indeed played an important role in the Chinese economy. Since 1978, the value of China's exports has increased from US$9.8 billion to US$593.4 billion in 2004, implying that the proportion of the value of exports over GDP rose from 4.6 per cent in 1978 to 54.9 per cent in 2004 (see Figure 1.4).[11]

Another commonly cited indicator of global integration is the level of foreign direct investment (FDI). It is now well known that China has scored well in terms of attracting FDI. China's FDI has risen from non-existence to about 60 billion dollars in 2004 (Figure 1.4). Since 1996, China has been the largest host of FDI among the developing economies and the world's largest recipient in some years. Recently, China has also become an increasingly important supplier of FDI. Chinese companies invested an average of about US$3 billion per annum during 2001-2004 and their accumulated outward investment stock reached about US$39 billion, which was almost on par with the amount invested by Korean companies (F.Wu 2005).

China's active participation in international trade and investment since 1978 has made the country's economy one of the world's most open ones. China became a WTO member in November 2001 after a lengthy process of negotiation lasting for sixteen years. According to the World Bank (2005), China's weighted mean tariff rate fell from 32.1 per cent in 1992 to 6.0 per cent in 2004 (World Bank 2005). In terms of trade liberalization, China is now ahead of India (with a weighted mean tariff rate of 28 per cent in 2004), Mexico (13.8 per cent in 2004), Korea (10 per cent in 2002) and Thailand (8.3 per cent in 2003).[12]

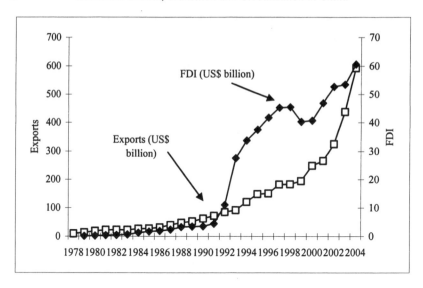

Sources: National Bureau of Statistics (1983, 1997 and 2005) and Wu (1999).

Figure 1.4 China's exports and FDI values, 1978-2004

OUTLINE OF THE CHAPTERS

The ten core chapters of the book are divided into three parts with each focussing on a topic, namely, economic growth and outlook (Part I), urban economy, migration and labour market (Part II) and banking, exchange rates and globalization (Part III). Part I begins with Chapter 2 by Nazrul Islam, Erbiao Dai and Hiroshi Sakamoto. This chapter examines the sources of economic growth in China using a dual approach to growth accounting. The existing growth accounting studies conducted on China so far have mainly followed the primal approach, which depends heavily on national income accounts data. The latter is still plagued with numerous problems, despite attempts to rectify them. The authors thus argued that the dual approach is useful because it allows independent price information to play a role. They found that the rate of China's TFP growth derived using the dual approach proves similar to the high TFP growth rates obtained by many researchers using the primal approach. The authors also found that the rate of TFP growth in China has slowed down a little, but still remains high.

Chapter 3 investigates inter-regional output spillovers in China. The authors, Nicolaas Groenewold, Guoping Lee and Anping Chen, considered a six-region vector-autoregressive model which is subjected to extensive sensitivity analysis. They found that the Yellow River and Yangtze River regions have spillover effects on other regions while the South West region has no significant spillover effects on the rest of the country. However, in contrast to expectations, the authors' findings show that shocks to the South East region affect mainly the region itself with little spillover to the other regions and the same is true for the North East region while the North West region has extensive spillovers to other regions.

In Chapter 4, Yanrui Wu attempts to understand the role of business-cycle volatility in China's growth, a topic which has not been addressed so far. This study thus fills the void in the literature by examining the relationship between business-cycle volatility and economic growth using data from Chinese regional economies. Both cross-sectional and panel data models are estimated in order to test the relationship between volatility and economic growth. This relationship is further investigated by incorporating standard control variables.

The final chapter of Part I (Chapter 5) explores China's growth prospects in the coming decades. The authors, Shantong Li, Yongzhi Hou, Yunzhong Liu and Jianwu He, applied a computable general equilibrium (CGE) model developed by the Development Research Center, the State Council, Beijing. Various forecast scenarios are presented. In general, the Chinese economy is projected to grow at a rate of 7.5 per cent during 2005-2010 and 5-6 per cent during 2010-2020. This growth will have important implications for urbanization, structural transformation and environments in China. The authors discuss these issues in detail.

Part II has three chapters, addressing the performance of urban economies (Chapter 6), rural migrants and public security (Chapter 7) and the efficiency of job-matching (Chapter 8), respectively. In Chapter 6, Yuk-shing Cheng and Sung-ko Li attempt to evaluate the relative performance of prefecture-level and county-level cities from the perspective of technical efficiency. The argument underlying their study is that different levels of governments have different powers and thus could have different abilities in the mobilization of resource and choice of technology. As a result, the administrative status of a city may have a substantial impact on its performance. However, they found that the prefecture-level cities in China are less efficient than county-level cities, although the former have bigger administrative power.

Chapter 7 by Ingrid Nielsen and Russell Smyth focuses on rural migrants and public security in urban China. This is an emerging issue in the Chinese society. The authors use a recent survey conducted in 32 Chinese cities to investigate the determinants of perceptions of public safety among the urban population. One of their major findings is that individuals who have a negative perception of rural-urban migrants living in their cities have a poor perception of public safety. The authors also found that perceptions of public safety are affected by many other factors such as the unemployment rate, the masculinity ratio and expenditure on armed police in the city in which the individual resides, whether the individual lives in the coastal region as opposed to the central or western region, and average changes in housing and rental prices in the city in which the individual lives.

Sheng Yu in Chapter 8 applied the stochastic frontier technique to examine the efficiency of job-matching in China's labour market. His study is based on seven year provincial data. His findings show that the estimated matching function is generally characterized by systematic matching inefficiency. He also examined the determinants of these inefficiencies and concluded that job-matching inefficiency was partly due to the rapid openness to trade and urbanization in China.

The final part of the book (Part III) presents surveys of three important topics associated with the Chinese economy, that is, banking reforms (Chapter 9), exchange rate policy (Chapter 10) and globalization (Chapter 11). As the Chinese economy becomes more competitive and global imbalances grow, both domestic and international pressures have been mounting for the Chinese government to adopt more flexible exchange rate policy and to free-up the capital account to foster greater integration with global markets. There is also a need for less regulated and more market driven interest rates in order to develop a more mature financial system to meet the needs of a growing market economy and unrestricted foreign bank entry in 2007. The need for continuing reform of China's currently fragile domestic banking system further influences the nature and timing of policy options. In Chapter 9 Michael Thorpe reviews recent macroeconomic management performance in China and assesses the options facing policy makers in reforming the banking sector.

Until July 2005, the Chinese currency *Renminbi* has been pegged to the US dollar. The growing deficit of US trade with China has triggered a heated debate on China's exchange rate policy, which is also the focus of Chapter 10. In this chapter James Laurenceson and Fengming Qin present a review of the key issues in debate. They argue that moving to a flexible regime is far from a proximate policy response to the problems that are in evidence in China's economy. They reckon that institutional realities make moving to a flexible regime difficult and should not be overlooked. They conclude the chapter by noting that in the longer term moving to a more flexible regime may be in China's best interests. But for now, the focus needs to be firmly in the area of domestic financial reform.

Finally, Chapter 11 by Abu Siddique examines issues involving the process and progress of globalization and its effects on the economy of China. He starts with a review of the concepts and measurements of globalization. He then presents an evaluation of the process and progress of globalization in China. He concludes the chapter by investigating the impacts of China's participation on development and growth in the past decades.

NOTES

1. See, for example, Perkins (1988), Lin (1992), Ash and Kueh (1996), Naughton (1996), World Bank (1997), Woo (1998), and Nolan (2001).
2. This rate of growth is calculated using gross capital formation data which are deflated by a price index for the secondary sector (manufacturing and construction combined). The source of the raw data is the National Bureau of Statistics (2005).
3. These statistics are derived using data from the National Bureau of Statistics (1983, 2005).
4. This rate is based on the US dollar values of exports during 1978-2004 (National Bureau of Statistics 1997, 2005).
5. These studies include Hu and Khan (1997), Maddison (1998), Chow and Li (2002), Bosworth and Collins (2003) and Y.Wu (2005), to cite a few.
6. The sources of the raw data are the National Bureau of Statistics (2005).
7. This figure is based on the revised GDP statistics released by the National Bureau of Statistics (Zhu 2005). The original statistics imply a share of 52.9 per cent for the manufacturing sector (National Bureau of Statistics 2005). The manufacturing sector is here defined to include mining, manufacturing and construction.
8. The figure for 2004 is based on the revised GDP statistics released by the National Bureau of Statistics (Zhu 2005). The original statistics imply a share of 15.2 per cent (National Bureau of Statistics 2005).
9. Author's own estimates using data from *China Statistical Abstract 2005* compiled by the National Bureau of Statistics and published by China Statistics Press, Beijing.
10. See Chapter 11 of this book for a review of the concepts.
11. In calculating the shares, the revised GDP figure for 2004 is employed.
12. These figures are drawn from the World Bank (2005).

REFERENCES

Ash, R. F. and Kueh, Y. Y. (eds), 1996. *The Chinese economy under Deng Xiaoping*, Clarendon Press, Oxford and Oxford University Press, New York.
Bosworth, B. and Collins, S. M., 2003. 'The empirics of growth: an update', unpublished, Washington: Brookings Institution.
Chow, G. C. and Li, K. W., 2002. 'China's economic growth: 1952-2010', *Economic Development and Cultural Change*, **51**, 247-56.
Hu, Z. F. and Khan, M. S., 1997. 'Why is China growing so fast?', *IMF Staff Papers*, **44(1)**, International Monetary Fund, Washington DC.
Lardy, N. R., 1995. 'The role of foreign trade and investment in China's economic transformation', *The China Quarterly*, **144**, 1065-82.
Lin, J. Y., 1992. 'Rural reforms and agricultural growth in China', *American Economic Review*, **82**, 34-51.
Maddison, A., 1998. *Chinese economic performance in the long run*, OECD Development Centre, Paris.
Maddison, A., 2003. *The world economy: historical statistics*, Development Centre Studies, OECD Development Centre, Paris.
National Bureau of Statistics, 1983. *China statistical yearbook 1983*, China Statistics Press, Beijing.
National Bureau of Statistics, 1997. *China statistical yearbook 1997*, China Statistics Press, Beijing.

National Bureau of Statistics, 2000. *China statistical yearbook 2000*, China Statistics Press, Beijing.

National Bureau of Statistics, 2005. *China statistical yearbook 2005*, China Statistics Press, Beijing.

Naughton, B., 1996. *Growing out of the plan: Chinese economic reform, 1978-1993*, Cambridge University Press, Cambridge and New York.

Nolan, P., 2001. *China and the global business revolution*, Palgrave, New York.

Perkins, D., 1988. 'Reforming China's economic system', *Journal of Economic Literature*, **26(2)**, 601-45.

Woo, W. T., 1998. 'Chinese economic growth: sources and prospects', in M. Fouquin and F. Lemoine (eds) *The Chinese economy*, Economica Ltd, Paris.

World Bank, 1997. *China 2020: development challenges in the new century*, The World Bank, Washington DC.

World Bank, 2005. *World Development Indicator 2005*, Washington DC.

Wu, F., 2005. 'Corporate China goes global', *World Economics*, **6**, 171-81.

Wu, Y., 1999. 'FDI and economic growth: an introduction', in Y. Wu (ed), *Foreign direct investment and economic growth in China*, Edward Elgar Publishing, Cheltenham, England, and Northampton, USA, chapter 1, pp. 1-8.

Wu, Y., 2005. *A tale of two giants: understanding economic growth in China and India*, unpublished manuscript, East Asian Institute, National University of Singapore.

Zhu, J., 2005. 'On economic aggregate and structural changes by the chief of the National Bureau of Statistics', *People's Daily*, December 21, p. 5.

PART I

Economic Growth and Outlook

2. Sources of Growth

Nazrul Islam, Erbiao Dai and Hiroshi Sakamoto

This chapter examines the sources of economic growth in China using the dual approach. This approach is useful because of numerous problems that continue to beset Chinese national income accounts data, despite attempts to rectify them. Almost all growth accounting studies conducted on China so far have followed the primal approach, which depends heavily on national income accounts (NIA) data. The dual approach, by contrast, allows independent price information to play a role. Recent research on Chinese growth has revolved around the following two questions: (a) How significant has total factor productivity (TFP)'s role been in post-reform Chinese growth? (b) Has TFP growth rate slowed in more recent years? Examination of Chinese growth using the dual approach provides the following answers to these questions: (a) In contrast to what Hsieh (2002) found for Singapore, the rate of TFP growth in China derived using the dual approach proves similar to the high rates obtained by many researchers using the primal approach. (b) The rate of TFP growth in China has slowed a little, but still remains high. These results however need to be viewed with some caution, mainly because of the weak nature of the data on the rate of returns to capital in China.

The discussion of the chapter is organized as follows. It first provides the background by reviewing the growth accounting exercises that have been conducted for China so far and by considering the problems of Chinese NIA data. This is followed by a description of the theory of the dual approach to growth accounting. Finally, it presents the implementation of the dual approach for China and discusses the results.

BACKGROUND

Very Different Estimates of TFP

A good number of researchers have previously examined the issue of sources of Chinese growth. One of the initial studies on this topic is by Chow (1993) who focuses on the period of 1952-1980. Chow's main finding for this pre-reform period is that growth was almost entirely capital accumulation driven and there was no TFP growth. Based on both graphical presentation and estimation of aggregate production functions, Chow concludes that "technological change was absent in the growth of the Chinese economy from 1952 to 1980".

Chow and Li (2002) return to this issue, following a similar methodology to Chow (1993), but updating the analysis to the more recent year of 1998. They find that in contrast to the pre-reform period, growth during the post-reform period was driven to a considerable degree by TFP growth. According to their estimation results, "there is an average increase in total factor productivity of about 2.6 per cent per year from 1978 to 1998".

Borensztein and Ostry (1996) offer a starker contrast of the pre- and post-reform periods. According to their computation, while TFP growth was negative, -0.7 per cent, during 1953-1978, it was an astoundingly positive rate of 3.8 per cent during 1979-1994. Hu and Khan (1997a, 1997b) provide an even more upbeat assessment of the role of TFP growth in the post-reform growth. They compute a translog productivity index taking the directly observed capital and labour income shares as the respective elasticities. According to their results, the TFP growth rate for the pre-reform 1953-78 period was 1.1 per cent, while it rose to 3.9 per cent during the post-reform period 1979-94.[1]

There is not much debate about the relative absence of TFP growth in the pre-reform Chinese economy. Similarly there is not much debate that TFP growth played an important role in the post-reform growth. The debate rather concerns the following two questions: (i) How much TFP played a role in the post-reform growth of China? (ii) Has TFP growth in China slowed in recent years?

With regard to the second question, Hu and Khan (1997a, 1997b), for example, conclude that TFP growth is rather accelerating. According to their computation, TFP growth for the last few years of the sample period (1990-1994) was 5.8 per cent per annum, and during this sub period TFP growth surpassed growth in capital stock as a source of output growth.[2] The authors attribute the higher TFP growth of more recent years to further deepening of economic reforms.[3] Nogami and Li (1995) reach similar conclusions. Confining their analysis to the industrial sector, they divide the post-reform period into the following three sub-periods: 1977-1984, 1985-1988 and 1989-1992. According to their computation, TFP growth rate for these sub-periods was 2.06, 2.14, and 5.14 per cent, contributing to 24.8, 19.6, and 44.2 per cent of the overall growth, respectively (The average growth rate of TFP for the whole period of 1977-1992 is 2.40 per cent, accounting for 25.6 per cent of the output growth). Ezaki and Sun (1999) also agree with a rising trend in the TFP growth rate. Based on their analysis, these authors conclude that "TFP growth has been fairly high at from 3 to 4 per cent with a slight tendency to increase, and its contribution to GDP growth is around 40 per cent".

However, there are contrasting opinions as to the significance of TFP in recent Chinese growth. Skepticism has been voiced with regard to both the extent of the role of TFP in general and the claimed increasing tendency of this role. Woo (1997), for example, suggests that Chinese TFP growth rates are not only lower in general, they are also declining as the post-reform period progresses. According to his computation, net TFP growth rates for the period of 1979-1993 range from 1.1 to 1.3 per cent.[4] He divides the post-reform period into two sub-periods, 1979-84 and 1985-93,[5] and shows that while TFP growth rate ranges from 2.76 to 3.76 per cent (depending on the chosen value of labour share in income) during the first sub-period, it ranges only from -0.11 to 1.58 per cent during the second sub-period. Woo interprets this slowdown as evidence that "the TFP growth unleashed by the 1978 reforms was a one-time recovery in efficiency from the decade-long Cultural Revolution and from the overregulation of the economy by central planning".[6]

Young (2000) also concludes that China's TFP growth rates have been over reported. He adopts a skeptical view of the Chinese official data, and undertakes a laborious effort to reconstruct this data using information from both Chinese NIA and non-NIA sources. Young focuses on the period 1978-1998 and considers only the industrial sector. He substitutes the official industrial output deflator by ex-factory price index.[7] He also uses the national income identity to derive a deflator for the investment series in a residual manner. He conducts a meticulous analysis of the demographic and labour force participation data to derive the labour force growth rate to be 2.2 per cent.[8]

A major advance in Chinese growth accounting that Young accomplishes in his paper is incorporation of labour quality into the analysis. In this regard, he uses the Jorgenson *et al.* (1987) approach of using the income earned by a particular category of labour as an indicator of its productivity. He uses various surveys to get data on income of labour of difference categories. Based on the exercise, he finds that "the growth of human capital in the non-agricultural sector of the Chinese economy between 1978 and 1998 to be 1.1 per cent per annum".[9]

On the basis of the reconstructed data, Young finds that the rate of TFP growth in the Chinese economy for the same period was 1.4 per cent per annum.[10] He comments that this is "a respectable performance, but by no means extraordinary". Young does not consider explicitly the issue of a slowdown of Chinese TFP growth with the progression of the post-reform period. However, the spirit of his analysis suggests that he would support the slowdown view.

In a recent paper, Wang and Yao (2001) also allow for improvement in labour quality in growth accounting for China. However, they voice doubts regarding Young's (2000) data on income for specific categories of labour, and instead use the number of schooling years as indicative of labour quality. They follow the Barro and Lee (1997) approach of using enrolment rates in a perpetual inventory framework to derive the number of people belonging to different education categories. Changes in these numbers are taken to reflect changes in the quality of labour. On the basis of this exercise, Wang and Yao find significant improvement in the quality of Chinese labour. However, they find that even after taking into account the role of labour quality improvement, the contribution of TFP remains high.[11] They offer results with alternative assumptions regarding labour share in income. For example, for the pre-reform period 1953-77, they assume the labour share to be 0.40, and find the output, physical capital, labour quantity, human capital stock, and TFP to grow at an annual rate of 6.46, 6.11, 2.63, 5.30, and -0.57 per cent, respectively, and the contribution to output growth of physical capital, labour, human capital, and TFP to be 56.8, 16.3, 32.8, and -5.9 per cent, respectively. For the reform period 1978-99, they assume a labour share of income of 0.50, and find output, physical capital, labour quantity, human capital stock, and TFP to grow at an annual rate of 9.72, 9.39, 2.73, 2.69, and 2.32 per cent, respectively, and the contribution to output growth of physical capital, labour, human capital, and TFP to be 48.3, 14.0, 13.8, and 23.9 per cent, respectively. Thus, while in the pre-reform period the TFP average growth rate is negative, -0.57 per cent, during the reform period it is 2.32 per cent.[12] The results regarding TFP estimates of Wang and Yao are therefore somewhere between the very high estimates of 4 to 5 per cent per annum offered by Hu and Khan, Nogami and Li, and others, and the very low estimates of 1.1 to 1.4 per cent of Woo and Young.[13]

This brief survey of Chinese growth accounting exercises shows that results differ widely regarding the relative importance of accumulation versus assimilation (represented by TFP growth) in the country's growth.[14] Results also differ widely with regard to whether TFP growth rates have slowed in recent years. More research is therefore necessary to resolve these disparate findings. The answer to the second question has wider ramifications, as Sachs and Woo (1997) expound. The purpose of the chapter is to make use of the dual approach to answer the two questions above. However, before embarking on that exercise it is worthwhile to explore possible reasons why TFP estimates have differed so much.

Reasons for Divergent TFP Estimates

Referring to the wide range of TFP estimates, Sachs and Woo (1997, p.21) offer the following observation: "The wide range of TFP estimates in the literature could be caused by a wide array of factors which include the choice of data set (e.g. geographical and sectoral representation, time period), the specification of the production function (e.g. Cobb-Douglas, Griliches-type), the assumption of technical change (e.g. Hicks-neutral, labour-augmenting), the estimation method (e.g. OLS, stochastic frontier), the selection of deflators for outputs and inputs, and ad hoc exclusion of observations". This is quite an apt description, and the authors concur with its sentiment.

However, a particular source for differences in TFP estimates is the problems that beset the Chinese NIA data. It may be noted that there are quite contrasting views regarding the merit of Chinese NIA statistics. At one extreme is Chow (1993, p.810), who relies entirely on Chinese official statistics viewing that these are by and large "...internally consistent and accurate enough for empirical work". He also adds that "...official statistical reporting in China is by and large honest". At the other extreme is Young (2000). He notes that under the Chinese system, there are inbuilt tendencies for local officials to "...overstate the growth of output, while understating investment and births".[15] Young wryly comments that "... while the Chinese government has conducted laudable campaigns against statistical misrepresentation, recording no less than 70 000 such cases in 1994 and 60 000 cases in 1997, this information has difficulty in finding its way into revisions of the GDP estimates".

In addition to the problems of honest reporting, Chinese national accounts data are also affected by several methodological problems. During the pre-reform period, China was following the Material Product System (MPS) under which output of many service sectors was not included in the measured national product. From 1985, China began its shift to the international System of National Accounts (SNA), and this shift was completed only in 1992. Despite this shift, Wang and Yao (2001), amongst others, note the following three problems. The first is the problem of compatibility of national income (GDP) measure before and after reform. The second is the problem of absence of deflator for national income of the pre-reform period 1952-77. And the third is the problem of absence of investment deflator for the period 1952-1990.[16] Attempts have been made to correct these statistical problems.[17] Hsueh and Li (1999) represent a significant contribution in this regard. Using historical data, they extrapolate to estimate the missing service sector output in the national income data for the pre-reform period 1952-77, so that the data is now more comparable with that of the reform period 1978-95. Hsueh and Li also provide deflators for both GDP and investment, so that real values of these variables are now available for the period 1952-1995.

Some researchers, such as Wang and Yao (2001), acclaim the contribution of Hsueh and Li (1999) and conclude that their work resolves all major methodological problems of Chinese national income accounts data.[18] Others have however voiced doubts. For example, Young (2000) notes that the way missing service sector output was incorporated into GDP is not proper, because it assumes that most of the service sector activities sprang up only during the post-reform period and almost nothing existed during earlier years.[19]

Young also has serious reservations about the deflators. He thinks that "Despite ...riders and exceptions, it is fair to say that overall the SSB (State Statistical Bureau) remains heavily dependent upon enterprise-provided output-based implicit deflators to deflate nominal value added". Echoing views expressed earlier by Ruoen (1995) and Woo (1998), Young (2000, p.8) also thinks that "implicit deflators provided by Chinese enterprises are systematically biased". He in fact formulates and estimates a sophisticated bi-factor latent variable model to prove this systematic bias. Young laments that SSB uses implicit deflators provided by the enterprises themselves instead of using 'independent price indices,' on which it collects data. This choice of deflator leads to the much discussed problem of underdeflation of the industrial output, particularly of the output of the township and village enterprises (TVEs). It is in view of this bias that Young uses for his own analysis the ex-factory price index as the deflator instead of the one provided by the national accounts.[20]

Young is similarly unhappy with the official deflator for gross fixed capital formation (GFCF). He thinks that "The official deflator for GFCF is presumably an inappropriate choice, as it relies upon enterprise output deflators and is, consequently, likely to be characterized by the same understatement of inflation that plagues the People's Republic's production estimates". As mentioned earlier, Young resorts to an elaborate exercise to derive an investment deflator via the income expenditure identity.

The above discussion makes it clear that, despite efforts to improve, Chinese national income accounts data continue to be affected by several problems. Yet growth accounting exercises using the primal approach generally depend heavily or entirely on national income accounts data. Almost all growth accounting exercises for China conducted so far have used the primal approach. It is therefore difficult for these exercises to extricate themselves from the impact of these data problems. Growth accounting using the dual approach however provides more scope for information other than that sourced from national accounts to be included. It is therefore useful to find out what kind of answer this approach can provide to the two questions mentioned above.

THE DUAL APPROACH TO GROWTH ACCOUNTING

The dual approach to growth accounting was proposed by Jorgenson and Griliches (1967).[21] Having presented the expressions for TFP from the primal and dual approach, they note that "These two definitions of total factor productivity are dual to each other and are equivalent. In general, any index of total factory productivity can be computed either from indexes of the quantity of total output and input or from the corresponding price indexes". There are many different ways in which the dual approach may be presented. A rather simple way is to proceed from the following national income accounting identity:[22]

$$Y = r K + w L, \tag{2.1}$$

where Y is the aggregate output (or aggregate income), r is the real rental price of capital, w is the real wage, L is labour, and K is capital. Upon differentiation with respect to time and dividing by Y, we get

$$\hat{Y} = s_K (\hat{r} + \hat{K}) + s_L (\hat{w} + \hat{L}) \tag{2.2}$$

where $s_k = rK/Y$ and $s_L = wL/Y$ are the factor income shares, and variables with "^" on top are the corresponding growth rates, so that $\hat{r} = dr/r$, and $\hat{w} = dw/w$. Rearranging equation (2.2), we get

$$\hat{Y} - s_K \hat{K} - s_L \hat{L} = s_K \hat{r} + s_L \hat{w}. \tag{2.3}$$

The left hand side of equation (2.3) represents the usual, primal representation of the Solow residual, so that we can write

$$SR_{primal} = \hat{Y} - s_K \hat{K} - s_L \hat{L} \tag{2.4}$$

However, equation (2.3) also shows that SR_{primal} is equal to the right hand side, which gives the dual representation of the Solow residual in terms of the share-weighted growth in factor prices, so that we can write

$$SR_{dual} = s_K \hat{r} + s_L \hat{w}. \tag{2.5a}$$

Note that this equality between SR_{primal} and SR_{dual} proceeds entirely from the national income identity and does not require any additional assumption.

Just as the SR_{primal} can be interpreted as a measure of shift in the production frontier, provided the efficiency parameter is Hicks neutral and equality between marginal products and factor returns hold, SR_{dual} can also be interpreted under these assumptions as a measure of shift in the corresponding factor price frontier. Samuelson (1962) provides an elaborate discussion of the relationship between the production frontier and factor price frontier. Diamond (1965) and Phelps and Phelps (1966) in fact use factor price frontier in defining changes in total factor productivity.[23]

The equality shown by equation (2.3) also makes it clear that if one computes the SR_{dual} using r and w obtained from capital and wage income data provided by national income accounts, SR_{dual} should be exactly equal to SR_{primal}. Such an exercise would therefore be redundant. However, the usefulness of SR_{dual} lies in the fact that it can be computed based on factor price information from alternative sources, and such TFP estimates can then provide a useful check on the validity of SR_{primal} estimates and/or the validity of national income accounts data.

As is known, both the primal and the dual version of the Solow residual, as given by equations (2.4) and (2.5a) above, are growth rates of continuous-time, Divisia-type indices. In order to compute Solow residual using discrete time data, Jorgenson and Griliches (1967) introduce a discrete time approximation to the Divisia index derived from Tornqvist index. Under this approximation, the TFP growth rate (TFPGR) between time t-1 and t, as measured by SR_{dual} is given by:

$$TFPGR_t = SR_{dual} = s_{L\tau}\hat{w}_t + s_{K\tau}\hat{r}_t \qquad (2.5b)$$

where $\hat{w}_t$ and $\hat{r}_t$ are growth rates of w and r, respectively, between t-1 and t, and

$$s_{L\tau} = \frac{1}{2}\left[s_{L,t-1} + s_{Lt}\right], \qquad (2.6a)$$

$$s_{K\tau} = \frac{1}{2}\left[s_{K,t-1} + s_{Kt}\right]. \qquad (2.6b)$$

In other words, continuous time (exponential) growth rates are replaced by growth rates between discrete time periods t-1 and t, and the continuous time shares (s) are replaced by averages of the shares of t-1 and t.[24]

Just as is the case with the primal approach, the dual approach to growth accounting can also be extended to take into account improvements in quality of the inputs. As is known, this is usually done by allowing for different types of labour and capital.[25] The Divisia index framework facilitates the task. For example, assuming that there are m different types of labour, an aggregate growth rate of the wages, $\hat{w}$, can be derived as a share-weighted average of the growth rates of the individual labour types, using the following formula:

$$\hat{w} = \sum_{j=1}^{m} s_{L_j}\hat{w}_j, \qquad (2.7)$$

where $\hat{w}_j$ is the growth rate of wages of a worker of type j, and s_{L_j} is the share of wage payments to workers of type j in total wage payments. Similarly, if there are n different types of capital, the aggregate rental price can be obtained as a weighted average of rental prices of these different types of capital, using the formula:

$$\hat{r} = \sum_{i=1}^{n} s_{k_i} \hat{r}_i, \tag{2.8}$$

where $\hat{r}_i$ is the growth rate of the rental price of type i capital, and s_{k_i} is the share of payments to capital type i in total payments to capital. This property of the Divisia index can be used to compute $\hat{w}_j$ and $\hat{r}_i$ based on sub-types into which labour of type j and capital of type i can be further disaggregated. In all cases, the Tornqvist approximation helps in estimating the Divisia growth rates using discrete (annual) data.

The importance of accounting for input quality improvements while computing TFP can not be overemphasized. Note that TFP represents the costless part of the growth in output (in the primal approach) and returns to factors (in the dual approach).[26] We know that high educational attainments have been a key characteristic of East Asian growth. However, these societies had to incur substantial costs in order to have these educational attainments. Unless improvement in the quality of labour arising from higher educational levels is accounted for (instead of measuring the labour input only by the number of bodies or even hours), the TFPGR will be overestimated. From the dual point of view, wage growth achieved by having more people with higher education than before should not count as TFP growth. Only wage growth with unchanged labour quality (education) can be taken as reflective of TFP growth. Equation (2.7) allows us to capture that part of wage growth. If wages for workers of given levels of education do not increase, the value of $\hat{w}$ will be zero, even though the unweighted growth rate is positive. Similarly, the aggregate rental price of capital may be higher just because of relatively more productive capital goods being in place than before. However, the society has to incur costs in order to bring about the changed composition of its capital stock. Equation (2.8) allows us to capture the change in the rental rate for a constant quality (composition) of capital stock. Thus unless rental prices change for given types of capital, the value of $\hat{r}$ computed using equation (2.8) will be zero even though the unweighted average rate of change of the rental price may change.[27]

Although in terms of algebra the above framework is symmetric with respect to labour and capital, it differs in terms of actual capability to capture their quality changes. This is because while there are independent physical measures of both quantity and quality of the labour input, such measures are generally absent for capital. Thus, the quantity aspect of the labour input can be measured by the number of bodies or hours, and the quality aspect of the labour input can be measured by the number of schooling years. By contrast, given the heterogeneity of capital goods, there is no physical measure of aggregate capital, either at the national, sectoral, or even plant level. The Jorgenson-Griliches approach of taking the rate of return earned by a particular type of capital as a measure of its quality can ideally provide a way around the problem. However, data on such rates of return are often difficult to obtain. More importantly, this does not obviate the problem of absence of a physical measure of the quantity of capital. We will encounter these problems in our growth accounting for China too.

There have been several prominent applications of the dual approach growth accounting in recent years. For example, Shapiro (1987) uses this approach to show that TFP movements are not caused by demand side shocks. Hsieh (1999, 2002) provides a more important recent application that is closely related to the present study. Hsieh's work is a response to Young's (1992, 1995) earlier work showing that Singapore experienced negative TFP growth. Hsieh notes that constant capital share and spectacular capital stock growth suggested by Young's data (obtained from Singapore's national income accounts) would imply a significant fall in the rental rate of capital in Singapore.[28] Hence looking at the dynamics of factor prices can provide an additional check on the validity of the national accounts data on capital accumulation. Accordingly, Hsieh conducts a dual approach growth accounting exercise for the East Asian Tigers (namely Hong Kong, Korea, Singapore, and Taiwan) and produces TFP growth rates for these economies. He finds that while for Korea and Hong Kong the dual estimates of TFP growth are similar to the primal estimates, they exceed the primal estimates by more than 2 percentage points for Singapore. Hsieh shows that the reason for this large discrepancy lies in the fact that while Singapore national income accounts data imply a large decline in the rate of return to capital, independent information on these returns do not indicate any such a fall.[29] He notes that such a fall is not likely given the openness of the Singaporean economy to cross border capital mobility and given the already low level of the rate of return to capital at the beginning of the period.[30] This suggests that Singaporean national income accounts must have over reported capital accumulation.

Hsieh's use of the dual approach was therefore prompted to a large extent by problems in the Singaporean national accounts data.[31] There is therefore a parallel with the Chinese situation in this regard. As seen in the discussion of the preceding section, there are considerable problems with Chinese national accounts data too, though of different type and extent. Problems in national income accounts data are not uncommon, and it is not easy to completely eradicate these problems.[32] The use of the dual approach to growth accounting can therefore provide a useful alternative check on the results produced so far for China by the primal approach.

IMPLEMENTING DUAL APPROACH GROWTH ACCOUNTING FOR CHINA

In conducting the growth accounting exercise for China, this chapter focuses entirely on the post-reform period 1978-2002. One question that is often asked in this regard is whether actual conditions of developing economies such as China satisfy the neoclassical assumptions of competition and equality between factor prices and their marginal value products. While most authors of Chinese growth accounting studies do not discuss this question explicitly, some do. For example, Nogami and Li (1995, p.1) note that "It has been a long controversy whether or not neo-classical model is applicable for the Chinese economy". They respond to the question by providing the following quote from Rawski and Zheng (1993, pp.320-21):

> ...The absolutely complete market economy doesn't exist in reality....It can not be obstructed that we describe the basic trends of the Chinese economy with the simple theory model. The practice proves that the Chinese economy which is changing into a market economy can be described with such simple theory model to some extent, and the results are basically fitted the reality....and the practice also proved that the result is more sensitive to different data than to different methods. So we should pay more attention to data handling.

Be that as it may, the important point to note is that the equality of prices with marginal products is required for the interpretation of the Solow residual as shifts of the production frontier (in the primal approach) and of the factor price frontier (in the dual approach). Even if this interpretation does not hold exactly because of departures from competitive equilibrium conditions, it is still possible to compute Solow residual and treat it as the measured productivity growth. Also, our choice of sample period (consisting entirely of post-reform years), makes it likely that competitive market equilibrium conditions will be satisfied to a greater extent.

Measuring Wage Growth

In implementing the dual approach, we first focus on the wage growth part of SR_{dual}. In other words, we want to obtain $s_L \hat{w}$, where we compute $\hat{w}$ using equation 2.7, in order to take into account different types of labour. We consider disaggregation in terms of both education level and residence (urban vs. rural). The disaggregation along these two lines for China turns out to be intertwined, as we shall see. Very few studies on China's TFP have attempted to incorporate changes in quality of labour, with Young (2000) and Wang and Yao (2001) being exceptions. Both these studies have however, conducted growth accounting following the primal approach. They both therefore needed to construct a quantity index of the labour input. In our case, we do not need the quantity index. All we need is a measure of wage growth that is net of the impact of growth in quality (of labour). However, in order for that we need data on wages differentiated by quality types (education categories) and also the distribution of the labour force among these quality types (education categories).

Distribution of Labour into Different Education Types

The distribution data of educational attainment by levels of schooling in the total Chinese population or total labour are available only in three recent censuses (1982, 1990 and 2000) and in several small sample-based Surveys on Population Change in recent years. In order to get such distribution for all years of the sample period, we follow the perpetual inventory method introduced by Barro and Lee (2000) and implemented recently for China by Wang and Yao (2001). We use annual enrolment and graduate flow data from Comprehensive Statistical Data and Materials on 50 Years of New China, 1949-98 and China Statistical Yearbooks for this purpose. The formulas for such perpetual inventory computation are as follows.

$$SP_{0,t} = (1-d_t)SP_{0,t-1} + (PRI\_ENROLLED_{0,t} - PRI\_GRADUATED_{0,t+6}) \qquad (2.9)$$

$$SP_{1,t} = (1-d_t)SP_{1,t-1} + (PRI_t - JUNIOR_{t+3}) \qquad (2.10)$$

$$SP_{2,t} = (1-d_t)SP_{2,t-1} + (JUNIOR_t - SENIOR_{t+3} - SPECIAL_{t+3}) \qquad (2.11)$$

$$SP_{3,t} = (1-d_t)SP_{3,t-1} + (SENIOR_t - HIGHER_{t+3.5}) \qquad (2.12)$$

$$SP_{4,t} = (1-d_t)SP_{4,t-1} + SPECIAL_t \qquad (2.13)$$

$$SP_{5,t} = (1-d_t)SP_{5,t-1} + HIGHER_t \qquad (2.14)$$

where $SP_{j,t}$ is the number of persons in the population for whom j is the highest level of schooling attained, so that $j = 0$ for incomplete primary, 1 for primary, 2 for junior secondary school, 3 for senior secondary school, 4 for specialized secondary school, and 5 for higher education. If a person cannot complete the enrolled education level, we take that person as belonging to the schooling level he had before. The variable d_t is the annual mortality rate of the population, which is drawn from Comprehensive Statistical Data and Materials on 50 Years of New China 1949-1998 and China Statistical Yearbook 2003.

These equations are broadly similar to those of Wang and Yao (2001). However there are a few differences. First, we allow for a different category for "incomplete primary education". In the classification of Wang and Yao, people with incomplete primary education are lumped with people with no schooling at all. Second, we take the number of years required to complete "specialized secondary school" to be three, instead of two which was used by Wang and Yao and which may not be correct.

Implementation of the above perpetual inventory method requires some information or assumption regarding the distribution in the initial year. Following Wang and Yao, we take India's distribution for 1960 to apply for China in 1951. According to this distribution, 16 per cent had incomplete primary, 8.4 per cent completed primary, 2.7 per cent had incomplete secondary, 0.1 per cent completed high school, 0.06 per cent completed higher education, and the rest was illiterate (see Barro and Lee 1997, 2000.) Although this assumed distribution may not be entirely accurate, the influence of the inaccuracy will wear off significantly by 1978, the beginning year of the sample period of this study.

After obtaining the education distribution of population, we compute the education distribution of labour, using the following formula:

$$SL_{jt} = TL_t \left(SP_{jt} / TP_t \right), \qquad (2.15)$$

where TL_t and TP_t are the total size of labour and educated population, respectively, in year t, and SL_{jt} and SP_{jt} are the size of labour and educated population, respectively, in that year for whom j is the highest level of schooling attained. The formula is based on the assumption that in a particular year, education distribution of population (in percentage form) is the same as the education distribution of labour (in percentage form).

In view of absence of any other more reliable source, we depend on the Chinese Statistical Yearbook (CSY) for the labour force data. However, we make a few adjustments to the pre-1990 labour force data. Based on the result of 2000 Population Census, the Chinese statistical authority has revised labour data for 1990-2000 significantly upwards, creating a huge jump (of 94.2 million) between the labour force figures of 1989 and 1990. Such a large increase in labour force in one year is unlikely. We therefore smooth out this jump by taking new 1990 labour data as the base and calculating backwards the labour force figures for 1978-1990 using the labour growth rates calculated from old data series for this period. This adjustment is made to total, urban, and rural labour figures.

Although the perpetual inventory exercise described above allows us to distinguish six different categories of education, corresponding data on wages are difficult to get, as noted earlier by Young (2000) and Wang and Yao (2001). In view of this difficulty, we collapse the education categories into three broad categories, namely "junior secondary school and below (Type-*E1*)," "high secondary school (including specialized secondary school and vocational school) (Type-*E2*)," and "higher education (university and college) (Type-*E3*)".

The results of the above perpetual inventory calculation can be seen in Table 2.1. Column 2 shows the total population, while columns 3, 4, and 5 show population, P1, P2, and P3, belonging to the three education types E1, E2, and E3, respectively. Similarly column 7 shows the size of the total labour force, while columns 8, 9, and 10 show labour force L1, L2, and L3 belonging to education type E1, E2, and E3, respectively.

Wage Data for Urban Labour

In order to proceed further we need information on wages distinguished by these three education types. There is some urban wage data by education level (for 1993-2001) reported in post-1994 issues of China Labour Statistical Yearbook (CLSY). However, the wage data is based on small sample surveys, usually covering only four to five cities, and its quality is questioned. For example, the data shows that in 1995 average wage rates for all education types are lower than those in 1994. This is highly unlikely. The probable reason for this anomaly is that the 1994 survey included more coastal cities and the 1995 survey included more inland cities.

In view of these difficulties with CLSY data, we instead use CSY data to get education specific labour incomes. We first consider wage rates of the urban labour force. Let w_{L1}, w_{L2}, and w_{L3} be the wage rates of urban labour of education type E1, E2, and E3, respectively. To the extent that E3 represents higher education, we take the wage rate in state-owned science and technology research sector (institutes), which has the highest share of labour with completed higher education, as a measure of w_{L3}. By analogous reasoning, we use the average wage data of state-owned enterprises (SOEs) as a measure of w_{L2}. Since the end of the 1970s, the labour growth in SOEs has been very slow. Usually only persons with completed senior secondary or special secondary education find employment in SOEs. On the other hand, except in some selected professional fields, SOEs do not attract and employ persons with completed higher education. Thus, employees of SOEs can be regarded as representing labour of education type E2. Finally, we use the average wage of collectively owned enterprises (COE) as w_{L1}. In China's Statistical system, COE is a type of small scale cooperatively owned enterprises, which (particularly the ones in the service sector) generally employ less educated urban labour and some of migrant rural labour. Information on urban wages obtained as above is provided in Table 2.2.

With the above information in hand, we can now compute the weighted average urban wage growth rate. However, before going ahead with this computation, we need to take note of the situation in the rural areas.

Special Situation with Rural Labour

The education distributions of population and labour force shown in Table 2.1 apply to the nation as a whole, i.e. including both urban and rural areas. Ideally, both urban and rural population and labour should fall into different education categories. However, data from surveys on population change (China Labour Statistical Yearbook 2003) show that less than five per cent of rural labour has completed senior secondary school or above. This would put 95 per cent of the rural labour into education type E1. Furthermore, the quality of high school education in rural areas is much lower than that in urban areas, so that rural labour nominally belonging to type E2 does actually belong to type E1, when quality of school education is taken into consideration (As we shall soon see, the wage data for rural labour also validates this observation). Also, though there are some official sample surveys on rural labour in China, none of these provide wage data distinguished by education categories. Thus even if we wanted to distinguish education type E2 and E3 in rural labour, we would not have corresponding data on wages. In view of this situation, we classify the entire rural labour (L_R) into education type E1.

Table 2.3 shows information on rural labour and wages. It gives total nominal rural wage, rural labour, nominal rural wage, national CPI, and rural CPI. It would seem proper to deflate nominal rural wage using rural CPI. Unfortunately, the rural CPI is generally regarded as very problematic, so that the use of the national CPI is preferred for this purpose. These average real rural wages (at 1978 prices), denoted by w_R, are given in column 8 of Table 2.3. For comparison, we also compute average rural real wage using the rural CPI as the deflator. This series, denoted by w_{R2}, is given in column 9. The year-to-year growth rates of w_R, denoted as $\hat{w}_R$, are given in column 10. On the other hand, year-to-year growth rates of w_{R2}, denoted as $\hat{w}_{R2}$, are shown in column 11. By comparing w_R with w_{L1} in Table 2.2, the urban wage of labour of education type E1, we see that indeed the former is much lower than the latter, supporting our earlier observation about inferior quality of rural education and the decision to classify all rural labour into education type E1. In fact, rural labour can be thought to belong to a separate, lower education type, say E0. However, doing so would not affect the computation, because in either case we will be using the rural wage to construct the weight for rural labour. We therefore refrain from introducing E0 in order to minimize notations and also to reflect the fact that nominally rural labour does belong to E1.

Table 2.1 Labour stock by education level (10,000 persons)

	(2)	(3)	(4)	(5)	(6)	(7)	(8)	(9)	(10)
Year	Total population	Educated population					Educated labour		
		E1	E2	E3	SUM	L	L1	L2	L3
1951	56300	10942	56	34	11032	45820	41612	3927	281
1978	95617	42538	4014	288	46840	46815	42226	4318	271
1979	96901	45901	4694	294	50889	48340	43339	4728	274
1980	98124	48570	5298	307	54175	49897	44611	5010	276
1981	99389	51561	5791	319	57671	51689	46187	5192	310
1982	100863	54135	6085	363	60583	52991	47379	5281	331
1983	102331	56445	6291	394	63130	55000	49250	5399	351
1984	103683	58829	6449	420	65698	56913	50994	5544	375
1985	105104	60982	6630	449	68060	58521	52417	5701	403
1986	106679	63040	6856	485	70381	60233	53880	5910	443
1987	108404	64985	7128	535	72648	62003	55383	6135	485
1988	110163	66906	7411	586	74904	63139	56304	6310	525
1989	112704	68647	7693	640	76980	64749	57636	6540	572
1990	114333	70229	7970	697	78896	65491	58186	6693	613
1991	115823	71600	8235	754	80589				

Year									
1992	117171	72848	8496	810	82153	66152	58659	6841	652
1993	118517	73868	8764	861	83493	66808	59107	7012	689
1994	119850	74734	9014	919	84667	67455	59541	7181	732
1995	121121	75498	9280	994	85772	68065	59912	7364	789
1996	122389	76176	9576	1071	86823	68950	60495	7604	851
1997	123626	76960	9901	1147	88008	69820	61055	7855	910
1998	124761	77859	10262	1223	89344	70637	61557	8114	967
1999	125786	78755	10700	1300	90754	71394	61954	8417	1022
2000	126743	82391	11260	1386	95036	72085	62493	8540	1051
2001	127627	86100	11844	1481	99425	73025	63238	8699	1088
2002	128453	89952	12442	1605	103999	73740	63780	8822	1138

Notes: E1=SP0+SP1+SP2; E2=SP3+SP4; E3=SP5. SP5, SP4, SP3, SP2, SP1, SP0 is the number of educated population for whom the highest level of schooling attained is higher education, special secondary, senior secondary, junior secondary, primary, and incomplete primary, respectively.

The percentage of population stock of each education level (SP5, SP4, SP3, SP2, SP1, SP0) to total population in 1951 is assumed as 0.06, 0.03, 0.07, 2.7, 8.4, and 16, respectively.

L is the size of the total labour force; L1 is the category of labour who received education lower than senior secondary school; L2 is the category of labour who completed senior secondary school education; L3 is the category of labour who completed higher education. L1= L (E1/SUM); L2= L (E2/SUM); L3= L (E3/SUM).

Sources: China Labour Statistical Yearbook (various years), China Statistical Yearbook (various years) and authors' calculations.

Table 2.2 Urban labour and wage by education level

(1)	(2)	(3)	(4)	(5)	(6)	(7)	(8)	(9)	(10)
	Nominal wage rate			Composition of L1		Real wage rate			Total real wage
Year	W_{L1}	W_{L2} (yuan)	W_{L3}	$L1_u$ (10,000)	L_R	W_{L1}	W_{L2} (yuan)	W_{L3}	(100 MY)
1978	506	644	670	6791	34794	506	644	670	615
1979	542	705	719	6971	35233	532	692	706	689
1980	623	803	853	7166	36154	569	733	779	775
1981	642	812	852	7492	37103	572	723	759	812
1982	671	836	860	7711	38461	586	730	751	854
1983	698	865	992	7968	39395	598	740	849	895
1984	811	1034	1074	8387	40846	676	862	895	1064
1985	967	1213	1268	8888	42092	737	925	967	1205
1986	1092	1414	1494	9263	43143	782	1013	1070	1345
1987	1207	1546	1624	9581	44290	805	1032	1084	1430
1988	1426	1853	1935	9874	45501	801	1041	1087	1482
1989	1557	2055	2123	9802	46492	741	978	1011	1397
1990	1681	2284	2411	9928	47708	776	1055	1113	1524
1991	1866	2477	2580	10160	48026	833	1106	1152	1657

Year									
1992	2109	2878	3130	10368	48291	885	1208	1314	1830
1993	2592	3532	3989	10561	48546	948	1292	1460	2008
1994	3245	4797	6212	10739	48802	957	1414	1832	2177
1995	3931	5625	6835	10887	49025	990	1416	1721	2256
1996	4302	6280	7984	11467	49028	1000	1460	1856	2415
1997	4512	6747	8974	12016	49039	1020	1526	2030	2609
1998	5331	7668	10146	12536	49021	1215	1748	2313	3166
1999	5774	8543	11543	12972	48982	1335	1975	2669	3667
2000	6262	9552	13221	13559	48934	1442	2200	3045	4154
2001	6867	11178	16218	14153	49085	1570	2556	3709	4850
2002	7667	12869	19006	14820	48960	1768	2967	4382	5736

Notes: $L1 = L1_u + L_R$ (total rural labour). Thus, $L1_u = L1 - L_R$.
W_{L1} in the column 2 is the weighted average wage of $L1_u$. The average wage of collectively-owned enterprises is used as proxy of w_{L1}.
W_{L2} is the average wage of L2, using the average wage data of SOEs.
W_{L3} is the average wage of L3. The average wage for labour of state-owned science and research sector is used as proxy of W_{L3}.
MY refers to million yuan.
Total real wage for year $i = L1_i \cdot W_{L1i} + L2_i \cdot W_{L2i} + L3_i \cdot W_{L3i}$.

Sources: China Labour Statistical Yearbook (various years) and authors' calculations.

Table 2.3 Rural wage growth rate

(1)	(2)	(3)	(4)	(5)	(6)	(7)	(8)	(9)	(10)	(11)
	Total rural nominal wage	Rural labour	Nominal wage rate	CPI	Rural CPI	Total rural real wage	Real wage rate		Wage growth rate	
							w_R	w_{R2}	$\hat{w}_R$	$\hat{w}_{R2}$
Year	(100 MY)	(10,000)	(yuan)	(1978=100)	(1978=100)	(100 MY)	(yuan)	(yuan)	(%)	(%)
1978	1055	34794	303	100.0	100.0	1055	303	303		
1979	1266	35233	359	101.9	101.9	1242	353	353	16.3	16.3
1980	1522	36154	421	109.5	109.5	1390	384	385	9.0	9.0
1981	1785	37103	481	112.3	112.2	1590	429	429	11.5	11.5
1982	2166	38461	563	114.5	114.4	1891	492	492	14.7	14.8
1983	2501	39395	635	116.8	116.7	2141	543	544	10.5	10.5
1984	2855	40846	699	120.0	119.9	2380	583	583	7.2	7.2
1985	3211	42092	763	131.1	134.2	2449	582	568	-0.1	-2.5
1986	3438	43143	797	139.7	142.4	2462	571	560	-1.9	-1.5
1987	3776	44290	852	149.8	151.2	2520	569	564	-0.3	0.7
1988	4488	45501	986	178.0	177.7	2521	554	555	-2.6	-1.5
1989	5002	46492	1076	210.1	211.9	2381	512	508	-7.6	-8.5

1990	5774	47708	1210	216.6	221.6	2666	559	546	9.1	7.6
1991	5996	48026	1248	223.9	226.7	2677	557	551	-0.2	0.8
1992	6664	48291	1380	238.3	237.3	2797	579	582	3.9	5.6
1993	7865	48546	1620	273.3	269.7	2878	593	601	2.4	3.3
1994	10461	48802	2144	339.2	332.8	3085	632	644	6.6	7.2
1995	13560	49025	2766	397.2	391.1	3414	696	707	10.2	9.8
1996	16388	49028	3343	430.1	421.9	3810	777	792	11.6	12.0
1997	17594	49039	3588	442.2	432.5	3979	811	829	4.4	4.7
1998	17978	49021	3667	438.6	428.2	4099	836	856	3.0	3.2
1999	18133	48982	3702	432.5	421.8	4193	856	878	2.4	2.5
2000	18216	48934	3723	434.2	421.4	4195	857	883	0.2	0.7
2001	18828	49085	3836	437.3	424.7	4306	877	903	2.3	2.2
2002	19370	48960	3956	433.8	423.0	4466	912	935	4.0	3.6

Notes: Total nominal rural wage = rural population * Per capita income of rural population. MY refers to million yuan. Data in columns 7, 8 and 10 are calculated using CPI, and data in columns 9 and 11 are calculated using rural CPI.

Source: China Statistical Yearbook (various years) for rural population, per capita income of rural population, rural labour, CPI, rural CPI and authors' calculations.

Aggregation over Education and Residence Types

We first subtract L_R from L1, the total labour of education type E1, in order to get $L1_U$, the urban labour belonging to education type E1. Column 5 of Table 2.2 shows $L1_U$. The rest of the computation of the urban wage growth rate is shown in Table 2.4, and is carried out using the following equation:

$$\hat{w}_U = s_{L1}\hat{w}_{L1} + s_{L2}\hat{w}_{L2} + s_{L3}\hat{w}_{L3}, \tag{2.16}$$

where $\hat{w}_{L1}$, $\hat{w}_{L2}$, and $\hat{w}_{L3}$ are the growth rates of w_{L1}, w_{L2}, and w_{L3}, respectively, and s_{L1}, s_{L2}, and s_{L3} are share of wage payments made to E1, E2, and E3 type labour in the total urban wage-payments. Columns 2, 3, and 4 show $\hat{w}_{L1}$, $\hat{w}_{L2}$, and $\hat{w}_{L3}$, while columns 5, 6, and 7 show the values of s_{L1}, s_{L2}, and s_{L3}, respectively. The values of $\hat{w}_U$ are presented in column 8. These values may be compared with unweighted average growth rates of urban wages shown in column 9.

We can now compute the weighted average of the wage growth rate for the economy as a whole ($\hat{w}$), using the formula:

$$\hat{w} = s_U \hat{w}_U + s_R \hat{w}_R. \tag{2.17}$$

The results are shown in Table 2.5. Columns 9 and 11 show the values of $\hat{w}_U$ and $\hat{w}_R$, respectively from earlier tables. Columns 8 and 10 show the values of s_U and s_R, respectively. The values of $\hat{w}$ can be seen in column 12. These values may be compared with unweighted average growth rates shown in columns 4 and 7.

Measuring Changes in the Capital Rental Rate

Measuring the capital rental rate in China is a challenging task. This is because capital markets were until recently either non-existent or very weak. The following therefore outlines possibilities for ascertaining movements in the capital rental rate for the period 1978-2002.

Estimating Capital Stock

The first task in measuring capital rental rate is to construct the capital stock figures. As noted in the preceding section, this remains a thorny issue. Our capital construction exercise is presented in Table 2.6. It begins with the gross investment series in current prices, shown in column 2. To bring these to constant 1978 prices, we use the GDP deflator, shown in column 3. We noted earlier that the deflator to be used for this purpose has been a point of conjecture, and we will comment on this later. The constant (1978) price investment figures are in column 4 of the Table. This investment series is then used to compute the capital stock using the perpetual inventory method using the following familiar equation:

$$K_t = (1-\delta)K_{t-1} + I_t \qquad (2.18)$$

where notations are obvious. The capital stock for the initial year, K_0, is computed using the formula:

$$K_0 = I_0 / [g_0 + \delta_0] \qquad (2.19)$$

where I_0 is the investment for the initial period, δ_0 is the rate of depreciation applicable for the initial year, and g_0 is ideally the rate of growth of capital around the initial year. To the extent that value of capital stock is unknown, various proxies are used. For example, in computing initial capital stock for 1960, Hall and Jones (1999, p.89, ff 5) takes g_0 to be "the average geometric growth rate from 1960 to 1970 of the investment series". In our case, we take 1957 as the initial year, and g_0 is taken to be 0.13, the average growth rate of investment during 1952-1957. As for the depreciation rate, it ranges between 0.02 and 0.04 in the Chinese official documents. We therefore take δ_0 to be equal to 0.03, the mid-point of this range. Note that since the period analyzed in this chapter is 1978-2002, the assumptions made in computing capital stock for 1957 will not have much influence in the capital stock data actually used.

It may be noted that the composition of the Chinese capital stock changed substantially over the last decades. In general, the share of "machinery and equipment," which depreciate faster, has increased relative to the share of "buildings and structures," which depreciate at a slower pace. This implies that the depreciation rate of the aggregate Chinese capital stock has increased over time. To reflect this trend, we take the depreciation rate to be 0.03 for 1952-1978, 0.04 for 1979-1992, and 0.05 for 1993-2002. The rates assumed for the first two sub-periods are based on Chinese statistical authorities (NBSC 1997). The assumed rate for the more recent sub-period is based on the past rates and some recent literature (see Ezaki and Sun 1999, Hu and Khan 1997b).

Table 2.4 Urban wage growth rate

(1)	(2)	(3)	(4)	(5)	(6)	(7)	(8)	(9)
	Growth rate by education			Share in total wage			Urban growth rate	
Year	$\hat{w}_{L1}$	$\hat{w}_{L2}$	$\hat{w}_{L3}$	S_{L1}	S_{L2}	S_{L3}	$\hat{w}_U$	$\hat{w}_U^{UN}$
	(%)	(%)	(%)				(%)	(%)
1978				0.56	0.41	0.03		
1979	5.1	7.4	5.3	0.54	0.43	0.03	6.1	6.5
1980	6.9	6.0	10.4	0.53	0.45	0.03	6.6	7.0
1981	0.5	-1.3	-2.6	0.53	0.45	0.03	-0.4	-0.3
1982	2.5	0.9	-1.0	0.53	0.44	0.03	1.7	1.8
1983	2.0	1.4	13.1	0.53	0.44	0.03	2.1	2.0
1984	13.1	16.4	5.4	0.53	0.44	0.03	14.3	14.1
1985	9.1	7.3	8.0	0.54	0.43	0.03	8.3	8.1
1986	6.0	9.5	10.6	0.54	0.43	0.03	7.6	7.6
1987	3.0	1.9	1.3	0.54	0.43	0.03	2.5	2.5
1988	-0.6	0.9	0.3	0.53	0.43	0.04	0.1	0.2
1989	-7.5	-6.0	-7.0	0.52	0.44	0.04	-6.8	-6.6
1990	4.7	7.8	10.2	0.51	0.45	0.04	6.3	6.5
1991	7.4	4.9	3.5	0.51	0.45	0.04	6.1	6.1

1992	6.2	9.2	14.0	0.50	0.45	0.05	7.9	7.9
1993	7.2	7.0	11.1	0.50	0.45	0.05	7.3	7.4
1994	0.9	9.4	25.5	0.47	0.47	0.06	6.2	6.1
1995	3.5	0.1	-6.0	0.48	0.46	0.06	1.3	1.5
1996	1.1	3.1	7.9	0.47	0.46	0.07	2.4	2.3
1997	2.0	4.5	9.3	0.47	0.46	0.07	3.7	3.6
1998	19.1	14.6	14.0	0.48	0.45	0.07	16.7	16.6
1999	9.8	13.0	15.4	0.47	0.45	0.07	11.7	11.7
2000	8.0	11.4	14.1	0.47	0.45	0.08	10.0	9.7
2001	8.9	16.2	21.8	0.46	0.46	0.08	13.3	12.9
2002	12.6	16.1	18.1	0.46	0.46	0.09	14.6	14.2
				Mean				
1978-2002	5.5	6.7	8.4	0.53	0.46	0.05	6.2	6.2
1978-1984	5.0	5.1	5.1	0.62	0.51	0.03	5.1	5.2
1985-1991	3.2	3.7	3.8	0.53	0.44	0.04	3.4	3.5
1992-2002	7.2	9.5	13.2	0.48	0.46	0.07	8.6	8.5

Notes: $\hat{w}_{L1}$, $\hat{w}_{L2}$, and $\hat{w}_{L3}$ are wage growth rates of labour categories, L1, L2, and L3, respectively. $\hat{w}_u$ is the weighted urban overall wage growth rate, while $\hat{w}_u^{UN}$ is an unweighted rate, which is calculated from the data of total urban labour and total real urban wage (column 10 of Table 2.2). Growth rates for 1978-2002, 1978-1984, 1985-1991, and 1992-2002 are arithmetic averages of annual wage growth rates of each period, respectively.

Source: Authors' calculations.

Table 2.5 Overall wage growth rate

(1)	(2)	(3)	(4)	(5)	(6)	(7)	(8)	(9)	(10)	(11)	(12)
Year	TWNIA	WNIA	$\hat{w}_{NIA}^{UN}$	TWCLSY	WCLSY	$\hat{w}_{CLSY}^{UN}$	S_U	$\hat{w}_U$	S_R	$\hat{w}_R$	$\hat{w}$
	(100MY)	(yuan)	(%)	(100MY)	(yuan)	(%)					(%)
1978	1800	393		1671	365		0.37		0.63		
1979	2004	428	9.0	1931	413	13.1	0.36		0.64	16.3	12.6
1980	2150	445	3.9	2165	448	8.6	0.36	6.6	0.64	9.0	8.1
1981	2331	467	5.0	2402	481	7.5	0.34	-0.4	0.66	11.5	7.4
1982	2584	500	7.0	2745	531	10.3	0.31	1.7	0.69	14.7	10.5
1983	2864	541	8.1	3036	573	7.9	0.29	2.1	0.71	10.5	8.0
1984	3301	600	11.0	3443	626	9.3	0.31	14.3	0.69	7.2	9.3
1985	3698	650	8.3	3653	642	2.5	0.33	8.3	0.67	-0.1	2.6
1986	4020	687	5.7	3807	651	1.3	0.35	7.6	0.65	-1.9	1.4
1987	4417	733	6.8	3949	656	0.8	0.36	2.5	0.64	-0.3	0.7
1988	4887	788	7.5	4004	646	-1.5	0.37	0.1	0.63	-2.6	-1.6
1989	5065	802	1.8	3778	598	-7.3	0.37	-6.8	0.63	-7.6	-7.3
1990	5454	842	5.0	4190	647	8.2	0.36	6.3	0.64	9.1	8.1
1991	5815	888	5.4	4335	662	2.3	0.38	6.1	0.62	-0.2	2.1
1992	6380	964	8.6	4626	699	5.7	0.40	7.9	0.60	3.9	5.4
1993	7323	1096	13.7	4886	731	4.6	0.41	7.3	0.59	2.4	4.3

1994	8337	1236	12.8	5262	780	6.7	0.41	6.2	0.59	6.6	6.4
1995	9508	1397	13.0	5671	833	6.8	0.40	1.3	0.60	10.2	6.6
1996	10529	1527	9.3	6225	903	8.4	0.39	2.4	0.61	11.6	8.0
1997	11331	1623	6.3	6589	944	4.5	0.40	3.7	0.60	4.4	4.1
1998	12296	1741	7.3	7264	1028	9.0	0.44	16.7	0.56	3.0	8.7
1999	12988	1819	4.5	7860	1101	7.1	0.47	11.7	0.53	2.4	6.6
2000	13757	1909	4.9	8350	1158	5.2	0.50	10.0	0.50	0.2	4.9
2001	14810	2028	6.3	9156	1254	8.2	0.53	13.3	0.47	2.3	7.9
2002	15823	2146	5.8	10201	1383	10.3	0.56	14.6	0.44	4.0	9.8
Mean											
1978-2002			7.4			5.8	0.4	6.2	0.6	4.9	5.6
1978-1984			7.3			9.4	0.3	5.1	0.7	11.5	9.3
1985-1991			5.8			0.9	0.4	3.4	0.6	-0.5	0.8
1992-2002			8.4			6.9	0.4	8.6	0.6	4.6	6.6

Notes: TW$_{NIA}$ (total labour compensation) and W$_{NIA}$ are calculated from national income account data; TW$_{CYSY}$ (total national wages) and W$_{CYSY}$ are calculated from wage data for rural sector and urban sector in *China Labour Statistical Yearbook*. All of these wage data (in1978 price) are deflated from nominal data by CPI. $\hat{w}$ in column 12 is the weighted overall wage growth rate, and data in columns 4 and 7 are two unweighted rates. Data for 1978-2002, 1978-84, 1985-91, and 1992-2002 are arithmetic averages for each period, respectively.

Source: Authors' calculations.

Table 2.6 Estimation of China's capital stock (hundred million yuan - 1978 price, unless otherwise indicated)

(1)	(2)	(3)	(4)	(5)	(6)	(7)	(8)	(9)
						Comparison of several estimations		
Year	Gross fixed investment (current prices)	GDP deflator (1978=100)	Gross fixed investment	Capital stock	Our estimation[1]	Hu and Khan (1997)[2]	Ezaki and Sun (1999)[3]	Chow and Li (2002)[4]
1978	1378	100.0	1378	12290	12290	8239		14112
1979	1474	103.6	1424	13222	13222	8850		15273
1980	1590	107.5	1480	14172	14172	9489	8325	16438
1981	1581	109.9	1439	15044	15044	9993	8948	17268
1982	1760	109.8	1604	16046	16046	10699	9681	18297
1983	2005	110.9	1807	17211	17211	11525	10606	19515
1984	2469	116.4	2121	18644	18644	12629	11753	20928
1985	3386	128.2	2641	20539	20539	13984	13253	22755
1986	3846	134.1	2869	22586	22586	15321	15079	24822
1987	4322	140.9	3068	24751	24751	16847	17155	27123
1988	5495	158.0	3478	27238	27238	18502	19466	30085
1989	6095	172.0	3544	29693	29693	19423	21507	33445
1990	6444	181.7	3547	32052	32052	20445	23090	36565
1991	7517	193.9	3876	34646	34646	21718	24726	39776

Year								
1992	9636	209.2	4607	37867	37867	23311	26823	43589
1993	14998	239.6	6259	42232	42232	25532	29700	48994
1994	19261	287.2	6707	46828	46828	28297	33373	55006
1995	23877	325.0	7347	51834	51834		37594	61856
1996	26867	344.3	7804	57046	57046			69304
1997	28458	347.0	8202	62396	62396			77218
1998	29546	338.6	8727	68003	68003			85692
1999	30702	331.0	9275	73878	73878			
2000	32500	334.1	9726	79910	79910			
2001	37461	338.1	11080	86994	86994			
2002	42355	337.2	12559	95204	95204			

Notes:

1. The gross fixed investment series is used to compute the capital stock using the perpetual inventory method, $K_t = (1-\delta)K_{t-1} + I_t$. The capital stock for the initial year (1957), K_0, is computed using the formula $K_0 = I_0 / (g_0 + \delta_0)$, where I_0 is the investment for the initial period, δ_0 is the rate of depreciation applicable for the initial year, and g_0 is ideally the rate of growth of capital around the initial year. In this study, g_0 is taken as 0.13, which is the average growth rate of investment during 1952-1957, and δ_0 is 0.03, which is the average value of rate of depreciation usually used by China government. After 1978, δ is taken as 0.04 for 1978-92, and 0.05 for 1993-2002.

2. They assume the depreciation rate as 0.036 for 1978-94. The investment deflator they used is not shown in their paper, but seems to be obviously higher than those used in Ezaki and Sun (1999) and Chow and Li (2002).

3. They assume the depreciation rate as 0.049 for 1980-1995. For comparison, we converted the original data series of Ezaki and Suns's estimation, which is in 1995 prices, into present data in 1978 prices.

4. They assume the depreciation rate as 0.04 for 1978-1998. Land is included in the estimated capital stock.

Sources: China Statistical Yearbook (various issues) and authors' calculations.

The estimated values of capital stock are influenced by the assumptions concerning deflators, initial capital stock, and depreciation rates. Table 2.6 therefore also offers a comparison of our estimated values of capital stock with those offered recently by other researchers. The comparison shows our capital stock figures to be larger than those of Hu and Khan (1997b) and Ezaki and Sun (1999). However, they prove smaller than those of Chow and Li (2002), who include land in their capital stock.

Rental Rate of Capital According to NIA Data

Before we compute capital rental rate using alternative sources information, we first check what these rates turn out to be when computed on the basis of NIA data. This exercise is presented in Table 2.7. Column 2 gives the GDP in current prices, while column 3 gives total wage payments aggregated for the national economy from provincial data (note that in China's national income account, only provincial data of wage payments are reported).[33] Payments to capital are shown in column 4, and are obtained by subtracting wage payments from GDP. The GDP deflator (shown in Table 2.6) is used to convert the capital payments data in current prices into constant 1978 prices. These are then divided by the capital stock data to obtain the capital rental rate, shown in column 6 of Table 2.7. The year-to-year changes (as percentages of the base years' values) are shown in column 7.

The main feature of the results regarding NIA-based rental rate is that this rate seems to have gone up from around 14 per cent to about 16 per cent. Such an increasing trend contradicts the expectation that capital deepening will pull down the rental rate via diminishing returns. As data in Table 2.6 shows, between 1978 and 2002, the aggregate capital stock has increased 7.8 fold, and per labour capital stock has increased 4.8 fold. It is remarkable that the capital rental rate has remained constant or even increased despite this enormous increase in capital.

Hsieh (2002) has argued in the context of Singapore that such an outcome is untenable if capital-output ratio has increased and the share of capital in national income has remained unchanged.[34] However, unlike Singapore, data for China does not show significant rise in the capital-output ratio. Based on our capital stock estimates, the capital-output ratio (K/Y) for 1978 and 2002 is 3.39 and 3.06 respectively. Thus, instead of increasing, the capital-output ratio has declined somewhat.[35] In the mean time, the national accounts data shows that the value of capital share β has also remained almost constant. This would suggest that marginal product of capital, MP_K, also remains constant. Thus unlike that of Singapore, the NIA data for China does not suggest any decline in the capital rental rate. We now check what evidence about capital rental rate can be obtained from alternative sources of information.

Rental Rate of Capital According to Industry Level Data

For one such alternative source of information, we turn to industrial level data to be found in "China Industry Economy Statistical Yearbook (CIESY)". This data also allows a two-level disaggregation. At the first level we distinguish two sectors, namely manufacturing and other. The latter consists mainly of agriculture and service sectors. At the second level, we distinguish capital by two ownership types, namely state owned enterprises (SOE) and non-state owned enterprises (Non-SOE). Since 1978 the Chinese economy has undergone a radical transformation of ownership type. The share of state-ownership of capital assets has considerably fallen. The share of various indigenous cooperative and individual ownerships has risen. In addition, there is now considerable intrusion of foreign ownership of various forms. It is often maintained that capital under these various types of ownership differs in quality, manifested in very different rates of return that they earn. A disaggregation in terms of ownership therefore will be helpful in netting out the impact of quality improvements in capital. Data limitations however restrict the second level disaggregation to the manufacturing sector only.

Table 2.8 shows the computation of the average rate of change in the rental rate of capital for the manufacturing sector based on disaggregation into SOE and non-SOE. Column 2 shows the rate of return for SOE part of the manufacturing sector, denoted as r_{SOE}. These rates are also computed from CIESY with "profit-plus-tax" as the numerator and the value of the fixed assets as the denominator. We see that r_{SOE} displays a strong declining trend. It falls from .25 per cent in 1978 to .10 per cent in 2002. The year-to-year changes of this rental rate (denoted as $\hat{r}_{SOE}$) are shown in column 4. Column 3 shows the rate of return to industrial capital in non-state owned enterprises (non-SOE), denoted as r_{NSOE}. The capital stock (value of fixed assets) of the non-SOEs is calculated by subtracting the value of fixed assets of the SOEs from the value of the total fixed assets of the manufacturing sector. Similarly, profit-plus-tax of the non-SOEs is computed by subtracting the "profit-plus-tax" of SOEs from the corresponding total for the industry. We see that r_{NSOE} also shows a strong declining trend. In fact, the declining trend is more pronounced for r_{NSOE} than for r_{SOE}. As column 3 shows, this rental rate has declined from a high of .44 per cent in 1978 to .18 per cent in 2002. The year-to-year changes in this rental rate (denoted as $\hat{r}_{NSOE}$) can be seen in column 5.

With this disaggregated data available, we can now calculate the rate of change in the rental rate in the manufacturing sector as a weighted average using the formula:

$$\hat{r}_M = s_{SOE,\tau}\hat{r}_{SOE,t} + s_{NSOE,\tau}\hat{r}_{NSOE,t}. \qquad (2.20)$$

Table 2.7 Return to capital according to national income accounts data

(1)	(2)	(3)	(4)	(5)	(6)	(7)
Year	GDP (current prices)	Payments to wages (current prices)	Payments to capital (current prices)	Payments to capital (1978 prices)	Rate of return to capital (%)	Year to year change (%)
1978	3624	1800	1825	1825	14.8	
1979	4038	2075	1963	1896	14.3	-3.41
1980	4518	2311	2207	2054	14.5	1.06
1981	4862	2562	2301	2094	13.9	-3.96
1982	5295	2836	2459	2240	14.0	0.30
1983	5935	3178	2757	2485	14.4	3.43
1984	7171	3842	3329	2860	15.3	6.26
1985	8964	4742	4222	3293	16.0	4.49
1986	10202	5389	4813	3591	15.9	-0.84
1987	11963	6223	5739	4074	16.5	3.54
1988	14928	7721	7207	4561	16.7	1.73
1989	16909	8710	8199	4767	16.1	-4.12

Year					
1990	18548	9908	8640	4755	14.8	-7.59
1991	21618	11276	10342	5333	15.4	3.75
1992	26638	13344	13294	6356	16.8	9.04
1993	34634	17548	17086	7130	16.9	0.59
1994	46759	23940	22819	7946	17.0	0.51
1995	58478	30900	27578	8486	16.4	-3.53
1996	67885	36249	31636	9189	16.1	-1.60
1997	74463	39312	35151	10131	16.2	0.80
1998	78345	41632	36713	10843	15.9	-1.80
1999	82068	42991	39077	11805	16.0	0.21
2000	89468	45970	43498	13017	16.3	1.95
2001	97315	50072	47243	13973	16.1	-1.40
2002	104791	53362	51429	15250	16.0	-0.27

Notes: Payments to wages is aggregated from provincial data in tables of national income account; Payments to capital (current price, in hundred million yuan) = GDP (current price) - Payments to wages (current price); Rate of return to capital is calculated as payments to capital (1978 price) / capital stock (1978 price).

Sources: National Bureau of Statistics of China, *The Gross Domestic Product of China 1952-1995*, and *China Statistical Yearbook* (various issues); Authors' calculations.

Table 2.8 Rate of return to capital in the manufacturing sector

(1)	(2)	(3)	(4)	(5)	(6)	(7)	(8)	(9)
	By ownership type (in manufacturing sector)						Overall change rate (%) (manufacturing sector)	
	Rate of return (%)		Year to year change (%)		Capital share			
Year	SOE (r_{SOE})	NSOE (r_{NSOE})	$\hat{r}_{SOE}$	$\hat{r}_{NSOE}$	SOE ($S_{SOE,t}$)	NSOE ($S_{NSOE,t}$)	$\hat{r}_M$	$\hat{r}_M^{UN}$
1978	24.8	44.1			0.92	0.08		
1979	24.9	38.5	0.70	-12.73	0.91	0.09	-0.44	-0.78
1980	24.3	38.1	-2.47	-1.09	0.90	0.10	-2.34	-1.81
1981	22.9	33.2	-5.84	-12.65	0.89	0.11	-6.53	-6.52
1982	22.2	30.7	-2.94	-7.69	0.89	0.11	-3.46	-3.40
1983	21.7	32.2	-2.53	4.84	0.88	0.12	-1.69	-1.21
1984	22.3	31.3	2.94	-2.71	0.87	0.13	2.25	2.37
1985	22.4	45.2	0.45	44.44	0.89	0.11	5.63	6.21
1986	19.9	27.5	-11.21	-39.15	0.85	0.15	-14.81	-15.54
1987	19.7	25.6	-0.84	-6.86	0.84	0.16	-1.78	-1.65
1988	20.2	27.8	2.33	8.65	0.83	0.17	3.39	4.04
1989	17.5	21.7	-13.53	-21.99	0.81	0.19	-15.05	-15.19
1990	12.9	15.9	-25.81	-26.65	0.81	0.19	-25.97	-25.87
1991	12.3	15.9	-5.35	-0.23	0.79	0.21	-4.32	-3.74

1992	12.4	20.1	1.06	26.31	0.79	0.21	6.40	7.75
1993	12.9	21.8	3.97	8.37	0.74	0.26	5.02	8.35
1994	12.5	19.9	-3.29	-8.47	0.69	0.31	-4.77	-2.89
1995	9.3	15.5	-25.38	-22.24	0.69	0.31	-24.40	-23.93
1996	7.9	14.0	-15.26	-9.83	0.67	0.33	-13.51	-11.87
1997	7.6	13.4	-3.72	-4.36	0.64	0.36	-3.94	-2.60
1998	7.0	12.7	-7.19	-4.79	0.74	0.26	-6.45	-11.62
1999	7.7	14.0	9.09	10.32	0.74	0.26	9.41	9.52
2000	10.3	17.0	33.69	21.35	0.73	0.27	30.41	29.67
2001	9.8	17.4	-4.60	2.06	0.72	0.28	-2.75	-1.27
2002	10.3	18.4	4.74	5.99	0.69	0.31	5.11	7.22
				Mean				
1978-2002	15.4	23.7	-2.96	-2.05	0.79	0.21	-2.69	-2.28
1978-1984	23.1	34.0	-1.69	-5.34	0.89	0.11	-2.03	-1.89
1985-1991	17.8	25.7	-7.71	-5.97	0.83	0.17	-7.56	-7.39
1992-2002	9.8	16.7	-0.63	2.25	0.71	0.29	0.05	0.76

Notes: The fixed asset for other enterprises (NSOEs) equals the gross fixed asset of the manufacturing sector minus that of state-owned enterprises, while profit and tax for NSOEs equals the gross profit and tax of the manufacturing sector minus that of SOEs. $\hat{r}_M^{UN}$ is the unweighted growth rate of return rate to capital for two kinds of enterprises in the manufacturing sector, SOEs and NSOEs, and $\hat{r}_M$ is the weighted growth rate.

The data for 1978-2002, 1978-84, 1985-91, and 1992-2002 are arithmetic averages for each period, respectively.

Sources: NBSC, *China Industry Economy Statistical Yearbook* (2003); Authors' calculations.

Columns 6 and 7 show the share of SOEs and non-SOE capital, denoted by $s_{SOE,t}$ and $s_{NSOE,t}$, respectively, in the total payments to capital in the manufacturing sector. We can see that $s_{NSOE,t}$ has steadily increased, from a mere eight per cent in 1978 to thirty-one per cent in 2002. Correspondingly, $s_{SOE,t}$ has decreased from 92 per cent in 1978 to 69 per cent in 2002. The weighted changes in the rental rate, $\hat{r}_M$, are shown in column 8.

As already mentioned, lack of data prevents disaggregation of the "other" sector by ownership type. We therefore next consider aggregation over manufacturing and other sector. The results from this exercise are provided in Table 2.9. Column 2 shows the rental rate of capital in the manufacturing sector, denoted as r_M. These rates are computed with "profit-plus-taxes paid" as the numerator and the value of the fixed assets as the denominator for the entire manufacturing sector. We again see that this rate of return displays a clear declining trend, from a value of .26 per cent in 1978 to .13 per cent in 2002. The rental rate of "other" sector, denoted by r_O, can be seen in column 3. The CIESY does not provide data on the capital stock of sectors other than the manufacturing sector. Hence the value of fixed assets for the "other" sector is calculated by subtracting the fixed asset of the manufacturing sector from the total capital stock of the economy, computed earlier through the perpetual inventory method. Similarly, we get the value of profit and taxes for the other sector by subtracting the profit and tax of the manufacturing sector from the total value of profit and tax (in the economy). The figures of column 3 show that, in contrast to what we saw for the manufacturing sector, the rental rate of capital for the "other" sector shows an upward trend. The year-to-year changes in these rates (denoted as $\hat{r}_{Ot}$) are shown in column 5. Column 4 reproduces the values of $\hat{r}_M$ obtained earlier in Table 2.8. Comparing, we see considerable differences between rental rates of capital in these two sectors, in terms of both level and trend.

We can now calculate the economy wide weighted average ($\hat{r}$) using the following formula:

$$\hat{r}_t = s_{M\tau}\hat{r}_{Mt} + s_{O\tau}\hat{r}_{Ot} \tag{2.21}$$

where $\hat{r}_M$ and $\hat{r}_{Ot}$ are as before and $s_{M\tau}$ and $s_{O\tau}$ are the share of payments to capital of the manufacturing and "other" sector, respectively, in the total payments to capital. Columns 6 and 7 in Table 2.9 show the values of s_{Mt} and s_{Ot}, respectively. Column 8 presents the computed values of $\hat{r}$. These may be compared with the unweighted rate of changes in the rate of return to capital, denoted by $\hat{r}^{UN}$ and shown in column 9. We note considerable differences between $\hat{r}$ and $\hat{r}^{UN}$, implying that disaggregation does influence the results.

Thus we see contrasting results regarding the rental rate of capital. The rental rate obtained on the basis of NIA data shows that this rate has remained relatively unchanged, despite very significant capital deepening as measured by capital stock per labour. This relatively unchanged rate is about 15 per cent. However, rental rate computed from industrial data shows a clear and marked declining trend. For the manufacturing sector as a whole this rate has come down from a high of 26 per cent in 1978 to about 12 per cent in 2002.[36]

Dual Estimates of TFP Growth Rates

We now collect the results to compute the SR_{dual}, or the dual approach TFPGR using equation (2.5b). This computation is presented in Table 2.10. The first few columns provide the ingredients for computation of SR_{primal}, or the primal TFPGR. Thus columns 2, 3, and 4 give the year-to-year growth rate in GDP, labour, and capital. Column 9 shows the share of labour income (S_L) in GDP, as per NIA data. These produce the primal TFPGR (TFP_p) shown in column 10.

The ingredients for computation of the dual TFPGR are in columns 5 and 7, which show the weighted growth rate of wage and rental rate. The corresponding unweighted averages can be seen in columns 6 and 8. The simple arithmetic average of $\hat{w}$ for 1978-2002 is 5.6 per cent, while analogous value for $\hat{w}_{CLSY}^{UN}$ is 5.8 per cent. Accounting for labour quality as measured by educational attainment does have some effect. Both these values are however much lower than the analogous average of $\hat{w}_{NIA}^{UN}$, the unweighted wage growth rate according to the NIA data. The latter has a value of 7.4 per cent.

The comparison of the weighted and unweighted average change in capital rental rate is more problematic, as noted earlier. The simple arithmetic average for 1978-2002 of $\hat{r}$ equals 1.05. The analogous average of $\hat{r}^{UN}$, the unweighted rate of change of capital rental rate according to NIA data equals 0.38. We may note that unweighted average is smaller in magnitude than the weighted average. We compute two alternative values of dual TFPGR. Column 11 shows TFP_d the dual TFPGR based on the weighted growth rates $\hat{w}$ and $\hat{r}$. Column 12 shows the dual TFPGR (denoted as TFP_d^{UN}) based on the unweighted averages $\hat{r}^{UN}$ and $\hat{r}^{UN}$. To conduct a rough and ready

Table 2.9 Rate of return to capital according to alternative sources of information

(1)	(2)	(3)	(4)	(5)	(6)	(7)	(8)	(9)
	Rate of return (%)		By sector Year to year change (%)		Capital share		Overall change rate (%)	
Year	Manufacturing sector (r_m)	Other sector	$\hat{r}_M$	$\hat{r}_{Ot}$	Manufacturing sector (S_{Mt})	Other sector (S_{ot})	$\hat{r}$	$\hat{r}^{UN}$
1978	26.3	10.3	—	—	0.28	0.72	—	—
1979	26.1	9.8	-0.44	-4.92	0.28	0.72	-3.67	-3.41
1980	25.7	10.3	-2.34	5.38	0.27	0.73	3.26	1.06
1981	24.0	10.1	-6.53	-1.80	0.27	0.73	-3.09	-3.96
1982	23.2	10.4	-3.46	2.34	0.28	0.72	0.74	0.30
1983	22.9	11.1	-1.69	6.98	0.28	0.72	4.54	3.43
1984	23.4	12.3	2.25	10.85	0.27	0.73	8.46	6.26
1985	24.9	13.0	5.63	5.75	0.25	0.75	5.72	4.49
1986	21.0	14.1	-14.81	8.18	0.26	0.74	2.25	-0.84
1987	20.7	15.0	-1.78	6.23	0.26	0.74	4.13	3.54
1988	21.5	15.2	3.39	1.48	0.25	0.75	1.97	1.73
1989	18.2	15.3	-15.05	1.10	0.24	0.76	-2.86	-4.12
1990	13.5	15.3	-25.97	-0.53	0.25	0.75	-6.78	-7.59
1991	13.0	16.2	-4.32	6.15	0.26	0.74	3.52	3.75
1992	14.0	17.7	6.40	9.29	0.25	0.75	8.56	9.04

Year								
1993	15.2	17.5	5.02	-1.43	0.26	0.74	0.21	0.59
1994	14.8	17.7	-4.77	1.38	0.25	0.75	-0.17	0.51
1995	11.2	18.2	-24.40	3.08	0.27	0.73	-4.01	-3.53
1996	9.9	18.3	-13.51	0.56	0.26	0.74	-3.18	-1.60
1997	9.6	18.7	-3.94	2.15	0.28	0.72	0.50	0.80
1998	8.5	18.9	-6.45	0.61	0.28	0.72	-1.36	-1.80
1999	9.3	18.7	9.41	-0.59	0.29	0.71	2.29	0.21
2000	12.1	18.0	30.41	-3.76	0.29	0.71	6.29	1.95
2001	11.9	17.8	-2.75	-1.49	0.29	0.71	-1.86	-1.40
2002	12.8	17.3	5.11	-2.40	0.29	0.71	-0.20	-0.27
Mean								
1978-2002	17.0	15.3	-2.69	2.27	0.27	0.73	1.05	0.38
1978-1984	24.2	10.7	-2.03	3.14	0.28	0.72	1.71	0.61
1985-1991	19.0	14.9	-7.56	4.05	0.25	0.75	1.14	0.14
1992-2002	11.8	18.1	0.05	0.67	0.27	0.73	0.64	0.41

Notes: Rate of return (to capital) = (gross profit and tax) / (fixed asset). The data on gross profit and tax, and fixed asset for the manufacturing sector are available in the *China Industry Economy Statistical Yearbook*. The value of fixed asset for the non-manufacturing sector is equal to gross capital stock minus fixed asset of the manufacturing sector, while the value of profit and tax for the Non-manufacturing sector is equal to gross capital income minus profit and tax of the manufacturing sector.

$\hat{r}$ is the weighted growth rate of return rate to capital for the economy comprising both the manufacturing and the non-manufacturing sectors, and $\hat{r}^{UN}$ is the unweighted growth rate.

The growth rates for 1978-2002, 1978-1984, 1985-1991, and 1992-2002 are arithmetic averages of annual growth rates for each period, respectively.

Sources: NBSC, *China Industry Economy Statistical Yearbook* (2003); Authors' calculations.

Table 2.10 TFPGR calculated by the two approaches

(1)	(2)	(3)	(4)	(5)	(6)	(7)	(8)	(9)	(10)	(11)	(12)
	Growth rate (%)							Labour share (S_L)	TFP(%)		
Year	GDP	Labour	Capital	$\hat{w}$	$\hat{w}_{CLSY}^{UN}$	$\hat{r}$	$\hat{r}^{UN}$		TFP_p	TFP_d	TFP_d^{UN}
1978	—	—	—	—	—	—	—	0.50	—	—	—
1979	7.60	2.17	7.58	12.58	13.1	-3.67	-3.41	0.51	2.83	4.68	5.09
1980	7.81	3.26	7.19	8.14	8.6	3.26	1.06	0.51	2.66	5.76	4.90
1981	5.26	3.22	6.15	7.35	7.5	-3.09	-3.96	0.53	0.63	2.41	2.06
1982	9.01	3.59	6.66	10.50	10.3	0.74	0.30	0.54	3.95	5.96	5.67
1983	10.89	2.52	7.26	7.97	7.9	4.54	3.43	0.54	6.10	6.38	5.82
1984	15.18	3.79	8.32	9.35	9.3	8.46	6.26	0.54	9.21	8.94	7.87
1985	13.47	3.48	10.16	2.56	2.5	5.72	4.49	0.53	6.78	4.04	3.45
1986	8.86	2.83	9.97	1.36	1.3	2.25	-0.84	0.53	2.61	1.78	0.31
1987	11.57	2.93	9.58	0.68	0.8	4.13	3.54	0.52	5.45	2.34	2.11
1988	11.27	2.94	10.05	-1.61	-1.5	1.97	1.73	0.52	4.92	0.12	0.05
1989	4.07	1.83	9.01	-7.29	-7.3	-2.86	-4.12	0.52	-1.21	-5.14	-5.77
1990	3.83	2.55	7.95	8.08	8.2	-6.78	-7.59	0.53	-1.31	1.16	0.82
1991	9.19	1.15	8.09	2.11	2.3	3.52	3.75	0.52	4.71	2.79	2.98
1992	14.24	1.01	9.30	5.45	5.7	8.56	9.04	0.50	9.25	7.00	7.34

1993	13.49	0.99	11.53	4.35	4.6	0.21	0.59	0.51	7.44	2.30	2.61
1994	12.66	0.97	10.88	6.44	6.7	-0.17	0.51	0.51	6.94	3.21	3.66
1995	10.51	0.90	10.69	6.59	6.8	-4.01	-3.53	0.53	4.90	1.59	1.93
1996	9.59	1.30	10.06	7.98	8.4	-3.18	-1.60	0.53	4.08	2.78	3.72
1997	8.84	1.26	9.38	4.12	4.5	0.50	0.80	0.53	3.68	2.41	2.76
1998	7.82	1.17	8.99	8.72	9.0	-1.36	-1.80	0.53	2.90	4.00	3.93
1999	7.14	1.07	8.64	6.57	7.1	2.29	0.21	0.52	2.44	4.53	3.80
2000	8.00	0.97	8.17	4.90	5.2	6.29	1.95	0.51	3.57	5.58	3.62
2001	7.50	1.30	8.87	7.94	8.2	-1.86	-1.40	0.51	2.57	3.18	3.56
2002	7.96	0.98	9.44	9.79	10.3	-0.20	-0.27	0.51	2.92	4.89	5.13
						Mean					
1978-2002	9.41	2.01	8.91	5.61	5.80	1.05	0.38	0.52	4.08	3.45	3.23
1978-1984	9.29	3.09	7.20	9.31	9.44	1.71	0.61	0.53	4.23	5.69	5.24
1985-1991	8.90	2.53	9.26	0.84	0.89	1.14	0.14	0.52	3.14	1.01	0.57
1992-2002	9.79	1.08	9.63	6.62	6.95	0.64	0.41	0.52	4.61	3.77	3.82

Notes: TFP$_p$ is calculated using the primal approach, while TFP$_d$ and TFP$_d^{UN}$ are calculated using the dual approach. TFP$_d$ is based on weighted wage growth rate and weighted growth rate of capital return rate (Columns 5 and 7), and TFP$_{d2}$ is based on two unweighted growth rates (Columns 6 and 8). The growth rates for 1978-2002, 1978-1984, 1985-1991, and 1992-2002 are arithmetic averages of annual growth rates for each period, respectively.

Source: Authors' calculations.

comparison, we may again look at the long-term averages of TFP_p, TFP_d, and TFP_d^{UN} provided in the bottom rows of Table 2.10. A simple arithmetic average of TFP_p equals 4.08, while those of TFP_d and TFP_d^{UN} equal 3.45 and 3.23, respectively. Thus we find the dual TFPGR to be only about half a percentage point less than the primal TFPGR. Unlike that for Singapore, the dual TFPGR for China do not appear to be that different from the primal TFPGR.

It may therefore be concluded that even after taking account of improvements in labour quality (through higher educational attainments), TFPGR in mainland China for the post-reform period 1978-2002 prove to be high, around 3 per cent per annum. In other words, the answer to the first question is that TFPGR did play a very important role in the post-reform growth. In fact our dual estimate of TFPGR proves higher than that of both Young (2000) and Woo (1997) and closer to that of Hu and Khan (1997a, b) and Wang and Yao (2001).[37] To answer the second question, we may look at the 1978-1984 and 1992-2002 averages of TFPGR. According to the primal measure, TFP_p, this average has increased from 4.23 per cent in the first sub-period to 4.61 per cent in the second sub-period. However, according to the dual TFPGR, TFP_d, this average has decreased from 5.69 to 3.77 per cent. The other measure of dual TFPGR, TFP_d^{UN}, also shows an analogous decrease from 5.24 to 3.82 per cent. Thus according to dual growth accounting, while the TFPGR still remains high, it has slowed to some extent. In this regard, we see a contrast between the results based on dual TFPGR and those based on primal TFPGR.

CONCLUDING REMARKS

This chapter shows that the dual approach to growth accounting can be applied to China, and such an application can help in answering difficult questions concerning sources of Chinese growth. However, there remain many weaknesses, particularly regarding the determination of rental prices of capital used in calculation. This is not surprising. Rental rates of capital, particularly disaggregated by capital types, are very hard to determine even for developed market economies. So we very much look forward to further improvement in this area. An alternative source of information regarding rate of return to capital in China is International Financial Statistics (IFS), which provide "deposit rate" and "lending rate". The former refers to "interest rates on institutional and individual deposits of one-year maturity". The latter refers to "rate on capital loans to state-owned industrial enterprises during 1980-1989 and to all enterprises thereafter". This information is more independent of NIA than the rental rates we used in our computation of dual

TFPGR above. However, most researchers think that the sphere of application of the IFS rates is very limited, and that these rates cannot be taken as representing the rental rate of capital for the broader Chinese economy. With time, as capital markets develop in coverage and depth in China, many other more representative rental rates will emerge. However, as of now, problems remain in getting capital rental rates that are completely independent of NIA. The situation with regard to wages is better in this respect. However, as we saw, there remain considerable problems in getting wages differentiated by education types, for both urban and in particular the rural sector.

The Chinese statistical authorities are making important progress in eliminating data deficiencies and weaknesses. Hopefully more of such improvements will take place soon and will help overcome many of the difficulties that were faced in this chapter in applying the dual approach growth accounting to China.

NOTES

1. This also implies that while TFP contributed only 18.0 per cent of the pre-reform growth, its contribution to the post-reform growth was 41.6 per cent.
2. As the authors put it, during this sub period, "productivity changes for the first time overtook capital as the predominant source of China's economic growth" (Hu and Khan 1997b, p.124).
3. In their words, "Instead of slowing down (as one might have expected), productivity growth reached stunning new highs as China moved forward on the reform path, albeit at an uneven pace" (Hu and Khan 1997b, p.124). They further add the following commentary in this regard: "Therefore, the evidence from this study points to a somewhat different conclusion from that reached by Sachs and Woo (1997). Even though the efficiency gains brought about by earlier agricultural reforms may have dissipated, the sharp growth in rural industry, the surge in foreign direct investment, the export boom, the further dismantling of the central planning system, and the increasing market orientation in the state-owned sector have combined to boost aggregate productivity growth in the 1985-94 period, and even more so during 1990-94" (Hu and Khan 1997b, p.124).
4. Inclusive of labour reallocation (from agriculture to industry) effect, TFP growth rate for this period would range from 2.2 to 2.4 per cent per annum (p.2).
5. He provides the following reasoning for the choice of the sub-periods: "The delineation of the sub-periods corresponds, one, to the policy regime change toward accelerating reforms in the non-agricultural sectors, and two, to the emergence of industry as the undisputed primary engine of growth. The growth performance of the 1985-93 subperiod may be a better guide (than that of the entire period) to understand the future growth prospects of China. This is because future Chinese growth is likely to be led by the (non) agricultural sectors as in 1985-93 period" (p.9).
6. He further adds that "The agricultural reforms may have accounted for a large part of the initial high net TFP growth" (p.10).
7. He notes that the use of this alternative deflator brings down the growth of real GDP between 1978 and 1998 from the official 9.1 per cent to 7.4 per cent for the aggregate and from 10.6 to 8.1 for the non-agricultural sector.
8. He thinks that "In sum working age population growth of 2.2 per cent per annum, in excess of the 1.3 per cent rate of population growth, is completely consistent with reasonable participation and demographic trends and may be deemed fairly accurate" (p.22).

9.   He however recognises that "… both slightly lower and moderately higher estimates are plausible, but all estimates are tolerably concentrated around a value of 1.1 per cent" (p.31).

10.   So far as factor shares are concerned, Young accepts the official data, stating that "…there is no reason to modify the reported Chinese estimates of the share of labour…In this paper I use the average share of labour reported in the Chinese national accounts, in preference over the more volatile figures of the input output tables" (p.41).

11.   "We found that, first, the accumulation of human capital was quite rapid and it contributes significantly to growth and welfare. Second, after incorporating human capital, the growth of TFP still plays a positive and significant role during the reform period 1978-1999. In contrast, productivity growth was negative in the pre-reform period. Results are robust to changes in labour shares in GDP" (Wang and Yao 2001, p.3).

12.   Wang and Yao (2001) present another Table (Table 2.2, p.16) where they impose the same value of labour share for the pre- and post-reform period and compute TFP growth rates. The pre- and post-reform TFP growth rate prove to be -0.87 and 2.98, -0.74 and 2.72, and -0.38 and 1.92 when labour income share is assumed to be 0.67, 0.60, and 0.40, respectively.

13.   In fact, that is exactly how they themselves view their results. They think that "Regarding the on-going debate, this paper proposes a middle-road answer to the sources of growth, and that is, both productivity growth and factor accumulation are very significant in accounting for China's growth performance during the reform period" (Wang and Yao 2001, p.3).

14.   For more on diverse TFP results on China, see Sachs and Woo (1997).

15.   Young (2000, p.5) observes that "Following a nationwide audit of statistical reports, the 1994 gross industrial output estimates were revised downwards by about 9 per cent, with most of the adjustment falling on township and village enterprises, whose output was deemed to have been exaggerated by about a third".

16.   State Statistical Board (SSB) of China began constructing fixed asset investment price index only in 1991.

17.   For example a Census of Services was conducted in 1991-1992 in order to gather data on the service sector, "which produced a dramatic revision of the national accounts" (Young 2000, p.6).

18.   "With the support and cooperation of the SSB, Hsueh and Li (1999) have made significant progresses and published the most complete set of Chinese national income from 1952 to 1995 based on SNA in 1999 both at the national and provincial level" (Wang and Yao 2001, p.5).

19.   "Beginning with the 1995 issue of the publication, the GDP estimates were revised on the basis of the data from the Census of Services. ….the estimated value of service sector output in 1993 was raised by about a third, while the estimates for 1978 were hardly changed at all. In other words, when the SSB improved its measure of the service sector, it concluded that virtually all the newly discovered, and hitherto unrecorded, value added had developed during the reform period. This assumption is retained, with minor revisions, in the most recent (1999) version of the national accounts. While the development of non-material sectors was neglected under the plan, so was their measurement. Consequently, the approach adopted by the SSB seems somewhat extreme, as it is likely that a fair amount of the newly discovered non-material output was present in 1978. As an alternative, one might assume that the ratio of unmeasured to measured activity found in 1993 existed in 1978 as well. If so, the SSB's adjustments overstate the growth of service sector nominal output between 1978 and 1993 by 1.6 per cent per annum" (Young 2000, pp.6-7).

20.   Young justifies his choice of deflator as follows: "… the joint stochastic behavior of the implicit GDP deflators and alternative price indices lends substantial support to Ruoen and Woo's argument that the implicit GDP deflators systematically understate price movements. Various attempts to allow the data to select its own inflation rate return estimates close to, if not exceeding, the growth of the alternative price indices. On this basis, I follow the suggestion of Ruoen, substituting the SSB price indices he recommends for the implicit deflators of the national accounts" (Young 2000, p.16). Young further

mentions that "Ruoen (1995) argues that these independent price indices can credibly substitute for the existing implicit deflators in the estimation of the growth of real output," and himself concludes that "For all these reasons, the Ex-Factory price index is arguably a superior choice as a replacement deflator" (p.10).

21. For even earlier discussion of the basic duality for indexes of total factory productivity, they refer to Siegel (1952).

22. This presentation of the dual approach follows Hsieh (2002).

23. As Hsieh (2002, p.503) explains, "In a simple model with two factors, say capital and labour, the outward shift of the factor price frontier is simply a share-weighted average of the growth rate of real wages and the rental rate of capital. According to the dual growth accounting formula, if real wage growth is entirely due to capital accumulation, the return to capital must fall by the same magnitude as the rate of real wage growth".

24. It is also known that the Tornqvist indices are not only a good approximation of the corresponding Divisia indices, they are also the exact indices if the underlying production function has the translog specification. To the extent that translog function can serve as the second order approximation to any other production function, the validity of the Tornqvist index is quite general. See Hulten (2000) for an excellent recent discussion of various issues regarding the theory and computation of TFP.

25. See Jorgenson, Gollop, and Fraumeni (1987, p.2) for elaboration.

26. See Abramovitz (1962, p.764), Griliches and Jorgenson (1967, pp.250-51), and Hulten (2000) for further elaboration of this point.

27. See Hsieh (2002, p.506) for further discussion.

28. "This evidence suggests that while the data on investment expenditures in the Korean national accounts are reasonably accurate, Singapore's national accounts significantly overstate the amount of investment spending" (p.503). Note that

$$r = \frac{rK/Y}{K/Y} = \frac{s_K}{K/Y} .$$

If s_K remains constant, r has to fall in exactly the same rate as rise of the capital-output ratio (K/Y). As Hsieh puts it, "Since the share of payments to capital in Korea and Singapore has remained roughly constant, the marginal product of capital implied by Korea's and Singapore's national accounts must have fallen by 3.4 per cent and 2.8 per cent a year respectively, the same rate as the increase in the capital-output ratio" (pp.502-3).

29. "This discrepancy is not explained by financial market controls, capital income taxes, risk premium changes, and public investment subsidies" (Hsieh 2002, p.502).

30. Actually, Hsieh's Figure 2 makes it clear that r did not have any further room to fall in Singapore. In 1962, r, as given by 'Average lending rate,' was already at the level of around 6-7 per cent. In contrast, Hsieh's Figure 1 shows that r in Korea, as measured by curb loan rate was at the level of around 16-17 per cent, and so there was considerable room to fall.

31. As Hsieh (2002, p.503) suggests, "As one solution to this problem, this paper presents price-based (dual) estimates of TFPG that do not rely on data from national accounts".

32. As Hsieh (2002) notes, "Of course, this simply reinforces what anybody who has worked with national accounts data knows: that the task of computing reliable national income statistics is an impossibly difficult one and that, even under the best of the circumstances, such statistics are riddled with large errors" (p.503).

33. These data series from 1978 are available in "The Gross Domestic Product of China 1952-1995" and "China Statistical Yearbook" (various years).

34. This can be clearly seen from the following expression of capital share, $\beta = MP_K \left(K/Y \right)$.

Clearly, if (K/Y) goes up while β remains unchanged, MP_K has to fall.

35. This finding regarding lack of capital deepening is not new. Earlier researchers have also been struck by this. For example, Hu and Khan (1997a, p.3) make the following comment in this regard: "... although the capital stock grew by nearly 7 per cent a year over 1979-94, the capital-output ratio has hardly budged. In other words, despite a huge expenditure on capital, production of goods and services per unit of capital remained about the same. This pronounced lack of capital deepening suggests a constrained role for capital".

36. What explains this discrepancy? The following observations by Hu and Khan (1997b) are pertinent in this regard: "The Chinese authorities regularly undertake fixed asset surveys for the state-owned sector, obtaining information on (1) gross stock of fixed assets valued at the original acquisition prices of the respective assets; and (2) the stock of fixed assets valued at current prices in the survey years, net of depreciation. In comparing the net stock value series, as reported by the official asset surveys, with the capital stock estimated using cumulated investment flows and the official depreciation table for the state-owned sector, large discrepancies emerge. One possible explanation is that the state owned enterprises (SOEs) and other state entities fail to use consistent price deflators for those asset surveys. Another possible reason is that official surveys suffer from serious reporting errors and omissions. In any event such official surveys are not conducted for urban collective and rural agricultural sectors, and thus do not cover the economy as a whole" (p.110). This difficulty was also mentioned in the shorter version of Hu and Khan (1997a, p.8): "Chinese asset surveys do not produce capital stock estimates consistent with the investment data in the national accounts. The difficulties of bridging this gap are considerable".

37. One thing that needs to be noted is that the contrast between the upbeat TFP growth rates of Hu and Khan and those of Young, Woo, and Wang and Yao may not be as great as they appear. This is because Hu and Khan's analysis does not take into account quality improvements of labour. Hence their estimates of TFP are inclusive of the contribution of human capital growth. On the other hand, both Young and Wang and Yao account for quality improvements in labour, and hence their TFP growth rates do not include the contribution of quality improvements in labour. As we can see from the results of Wang and Yao, presented above, the total of human capital growth and TFP growth rates prove to be 5.01 per cent for the post-reform period (analogous total for the pre-reform period proves to be 4.73 per cent per annum). This is a higher figure than even of Hu and Khan. Similarly, Young finds that while output per worker increases in the post-reform period by 3.6 per cent, output per effective worker increases by 2.6 per cent, suggesting a growth rate of human capital of about 1 per cent. Adding this to his TFP growth rate would raise it to 2.4 per cent, much higher than the measly 1.4 per cent.

REFERENCES

Abramovitz, M., 1962. 'Economic growth in the United States', *American Economic Review*, **52**, 762-782.

Barro, R. and Lee, J. W., 1996. 'International measures of schooling years and schooling quality', *American Economic Review (Papers and proceedings)*, **86**, 218-23

Barro, R. and Lee, J. W., 2000. 'International data on educational attainment: updates and implications', *CID Working Paper*, No. 42, Harvard, April.

Borensztein, E. and Ostry, J. D., 1996. 'Accounting for China's growth performance', *American Economic Review*, **86**, 224-228.

Chow, G., 1993. 'Capital formation and economic growth in China', *Quarterly Journal of Economics*, **3**, 809-842.

Chow, G. and Li, K. W., 2002. 'China's economic growth: 1952-2010', *Economic Development and Cultural Change*, **51**, 247-256.

Diamond, P. A., 1965. 'Technical change and the measurement of capital and output', *Review of Economic Studies*, **32**, 289-298.

Ezaki, M. and Sun, L., 1999. 'Growth accounting in China for national, regional, and provincial economies: 1981-1995', *Asian Economic Journal*, **13**, 39-73.

Griliches, Z. and Jorgenson, D. W., 1967. 'The explanation of productivity change', *Review of Economic Studies*, **34**, 249-283.

Hall, R. E. and Jones, C., 1999. 'Why do some countries produce so much more output than others?' *Quarterly Journal of Economics*, **114**, 83-116.

Hsieh, C. T., 1999. 'Productivity growth and factor prices in East Asia', *American Economic Review (Papers and Proceedings)*, **89**, 133-138.

Hsieh, C. T., 2002. 'What explains the industrial revolution in East Asia? Evidence from factor markets', *American Economic Review*, **92**, 502-526.

Hsueh, T. T. and Li, Q. eds., 1999. *China's National Income: 1952-1995*, Boulder: Westview Press.

Hulten, C. R., 2000. 'Total factor productivity: A short biography', *NBER Working Paper*, 7471.

Hu, Z. L. and Khan, M., 1997a. 'Why is China growing so fast?' *Economic Issues*, No. 8, International Monetary Fund, Washington, D. C.

Hu, Z. L. and Khan, M., 1997b. 'Why is China growing so fast?' *IMF Staff Papers*, The International Monetary Fund, Washington, DC.

Jorgenson, D. W. and Griliches, Z., 1967. 'The explanation of productivity change', *Review of Economic Studies*, **34**, 349-383.

Jorgenson, D. W., Gollop, F. and Fraumeni, B., 1987. *Productivity and US Economic Growth*, Cambridge: Harvard University Press.

NBSC (National Bureau of Statistics of China), 1997. *China Statistical Yearbook 1997*, China Statistics Press, Beijing.

Nogami, K. and Li, K., 1995. 'An analysis of China's economic growth: estimation of TFP in the Chinese industrial sector', *ICSEAD Working Paper 95-1*.

Phelps, E. S. and Phelps, C., 1966. 'Factor price frontier estimation of a vintage production model', *Review of Economics and Statistics*, **48**, 261-265.

Rawski, T. G. and Zheng, Y. J. (eds), 1993. *Productivity and Reform in Chinese Industry*, Beijing, Social Science Doc. Publishing Co.

Rouen, R., 1995. *China's Economic Performance in International Perspective*, OECD Development Centre, Manuscript.

Sachs, J. and Woo, W. T., 2000. 'Understanding China's economic performance', *Journal of Political Economy*, **4**, 1-50.

Samuelson, P. A., 1962. 'Parable and realism in capital theory; The surrogate production function', *Review of Economic Studies*, **29**, 193-206.

Shapiro, M. D., 1987. 'Are cyclical fluctuations in productivity due more to supply shocks or demand shocks?' *American Economic Review*, **77**, 118-24.

Siegel, I. H., 1952. *Concepts and Measurement of Production and Productivity*, US Bureau of Labour Statistics, Washington.

Wang, Y. and Yao, Y., 2001. 'Sources of China's economic growth: 1952-99: incorporating human capital accumulation', *Policy Research Working Paper 2650*, World Bank, Development Research Group, Washington, D.C.

Woo, W. T., 1998. 'Chinese economic growth: sources and prospects', in M. Fouquin and F. Lemoine (eds), *The Chinese Economy*, London: Economica.

Young, A., 1992. 'Tale of two cities: factor accumulation and technical change in Hong Kong and Singapore', *NBER Macroeconomics Annual 1992*, Cambridge, Massachusetts; and London: MIT Press.

Young, A., 1995. 'The tyranny of numbers: confronting the statistical realities of the East Asian growth experience', *Quarterly Journal of Economics*, **110**, 641-680.

Young, A., 2000. 'Gold into base metals: productivity growth in the People's Republic of China during the reform period', *Journal of Political Economy*, **111**, 1221-1261.

3. Inter-Regional Output Spillovers

Nicolaas Groenewold, Guoping Lee and Anping Chen

INTRODUCTION[1]

China's emergence as a major player in the world economy in the last 25 years has been spectacular. Between 1953 and 2004 real GDP increased by an average of approximately 8.0 per cent annually and since the beginning of reforms in 1978 the average rate has been about 9.5 per cent per annum; this is an outstanding record, even by the standards of the rapid growth experienced by many countries in the 20th century.

This rapid and sustained growth has, however, been far from smooth. Growth in the often tumultuous pre-reform years fell as low as -27.3 per cent in 1961 as a result of the disastrous Great Leap Forward, from a high of 21.3 per cent in 1958. Even the post-1978 period has seen substantial, albeit smaller fluctuations in the range of three to fifteen per cent per annum. The history of recent China's growth experience is illustrated in Figure 3.1.

Growth has fluctuated not only over time, as illustrated in Figure 3.1, but the spatial distribution has also been far from uniform. Figure 3.2 illustrates the weighted standard deviation as a measure of the regional (inter-provincial) distribution of growth rates over the period 1953-2004. It shows that growth rates have varied considerably across space and that this dispersion itself has fluctuated over time. Not surprisingly, the spatial distribution of economic activity and welfare has been the subject of considerable interest to both policy-makers and academic researchers.

From its inception, the government of the People's Republic of China has shown awareness of and concern for the effects of persistent regional economic disparities. At the beginning of its history, particularly during the first two Five-Year Plans (1953-57, 1958-62), the People's Republic of China emphasised industrialisation and initially favoured the north-eastern provinces which already had a relatively advanced industrial structure.[2] However, at least from the Third Five-Year Plan covering 1966-70, there has been a major focus on regional differences in economic policy formulation. As a result of the worsening relationships with the Soviet Union at that time, there were serious concerns for the national security of inland China which,

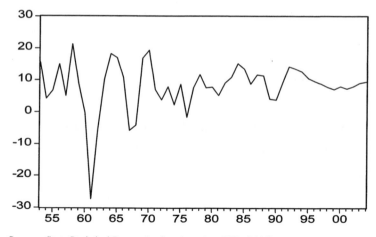

Sources: State Statistical Bureau (various issues) and Wu (2004).

Figure 3.1 Growth rate, 1953-2004

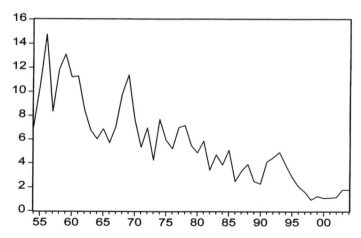

Sources: State Statistical Bureau (various issues) and Wu (2004)

Figure 3.2 Standard deviation of provincial growth rates, 1953-2004

coupled with a focus on Mao's principle of industrial self-sufficiency, resulted in a strong bias in favour of western and central regions at the expense of the more prosperous coastal region. Investment allocated to interior provinces increased to 71 per cent.

Emphasis began to shift, however, in the early 1970s with China's greater interaction with western economies and there was a gradual reduction in the discrimination in favour of the west. In the Fifth Five-Year Plan (1976-80) there was a shift of focus back to the coast with investment in coastal provinces being the highest since 1952; not surprisingly, growth in the east began to outstrip that in the rest of the country. By the Sixth Five-Year Plan (1981-85) there was an explicit policy of unbalanced growth, now favouring the coastal region under the argument that the limited development resources of the country should be allocated to those provinces with the natural characteristics which would benefit most from the investment.

This policy of unbalanced growth continued during the currency of the Seventh Five-Year Plan (1986-90) with an even higher proportion of government investment going to coastal provinces compared to the interior provinces. The basis of this strategy is the strong expectation that the faster-growing coastal region would act as a growth locomotive, taking the rest of the country with it.

More recent Plans have shifted the focus back towards the interior with growing concern about the implications for social instability of large and persistent differences in inter-provincial levels of economic welfare. In particular, in 1999 the central government announced the Great Western Development during the currency of the Ninth Five-Year Plan in which a considerable shift of resources to the western provinces was foreshadowed. It appears that there has been a noticeable increase in the resources going to the western region under this Development although, on the whole, the growth in the coastal provinces has continued to outstrip that in the west.

Most recently, during the Tenth Five-Year Plan the policy of 'Resurgence of North-Eastern Old Industry Base' was announced, focusing on the coastal province of Liaoning and the central provinces of Jilin and Heilongjiang. Historically, these three provinces had an industrial base considerably in advance of the rest of the country and were the location of many industries, such as automobiles, oil and chemicals which generated a per capita income level higher than most other provinces. By the late 1990s, however, they had fallen far behind the other coastal provinces.[3] The goal of the resurgence initiative is to reverse this long-term relative trend although, in contrast to the Great Western Development, it emphasizes the development of this region through a process of reforming corporate structure, renovating old technology and equipment and so on.

Notwithstanding the more recent shift in regional focus, there continues to be an expectation that the faster-growing coastal region will exert a beneficial influence on the remaining regions. This expectation depends on the existence of strong economic linkages between regions. While there has been much discussion of these inter-regional real output spillovers, there is remarkably little empirical work assessing their strength and timing. Three existing studies, Ying (2000), Brun, Combes and Renard (2002) and Zhang and Felmingham (2002), use annual provincial GDP data for the post-1978 period to assess the existence and strength of spillovers. More recently, the paper by Groenewold *et al.* (2005) uses data going back to 1953 in a vector autoregressive (VAR) model to assess these spillovers directly by simulating the effects of shocks in one region on other regions. They admit, though, that their results are sensitive to the order in which the regional output variables appear in the model, something that is inherently arbitrary although they argue that their order is a 'natural' one. They provide little information on the extent of the sensitivity nor do they explore methods of overcoming the sensitivity.

This chapter takes the Groenewold *et al.* paper as its point of departure and uses their three-region VAR framework to assess the sensitivity of their results as well as suggesting a range of alternative ways of reducing the sensitivity.

The remainder of the chapter is structured as follows. It first briefly reviews the literature on Chinese regional economic growth and, in more detail, on spillover analysis with a focus on work using Chinese data and justifies our choice of modelling strategy. It then describes the data. This is followed by the model estimation and simulation. The conclusions are presented in the final section.

THE LITERATURE

There is a rapidly growing literature on regional economic growth in China. Most of this literature is, however, concerned with long-run questions which are the traditional concern of growth theory. Thus much of the literature is cast in terms of the convergence debate which focuses on whether there are persistent disparities between regions (usually provinces in China), whether these disparities will disappear of their own accord (the 'convergence' question) and, if not, what are the factors that determine the equilibrium disparities (the conditioning variables in 'conditional convergence').[4]

While most of the discussion of Chinese regional economic activity has been in the convergence framework, little has focused on the short-term fluctuations in output and in particular on the dynamic interaction between regional output levels which is necessary to address the spillover issue identified in the first section as the focus of the present chapter. Indeed, there is little econometric work analysing spillovers for any country.

A set of papers using a modelling approach similar to the one used in Groenewold *et al.* (2005) and in the present chapter (VAR modelling) have been produced by researchers at the Federal Reserve Bank of San Francisco: Sherwood-Call (1988), Cromwell (1992) and Carlino and DeFina (1995). Of these, the last is a specific analysis of the inter-regional spillover question and applies the VAR model to eight US regions to assess the effects of shocks to income growth in one region on income growth in other regions. Carlino and DeFina use 60 years of annual per capita income growth data for eight US regions to estimate and simulate a VAR model, reporting tests of block exogeneity, impulse response functions (IRFs) and forecast error variance decompositions (FEVDs). They find significant and persistent spillover effects and suggest that an understanding of these is important to the formulation of effective regional economic policy.

Other more recent papers in the same analytical vein are by Clark (1998), Rissman (1999) and Kouparitsas (2002). Kouparitsas uses a model and data similar to that used by Carlino and DeFina but a more sophisticated decomposition of income into trend and cyclical components. In contrast to the earlier findings, he concludes that regional spillovers account for a negligible part of regional income fluctuations in the US. Thus, while the use of the VAR model is well-established in US regional research, results are far from clear.

To our knowledge, only four papers have explicitly examined inter-regional spillovers for China, each of which uses a different method of analysis. The first, by Ying (2000) applies 'exploratory spatial data analysis' which uses time-series data for provincial growth rates to compute (static) relationships between each province's growth rate with those geographically near to it. Both positive and negative relationships are found with the strongest significant influence being exerted by Guangdong province which was for this reason identified as the core. Four of the five adjacent provinces showed a significant relationship to Guangdong growth: there were positive spillovers to Hainan and Guangxi but negative ones to Hunan and Jiangxi. Thus Ying found significant growth relationships between the provinces. However, the technique of spatial data analysis is essentially one of static growth correlations which does not permit the analysis of the strength and timing of the relationships, questions that are also vital for policy-formulation and central to the interest of this chapter.

The second paper to explicitly assess the nature of regional spillovers in China is by Brun, Combes and Renard (2002). They use provincial-level time series data for real per capita growth rates for the period 1981-98 to estimate a set of conventional provincial growth equations which are modified to include the variables representing the coastal, central and western regions. This modification is designed to capture the inter-regional spillovers and allows them to test the significance of spillovers from the coastal region to individual provinces in the other two. They find significant spillovers from the coastal region to provinces in the central region but no effect on the western region. They do not, however, entertain the possibility of spillovers from central and western regions and, perhaps more importantly, they do not incorporate feedback effects but treat the regional variables as exogenous in their growth equations. They are therefore able only to test for significance and not to analyse the shape of dynamic interactions between the regions.

The third paper to analyse regional spillovers in China is by Zhang and Felmingham (2002) who analyse it as an addition to a study of the relationship between exports, foreign direct investment and growth in China at the provincial level. For their spillover work they group the provinces into three traditional regions of coast, centre and west and assess the significance of spillovers from the coast to the centre and the west and from the centre to the west. Their framework is similar to that of Brun *et al.* in that they simply add a regional spillover term to otherwise conventional growth equations. Their results are clear-cut and similar to Brun *et al.*'s in that they find spillovers from the coast to the centre but, in contrast to Brun *et al.*'s, they also find spillover to the west from both the coast and the centre. Like the previous papers, they do not include any dynamic effects, using just a contemporaneous spillover term, nor do they allow for endogenous feedback.

The final extant paper is by Groenewold *et al.* (2005) which uses annual data for three regions (conventionally defined as coastal, central and western) for the period 1953-2003 to estimate and simulate a VAR model. In that paper it is found that there are strong spillovers from the coastal region to both other regions, from the central region to the western region but that shocks to the western region have no flow-on effect for the other two regions. They thus reach a tentative policy conclusion that developing the coastal region is likely to indirectly benefit the other two regions.

In this chapter we follow the Groenewold *et al.* analysis by using a VAR model since it provides flexibility in the analysis of dynamic interactions between the regions. Moreover, it is parsimonious in its data requirements and does not require the imposition of a prior theoretical framework. As stated in the previous section, we extend their analysis by subjecting their results to sensitivity testing and assess a variety of possible ways in which the sensitivity may be reduced.

THE DATA

The data used are recently available annual series on real provincial GDP for the period 1953-2003.[5] The sources of the data are two-fold: the early data come from Wu (2004) who obtained the 1953-95 series from China's GDP Data 1952-95 (State Statistical Bureau, 1997). Data for 1996-2002 come from the Statistical Yearbook of China (State Statistical Bureau, various years) and for 2003 from the China Statistical Abstract (State Statistical Bureau, 2004). Population data used for the computation of per capita output were taken from Comprehensive Statistics Data and Materials on 50 Years of New China (State Statistical Bureau, 1999) for the period to 1998 and thereafter from the Statistical Yearbook of China.

We use the provincial real GDP series to compute three regional real GDP series for the conventionally defined coastal, central and western regions. The composition of these three regions is as follows. Coastal: Beijing, Tianjin, Hebei, Guangdong, Shandong, Fujian, Zhejiang, Jiangsu, Shanghai, Liaoning, Guangxi; Central: Shanxi, Inner Mongolia, Jilin, Heilongjiang, Anhui, Jiangxi, Henan, Hubei, Hunan; Western: Sichuan, Guizhou, Yunnan, Shaanxi, Gansu, Qinghai, Ningxia, Xinjiang.[6]

Before proceeding to the estimation and simulation results we need to attend to a preliminary matter. In empirical analysis based on time-series data it is customary to assess the stationarity of the data and to difference the data if non-stationary (unless the variables are cointegrated). Groenewold *et al.* (2005) contains an exhaustive discussion of the stationarity of the (logs of) real output for the three regions for the period 1953-2003. They find that all three series are trend stationary if the trend is allowed to break at 1978 with a further possible break at 1966. Without repeating their tests, we estimate our model in (log) levels with trend and breaks in trend and level at both 1966 and 1978 before eliminating possible irrelevant break terms.

THE RESULTS

In this section we report the results of our exploration. We begin by setting out the VAR framework and then report our estimation and simulation results, starting with the base case as reported in Groenewold *et al.* (2005) which is based on the use of log levels of the variables entered into the model in their 'natural ordering' of coastal, central and western regions. We then report the sensitivity of these results to the variable ordering before exploring various methods of reducing this sensitivity.

The VAR Model

Like Groenewold *et al.*, we use a vector-autoregressive (VAR) framework to explore the empirical relationship between the three regional output variables. Since we extend their analysis by paying particular attention to the sensitivity of the simulations to the model specification, it is useful first to set out the model and the derived impulse response functions (IRFs) in some detail.

We start from a general linear pth-order dynamic model in the n-vector of variables $\underline{x}_t$:

$$B(0)\underline{x}_t = \underline{b}_0 + B(L)\underline{x}_{t-1} + \underline{\varepsilon}_t \qquad (3.1)$$

where $B(0)$ is an *(n×n)* matrix of coefficients capturing the contemporaneous effects between the xs and $B(L)$ is a pth-order matrix polynomial in the lag operator, L:

$$B(L) \equiv B(1) + B(2)L + B(3)L^2 + .. + B(p)L^{p-1} \qquad (3.2)$$

and $L^j \underline{x}_t \equiv \underline{x}_{t-j}$. The εs are the structural error terms which are mutually independent. Our dynamic analysis consists of shocking one of these errors at a time and tracing the effects on all the *x*s over time, the results being captured in the impulse-response functions (IRFs).

The model in (3.1) cannot be estimated as it stands since it is not identified. Instead the (reduced-form) VAR is usually estimated. It is derived from (3.1) as:

$$\underline{x}_t = \underline{a}_0 + A(L)\underline{x}_{t-1} + \underline{e}_t \tag{3.3}$$

where $\underline{a}_0 \equiv B(0)^{-1}\underline{b}_0, A(L) \equiv B(0)^{-1}B(L)$ and $\underline{e}_t \equiv B(0)^{-1}\underline{\varepsilon}_t$. This system of equations can be validly estimated using OLS but, at best, we can obtain estimates of the reduced-form errors (rather than the structural errors) in the form of VAR residuals.

The moving-average (MA) form of the model is used for generating the IRFs and is derived from the (reduced-form) VAR model, equation (3.3), as:

$$\underline{x}_t = \underline{c}_0 + C(L)\underline{e}_t \tag{3.4}$$

where $C(L) \equiv (I - A(L)L)^{-1}$, $\underline{c}_0 \equiv C(L)\underline{a}_0$ and I is the identity matrix of appropriate order.

Since we wish to simulate the effects of shocks to the structural errors, we need to identify the εs. There are various ways of accomplishing this. The standard approach (the approach used in Groenewold *et al.*, 2005) is to use a Choleski decomposition of the contemporaneous covariance matrix of the VAR errors, Σ:

$$\Sigma = PP'$$

where P is a lower triangular n-matrix and P' denotes the transpose of P. The structural errors are then written as

$$\underline{\varepsilon}_t = P^{-1}\underline{e}_t \tag{3.5}$$

which are contemporaneously uncorrelated and have a unit variance, given the properties of the P matrix. The effect of a shock to the *j*th error on the *i*th *x* variable after an elapse of τ periods is given by the value of the relevant IRF at τ:

$$IRF_{ij\tau} = \underline{i}'_i C(\tau)P\underline{i}_j \tag{3.6}$$

where $\underline{i}_k$ is an n-vector of zeros except for a 1 in the *k*th position and $C(\tau)$ is the τth matrix in the matrix polynomial $C(L)$.

A potentially serious drawback of this approach, the effects of which we explore at some length in what follows, is that the P matrix is not unique and therefore the IRFs are not unique. In particular, in the standard applications of the Choleski approach the IRFs depend on the order in which the variables are listed in the model, an ordering which often has an arbitrary element. This weakness is mitigated where a particular ordering can be justified *a priori* or where the contemporaneous correlation between the VAR errors is weak.[7]

The Base Case

Before deriving the IRFs, we need to attend to the matter of lag length in the VAR model. Groenewold *et al.* found that two lags were sufficient to eliminate all autocorrelation in the equation residuals. Given that we use the same data and, initially, the same model specification, we focus on results derived from a model with two lags of the (logs of) three regional output variables as well as a trend, intercept and breaks at 1966 and 1978 if significant. The base case is for the variable ordering: coastal, central, western which Groenewold *et al.* call their 'natural ordering'.

The estimated coefficients for this model are taken from Groenewold *et al.* and are reported in Table 3.1. The degree of explanatory power of all the equations is very high which is not surprising since they are estimated in log levels and have a strong trend. The trend is significant in all equations. The level break terms are generally only of marginal significance but the trend breaks are significant in at least one equation, with the 1966 term significant in all three. We therefore retain all the break dummy variables.

The IRFs for shocks to coastal, central and western, again taken from the Groenewold *et al.* paper, are reproduced in Figures 3.3, 3.4 and 3.5. The effects appear quite plausible in the light of earlier work by Brun *et al.* (2002). The overall flow of spillovers is from the coast to the centre and from the centre to the west but with little return effect of the west on the other two regions. The greater part of the positive spillover in all three cases is completed in about 3 years although there are subsequent dampened cyclical effects for a further period of up to 10 years.

However, the results are not insensitive to the ordering of the variables in the model, a potential problem we highlighted when discussing the Choleski identification procedure above. While it may be argued that there is certain naturalness to the ordering of coastal, central and western regions which underlies the simulations reported in Figures 3.3, 3.4 and 3.5, there are plausible alternatives. When we consider these the results are quite dramatic: we find that the order of the second and third variables has little effect on the nature of the IRFs but that the identity of the first-ordered variable is crucial. Indeed, the shape of the IRFs for the effects of shocks to the coastal region are largely determined by the fact that coastal is first in the variable-ordering – the IRFs for shocks to the central region are very similar to those reported for the coastal region in Figure 3.3 if the central region is put first in the

Table 3.1 Estimated VAR model for the base case

Regressor	Coastal Coefficient	t-stat	Central Coefficient	t-stat	Western Coefficient	t-stat
Lco(-1)	0.4164	0.99	-0.3479	-0.83	-0.0744	-0.19
Lco(-2)	-0.3722	-0.99	-0.1680	-0.45	-0.4566	-1.32
Lce(-1)	0.7067	1.44	1.0905	2.26	0.3406	0.76
Lce(-2)	-0.2226	-0.48	-0.0845	-0.18	0.0995	0.23
Lwe(-1)	-0.1259	-0.46	0.1855	0.68	0.5901	2.33
Lwe(-2)	0.0396	0.15	-0.2410	-0.90	-0.2493	-1.00
Constant	2.2766	5.38	2.1079	5.06	2.3051	5.93
Trend	0.0168	2.41	0.0153	2.23	0.0181	2.83
DU1	-0.0440	-0.69	-0.0247	-0.39	-0.1093	-1.87
DU2	-0.1045	-1.72	-0.0604	-1.01	-0.0472	-0.85
DT1	0.0372	3.17	0.0289	2.50	0.0480	4.45
DT2	0.0128	1.58	0.0165	2.05	0.0100	1.34
$\bar{R}^2$	0.9967		0.9956		0.9964	
P-value	0.7560		0.3920		0.063[a]	

Notes: Lco is the log of real GDP for the coastal region, Lce is the log of real GDP for the central region and Lwe is the log of real GDP for the western region. The deterministic variables, in addition to the trend, are DU1, DU2 which are the level breaks at 1966 and 1978 and DT1 and DT2 which are the corresponding trend breaks. The p-value is that of Q(15) .
[a] Only the Q-statistics at lags 1 and 15 have p-values less than 0.1.

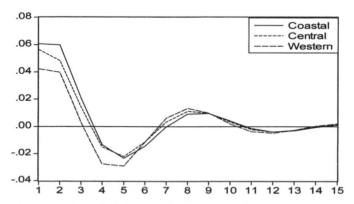

Figure 3.3 Response to one s.e. shock to coastal: base model

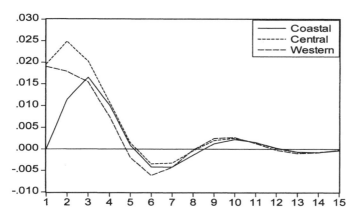

Figure 3.4 Response to one s.e. shock to central: base model

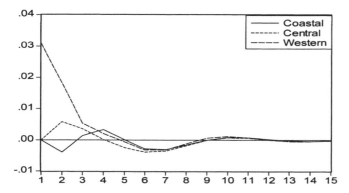

Figure 3.5 Response to one s.e. shock to western: base model

model; the same goes for the western region. This sensitivity to ordering results from the high contemporaneous correlation of the equation residuals which makes the data less informative about the effects of individual regional shocks than they would otherwise be. The correlations are reported in Table 3.2. The correlations are clearly very high and the sensitivity to ordering is therefore not surprising. Groenewold *et al.* (2005) resolved this problem by arguing that their ordering was a natural one based on the size and level of development of the three regions, as well as precedents in earlier literature. In this chapter we explore the possible source of such correlations and consequent re-specification of the model to reduce the correlation and, therefore, the sensitivity problem.

Table 3.2 Residual correlations for the base model

	Lco	Lce	Lwe
Lco	1.0000	0.9457	0.7685
Lce		1.0000	0.8378
Lwe			1.0000

Notes: Lco is the log of real GDP for the coastal region, Lce is the log of real GDP for
the central region and Lwe is the log of real GDP for the western region.

Alternative Specifications

We experiment with eight alternatives to the base case, labelled
unimaginatively but conveniently as models 1-8. They are as follows:

Model 1: We conjecture that the source of the high residual correlations is
the fact that historically the regional shocks have been dominated by
aggregate national shocks. The first alternative we try, therefore, is to include
the (log) national output level as an additional variable in the model with the
expectation that it will capture this common shock, leaving the regional
variables to capture just regional shocks.

Model 2: An alternative conjecture is that the high residual correlation is
the result of a common trend in the data which is evident from a casual
inspection of the data; in this case a transformation of the variables to (log)
first-differences (i.e., annual growth rates) should reduce the sensitivity. Our
second alternative is therefore to cast the model in terms of growth rates.

Model 3: An alternative transformation of the variables which may be used
to address the common trend problem is to cast it in terms of growth rates
relative to the national level. This is used in model 3.

Model 4: It is possible that the common trend reflects underlying
population growth in each region. One way to remove this effect is to use the
variables in per capita terms which we do in model 4.

Model 5: This model combines the approaches of models 1 and 4 and
specifies the model in terms of (log) per capita output and includes the
corresponding national variable.

Model 6: A sixth variant is to measure the regional outputs as ratios of
national output which we do in model 6 (in logs).

Model 7: In this model we combine characteristics of models 2 and 5 and
use variables in the form of growth rates of output per capita in the three
regions.

Model 8: Our final version specifies the model in terms of per capita output
growth rates relative to that of the nation as a whole.

In the interest of keeping the chapter within manageable limits, we do not
report the estimation and simulation results for all eight alternative models.
Instead, we begin by discarding the approaches which yielded no appreciable

Table 3.3 Residuals correlation matrices for models 1, 2, 4, 5 and 7

Model 1: Three regions and the nation: log outputs			
	Lna	Lco	Lce	Lwe
Lna	1.0000	0.9397	0.9503	0.8771
Lco		1.0000	0.9432	0.7396
Lce			1.0000	0.8242
Lwe				1.0000
Model 2: Three regions: output growth rates			
	Gco	Gce	Gwe	
Gco	1.0000	0.9560	0.8247	
Gce		1.0000	0.8750	
Gwe			1.0000	
Model 4: Three regions: per capita outputs			
	Lcop	Lcep	Lwep	
Lcop	1.0000	0.9407	0.7420	
Lcep		1.0000	0.7863	
Lwep			1.0000	
Model 5: Three regions and the nation: output per capita			
	Lnap	Lcop	Lcep	Lwep
Lnap	1.0000	0.9417	0.9519	0.8756
Lcop		1.0000	0.9474	0.7340
Lcep			1.0000	0.8052
Lwep				1.0000
Model 7: Three regions: growth rates per capita			
	Gcop	Gcep	Gwep	
Gcop	1.0000	0.9503	0.8148	
Gcep		1.0000	0.8546	
Gwep			1.0000	

Notes: Lco, Lce, Lwe and Lna are the log of real GDP for the coastal, central and western regions and for the nation, respectively; Gco, Gce and Gwe are the corresponding growth rates, Lcop, Lcep and Lwep are the log per capita outputs and Gcop, Gcep and Gwep are the corresponding per capita growth rates.

resolution of the sensitivity problem. They are models 1, 2 4, 5 and 7. In all these five cases, the residual correlations were not much reduced from the base case and the IRFs were still very sensitive to the ordering of the variables in the model. For these models we report only the residual correlation matrices. These are given in Table 3.3. Clearly in all cases the correlations are still quite substantial and it is not surprising that the IRFs still show considerable sensitivity to the ordering of the variables in the model.

The next group consists of three models: 3, 6 and 8, all of which showed limited improvements compared to the base case as is evident from their residual correlations shown in Table 3.4. The correlations are considerably reduced, some being negative. It is not surprising that there is also less sensitivity of the IRFs to the ordering of the variables in the model. It is no longer the case that the IRF is largely determined by the order rather than the identity of the variables. Nevertheless, there is still some sensitivity. Thus,

Table 3.4 Residual correlations for models 3, 6 and 8

Model 3: Three regions: relative growth rates			
	Rgco	Rgce	Rgwe
Rgco	1.0000	0.5130	-0.3456
Rgce		1.0000	-0.0954
Rgwe			1.0000
Model 6: Three regions: relative per capita output			
	Rlcop	Rlcep	Rlwep
Rlcop	1.0000	0.5370	-0.5632
Rlcep		1.0000	-0.3706
Rlwep			1.0000
Model 8: Three regions: relative per capita growth rates			
	Rgcop	Rgcep	Rgwep
Rgcop	1.0000	0.5465	-0.4692
Rgcep		1.0000	-0.3043
Rgwep			1.0000

Notes: Rgco, Rgce and Rgwe are the relative growth rates of output for the three regions: coastal, central and western; Rlcop, Rlcep and Rlwep are the corresponding relative per capita log outputs and Rgcop, Rgcep and Rgwep are the corresponding relative per capita growth rates.

for example, using model 3 (growth rates of relative outputs) a shock to the coastal region always has the largest effect on itself and a positive effect on the central region although almost no effect on the other two regions when it is not in the first position in the model.

Thus we searched for a further alternative. It was based on the output of model 1. Recall that this was simply the original model (log real outputs) with the national variable added to it. The estimated model is reported in Table 3.5. The log national output variable (Lna) is at least marginally significant in all the regional equations of the extended model and appears to have absorbed some of the explanatory role previously assigned to the trend term, the significance of which has been significantly reduced. It is interesting that the first trend break dummy variable is still consistently significant.

The IRFs generated using the estimated model in Table 3.5 are sensitive to the ordering as has been pointed out above. However, we have argued previously that the sensitivity is likely to be due to the presence of a strong national component in all regional shocks when the national variable is omitted from the model. If we then recognise that using the Choleski decomposition effectively loads the common component onto the first-listed variable, it seems reasonable to always list Lna as the first variable in the model and assess sensitivity only to variation in the ordering of the remaining three. Taking this approach, we find that there is very little sensitivity to the ordering of Lco, Lce and Lwe. The IRFs for the three regions for the order: coastal, central and western are reported in Figures 3.6, 3.7 and 3.8.

Table 3.5 Estimated VAR results for model 1

Regressor	National		Coastal		Central		Western	
	coefficient	t-value	coefficient	t-value	coefficient	t-value	coefficient	t-value
Lna(-1)	2.1835	2.70	1.7251	1.74	1.5023	1.54	1.5933	1.75
Lna(-2)	-1.1060	-1.34	-1.6153	-1.60	-1.7361	-1.75	-1.2647	-1.36
Lco(-1)	-0.8619	-1.71	-0.2764	-0.45	-0.8810	-1.45	-0.7629	-1.34
Lco(-2)	0.2564	0.51	0.5113	0.83	0.6766	1.11	0.3075	0.54
Lce(-1)	0.2741	0.62	0.4352	0.80	0.7410	1.39	0.1679	0.34
Lce(-2)	-0.0074	-0.02	-0.1180	-0.24	0.0996	0.20	0.1320	0.29
Lwe(-1)	-0.5410	-1.46	-0.6860	-1.52	-0.2522	-0.57	0.0384	0.09
Lwe(-2)	0.2336	0.69	0.4934	1.19	0.2764	0.68	0.0854	0.22
Const	1.9130	1.86	1.9216	1.53	2.3379	1.88	1.6053	1.39
Trend	0.0124	1.37	0.0091	0.82	0.0117	1.08	0.0088	0.87
DU1	-0.0506	-0.85	-0.0323	-0.44	0.0035	0.05	-0.1109	-1.66
DU2	-0.0505	-0.83	-0.1026	-1.37	-0.0803	-1.09	-0.0306	-0.44
DT1	0.0371	3.67	0.0428	3.46	0.0326	2.68	0.0539	4.74
DT2	0.0117	1.76	0.0100	1.23	0.0135	1.67	0.0078	1.03
$\overline{R}^2$	0.9973		0.9968		0.9957		0.9965	

Notes: Lco, Lce, Lwe and Lna are the log of real GDP for the coastal, central and western regions and for the nation, respectively. The deterministic variables, in addition to the trend, are DU1, DU2 which are the level breaks at 1966 and 1978 and DT1 and DT2 which are the corresponding trend breaks.

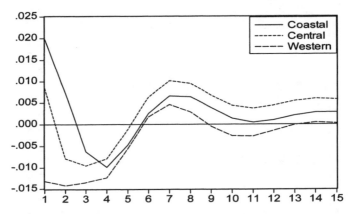

Figure 3.6 Response to one s.e. shock to coastal: model 1

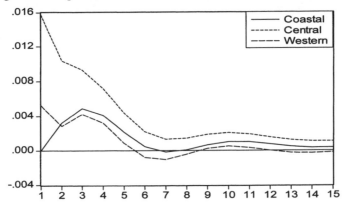

Figure 3.7 Response to one s.e. shock to central: model 1

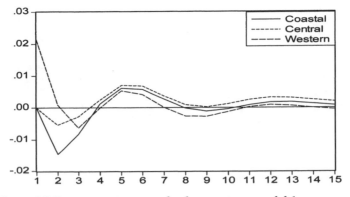

Figure 3.8 Response to one s.e. shock to western: model 1

The shock to the coastal region has the largest effect on that region itself. There is also a significant spillover to the central region (about half the size of the effect on Lco) but the initial effect on the western region is negative, perhaps reflecting resource diversion. Over time the relative magnitudes of the effects on Lco and Lce are reversed with the larger effect being consistently on the central region and still a negligible effect on the western region. A shock to the central region has less spillover effects than the coastal shock. Again, the largest effect is on the central region itself but there is also a positive spillover to the western region (the zero initial effect on the coastal region is forced by the Choleski orthogonalization). Over time the effect on the central region itself continues to dominate and there is a persistent effect on the coastal region but the effect on the western region is quickly dampened. Finally, there are only limited spillovers from the western region to the other two (again, the initial zero effects on the other two regions are forced by the Choleski orthogonalization). Over time there is a small negative effect on the other two regions followed by a largely offsetting positive effect after 4 or 5 years.

These results are similar but not identical to those reported by Groenewold *et al.*(2005), allowing us to conclude that, while it is important to assess the sensitivity of the spillovers to the model specification, it appears that in our preferred model there is not a significant reversal of the conclusions drawn from the simpler model.

From a policy perspective we may draw some tentative implications.[8] Since the spillover effects from the coastal region are the largest, particularly to the central region, stimulating the growth of the coast is not only beneficial for the region itself but also for the rest of the country, although the effect on the western region is at best modest. It appears that the spillover from the centre to the west is stronger so that stimulating the central region will have benefits for the west as well.

Notwithstanding these spillover effects, it is true that the own effects dominate in all regions. For this reason, while stimulating the coastal region has beneficial effects on the centre, the effect on the coast itself is greater and the already substantial disparities in output per capita between the two regions will be exacerbated if there is a primary reliance on the stimulation of the coastal region. This is even more so for the western region which received very small spillovers from the other two. From this perspective, policies which focus particularly on the west such as the Great Western Development will be needed if the west is to experience sustained catch-up or, indeed, even maintain its position relative to the country as a whole.

CONCLUSIONS

This chapter has reported on the empirical assessment of inter-regional spillovers in China. We used a three-region model, based on the common division of China into coastal, central and western regions. Our point of departure was a recent paper by Groenewold *et al.* (2005) which used a three-region VAR model to investigate inter-regional spillovers in China. While their results are interesting and suggestive, they admitted that they are sensitive to the order in which the variables appear in the model, a sensitivity which reflects the high contemporaneous correlations of the residuals of the estimated model. Although they argued that their ordering is a natural one, other orderings are possible and should be explored. This is the exercise we carried out in the research reported in this chapter.

We canvassed eight alternative models, many of which showed an improved performance in terms of the strength of residual correlations although they still retained some sensitivity to variable-ordering. Our preferred approach was to use a four-variable model, with the fourth variable being the (log of) national output. Then, on the argument that the high residual correlations are the result of a strong common component in the shocks to the individual regional equations, we always chose the national output variable as the first in the model so that it would be allocated the common component of the shocks. After this allocation was made, the results were relatively insensitive to the order of the three regional output variables and the impulse response functions were quite stable with respect to variable ordering.

The preferred model showed spillover effects not greatly at odds with the results reported in the Groenewold *et al.* paper and, indeed, with those reported in earlier papers by Brun *et al.* (2002) and Zhang and Felmingham (2002) using different modelling techniques. The overall results are that there are mild spillovers from the coastal and central regions but not from the western region.

Despite our resolution of the ordering problem, the results are sufficiently different from previous findings that further investigation is warranted of this important issue – perhaps with further disaggregation of the regions and, ultimately, using a more complicated structural model in contrast to the VAR model used in this study. While the VAR model is straightforward to estimate and simulate and it is parsimonious with respect to the data requirements (an important consideration when carrying out empirical research on the Chinese economy), it does not allow one to identify the channels of influence which are crucial for the formulation of policy designed to exploit the presence of spillovers.

NOTES

1. This section draws on the general discussion of regional development and policy in Wu (2004, particularly Chapters 5 and 6) and Demurger *et al.* (2002).
2. It has been argued that this was due to the earlier Japanese influence during their occupation before 1945. This is controversial, however; see, e.g., Demurger *et al.*(2002).
3. For example, the GDP of Liaoning was larger than Guangdong's in 1978 but in 2004 GDP in Guangdong is more than twice of that of Liaoning.
4. The literature goes back at least to the work of Kuznets (1955) and Williamson (1965); the concept was more recently developed in Barro and Sala-i-Martin (1992). There is a vast empirical literature. Some important papers with a bias to Chinese applications are: Chen and Fleisher (1996), Fleisher and Chen (1997), Kanbur and Zhang (1999), Yao and Zhang (2001a, 2001b), Demurger (2001), Chang (2002), Lu (2002), Cai, Wang and Du (2002), Yang (2002), Demurger *et al.* (2002) and Bao *et al.* (2002).
5. Since beginning this project, the 2004 data have become available. We have not updated our data set in the interests of preserving comparability with the results reported in Groenewold *et al.* (2005) whose sample period ends at 2003.
6. Note that Hainan, Chongqing and Tibet are missing. Hainan is included in Guangdong and Chongqing in Sichuan. Tibet has been omitted altogether due to missing data.
7. For an extensive discussion of this issue in a bivariate context, see Ender (2004).
8. It is important to stress that they are tentative since the analysis reported here is only a first step in the assessment of the evidence and, moreover, the model used has no structural features which would permit the identification of channels of influence or specific policies to be used for stimulation.

REFERENCES

Bao, S., Chang, G. H., Sachs, J. D. and Woo, W. T., 2002. 'Geographic factors and China's regional development under market reforms, 1978–1998', *China Economic Review*, **13**, 89-111.

Barro, R. J. and Sala-i-Martin, X., 1992. 'Convergence', *Journal of Political Economy*, **100**, 223-251.

Brun, J. F., Combes, J. L. and Renard, M. F., 2002. 'Are there spillover effects between the coastal and noncoastal regions in China?' *China Economic Review*, **13**, 161-169.

Cai, F., Wang, D. and Du, Y., 2002. 'Regional disparity and economic growth in China: the impact of labour market distortions', *China Economic Review*, **13**, 197-212.

Carlino, G. and DeFina, R., 1995. 'Regional income dynamics', *Journal of Urban Economics*, **37**, 88-106.

Chang, G. H., 2002, 'The cause and cure of China's widening income disparity', *China Economic Review*, **13**, 335-340.

Chen, J. and Fleisher, B. M., 1996. 'Regional inequality and economic growth in China', *Journal of Comparative Economics*, **22**, 141-164.

Clark, T. E., 1998. 'Employment fluctuations in the U.S. regions and industries: the roles of national, region-specific and industry-specific shocks', *Journal of Economics*, **16**, 202-229.

Cromwell, A. B., 1992. 'Does California drive the west? An econometric investigation of regional spillovers', *Federal Reserve Bank of San Francisco Economic Review*, **2**, 15-25.

Demurger, S., 2001. 'Infrastructure development and economic growth: an explanation for regional disparities in China?' *Journal of Comparative Economics*, **29**, 95-117.

Demurger, S., Sachs, J. D., Woo, W. T., Bao, S. and Chang, G., 2002. 'The relative contributions of location and preferential policies in China's regional development: being in the right place and having the right incentives', *China Economic Review*, **13**, 444-465.

Enders, W., 2004. *Applied Econometric Time Series*, 2nd ed., Wiley, New York.

Fleisher, B. M. and Chen, J., 1997. 'The coast-noncoast income gap, productivity and regional economic policy in China', *Journal of Comparative Economics*, **25**, 220-236.

Groenewold, N., Lee, G. and Chen, A., 2005. 'Regional output spillovers in China: estimates from a VAR model', *Discussion Paper No.05-05*, Department of Economics, University of Western Australia.

Kanbur, R. and Zhang, X., 1999. 'Which regional inequality? The evolution of rural-urban and inland-coastal inequality in China from 1983 to 1995', *Journal of Comparative Economics*, **27**, 686-701.

Kouparitsas, M. A., 2002. 'Understanding US regional cyclical comovement: how important are spillovers and common shocks?' *Federal Reserve Bank of Chicago Economic Perspectives*, 4th quarter, 30-41.

Kuznets, S., 1955. 'Economic growth and income inequality', *American Economic Review*, **45**, 1-28.

Lu, D., 2002. 'Rural-urban income disparity: impact of growth, allocative efficiency and local growth welfare', *China Economic Review*, **13**, 419-429.

Rissman, E. R., 1999. 'Regional employment growth and the business cycle', *Federal Reserve Bank of Chicago Economic Perspectives*, 4th quarter, 21-39.

Sherwood-Call, C., 1988. 'Exploring the relationship between national and economic fluctuations', *Federal Reserve Bank of San Francisco Economic Review*, summer, 15-25.

State Statistical Bureau, 2004. *China Statistical Abstract*, Statistical Publishing House of China, Beijing.

State Statistical Bureau, 1999. *Comprehensive Statistics Data and Materials on 50 Year of New China*, Statistical Publishing House of China, Beijing.

State Statistical Bureau, 1997. *China's GDP data 1952-95*, Dongbei University of Economics and Finance Press, Daliang.

State Statistical Bureau, various issues. *Statistical Yearbook of China*, Statistical Publishing House of China, Beijing.

Williamson, J., 1965. 'Regional inequality in the process of national development', *Economic Development and Cultural Change*, **17**, 3-84.

Wu, Y., 2004. *China's Economic Growth: A Miracle with Chinese Characteristics*, London: Routledge Curzon.

Yang, D. T., 2002. 'What has caused regional inequality in China?' *China Economic Review*, **13**, 331-334.

Yao, S. and Zhang, Z., 2001a. 'Regional growth in China under economic reforms', *Journal of Development Studies*, **38**, 167-186.

Yao, S. and Zhang, Z., 2001b. 'On regional inequality and diverging clubs: a case study of contemporary China', *Journal of Comparative Economics*, **29**, 466-484.

Ying, L. G., 2000. 'Measuring the spillover effects: some Chinese evidence', *Papers in Regional Science*, **79**, 75-89.

Zhang Q. and Felmingham, B., 2002. 'The role of FDI, exports and spillover effects in the regional development of China', *Journal of Development Studies*, **38**, 157-178.

4.   Business Cycle and Growth

Yanrui Wu

Volatility in economic growth has often been viewed as undesirable because of its negative effect on social welfare (Rafferty 2004). Consequently, macroeconomic stability has for decades been an objective of government economic policy. However, if business cycle volatility is good for economic growth, gains associated with growth may overwhelm losses in welfare due to volatility and hence government policy to control volatility may actually harm growth (Kneller and Young 2001). In this case, government policy to reduce cyclical volatility might interfere with efforts to improve an economy's growth performance. On the contrary, if growth and volatility are negatively related, the welfare effect of business cycle could be very large and policy makers need to take this into consideration.

China's rapid economic growth in recent years has triggered a surge of interest in the Chinese economy. As a result, a huge literature has emerged.[1] There is however a major ignorance in the literature. The role of business cycle in China's economic growth has so far not been addressed by researchers. The objective of this study is to contribute to the understanding of the relationship between business cycle volatility and economic growth in China. This study thus enhances our knowledge of the rapidly growing Chinese economy. Some background issues about volatility and economic growth are presented first. This is followed by discussion of the analytical framework. The data issues and preliminary results are then described. Subsequently, some further analysis is reported. Finally, the chapter concludes with some summary remarks.

VOLATILITY AND GROWTH: THE BACKGROUND

Research on the relationship between volatility and growth has shifted from denial in the theoretical work (Lucas 1987) to fact-finding in the empirical literature (Ramey and Ramey 1995, Dawson and Stephenson 1997, and Dejuan and Gurr 2004). Traditionally, business cycle theory and growth theory have been treated as unrelated areas of macroeconomics (Ramey and Ramey 1995). This perspective was not changed until the appearance of several studies which noted the existence of a statistical relationship between growth and volatility (Zarnowitz and Moore 1986, Hamilton 1989 and Aizenman and Marion 1993). More recently, several authors have presented case studies of the OECD economies (Ramey and Ramey 1995), the US States (Dawson and Stephenson 1997) and the Canadian provinces (Dejuan and Gurr, 2004). While Kormendi and Meguire (1985) and Ramey and Ramey (1995) showed a significant relationship between growth and volatility, Dawson and Stephenson (1997) and Dejuan and Gurr (2004) provided inconclusive findings. The issue thus remains unresolved.

Current debate has focused on whether growth and volatility are positively or negatively related. Black (1987) argued that there may be two types of technologies, ie. high volatility, high growth and low volatility, low growth, and either can be adopted by a country. In either case, volatility and growth are positively related. Alternatively, Sandmo (1970) and Mirman (1971) showed that income uncertainty leads to increased saving and hence capital formation. To the extent that the latter leads to higher growth, a positive relationship between growth and volatility should be observed. Using a growth model emphasising learning-by-doing technology, Blackburn (1999) found that increased business cycle volatility actually raises the long-run growth potential of an economy. There are also reasons to believe the existence of a negative relationship between growth and volatility. For example, if there are irreversibilities in investment, then increased volatility can lead to lower investment and therefore slow growth (Pindyck 1991, Aizenman and Marion 1993). This negative relationship between volatility and growth is also confirmed in models proposed by Bean (1990) and Saint-Paul (1993).

Theoretical controversies are reflected in empirical findings. Kormendi and Meguire (1985) is one of the earlier studies which consider the relationship between volatility and growth. As part of their cross-country growth analysis, Kormendi and Meguire found that volatility is positively related to economic growth. They concluded that 1 per cent increase in the standard deviation of the rate of growth leads to 0.5 per cent increase in growth on average. Dejuan and Gurr (2004) also found a weak positive growth-volatility relationship using Canadian regional data. Other authors in the same camp include Grier and Tullock (1989) and Caporale and McKiernan (1996). The opposite conclusion was however drawn by Ramey and Ramey (1995). Their finding was disputed by Dawson *et al.* (2001) who argued that Ramey and Ramey's result might be biased due to measurement errors in cross-country data from the Penn World Tables (PWT). In addition, Lensink *et al.* (1999), Martin and Rogers (2000) and Kneller and Young (2001) also derived a significant negative relationship between growth and volatility.

Mainland China is divided into 31 administrative regions, i.e. provinces, autonomous regions and municipalities. Given the diversity and distance among the regions, cross-sectional variation in growth and volatility is expected. In addition, China has undertaken an ambitious reform programme since 1979. Changes associated with economic reform have caused great uncertainties in society. These uncertainties have been partly responsible for China's continuously high rate of domestic savings (see Figure 4.1). The latter may not be trivial in boosting China's economic growth which is still largely driven by factor accumulation (Wu 2003). Thus, it can be anticipated that volatility and growth in China may be positively related, in particular during the reform period.

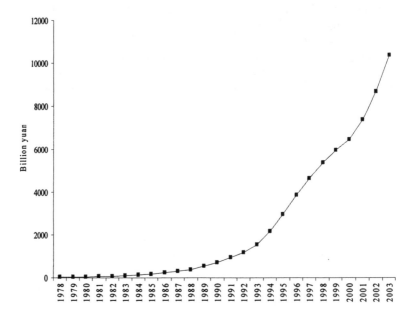

Sources: National Bureau of Statistics of China (2001, 2004).

Figure 4.1 China's household deposit 1978-2003

ANALYTICAL FRAMEWORK

The relationship between growth and volatility can be examined by the following growth equations, that is, equations (4.1), (4.2) and (4.3).[2] They are also called models I, II and III, respectively:

$$y_i = \alpha_0 + \alpha_1 s_i + \varepsilon_i \tag{4.1}$$

$$y_{it} = \beta_0 + \beta_1 \sigma_i + \sum_j^n \beta_j z_{jt} + \varepsilon_{it} \tag{4.2}$$

$$y_{it} = \lambda_0 + \lambda_1 \sigma_{it} + \sum_j^n \lambda_j z_{jt} + e_{it} \qquad (4.3)$$

where y_{it} is the rate of annual growth in per capita gross regional product (GRP) of the ith region over the period t; y_i and s_i are the mean and standard deviation of y_{it}, respectively; ε_i represents the white noise; ε_{it} is the disturbance term for equation (4.2) and normally distributed with zero mean and variance σ_i^2 and z_{jt}'s are the control variables; and e_{it} is a random error with a normal distribution of zero mean and variance σ_{it}^2.

Equation (4.1) is employed to examine the relationship between the mean rate and the standard deviation of annual growth among the regions. It can be estimated using the ordinary least square method. The sign and t-value of the estimated α_1 indicate the direction and significance of the relationship between growth and volatility.

Equation (4.2) is the panel data version of equation (4.1). In equation (4.2), it is assumed that the variance of the residual ε_{it} differs across regions but not across time. This assumption is relaxed in equation (4.3). Another feature of equation (4.2) is the introduction of region-specific control variables. It thus investigates the relationship between growth and volatility conditional on these regional characteristics. Equation (4.2) can be estimated using the maximum likelihood procedure.

The final model presented in equation (4.3) is the full version of the panel data model which of course removes some of the restrictive assumptions imposed on models I and II. In particular, it is assumed that the variance of the error term in equation (4.3) is different across regions as well as over time. This equation can also be estimated using the maximum likelihood procedure.

DATA ISSUES AND PRELIMINARY RESULTS

The annual rates of economic growth for Chinese regions are available for the period of 1954-2003. The first model is estimated using three samples which correspond to three periods of economic development in China. The purpose of looking at three time periods is to explore the variation over time while the regressions are still based on samples with a reasonable size. China's economic reform began in the rural sector in 1979 and in the urban sector in the middle 1980s. The division of the sample reflects these developments over time. The ordinary least square estimation results presented in Table 4.1 suggest a significantly positive relationship between volatility and growth across Chinese regions during the periods of 1979-2003 and 1984-2003. This relation for the entire sample period 1954-2003 is not statistically significant. These findings are consistent with a more even development strategy adopted by the Chinese government before economic reform took off in 1979. During the reform era, policy priority has been given to the development of the coastal areas, and the promotion of international trade and foreign direct investment. The findings in Table 4.1 imply that, during the period of economic transition, regions with higher year-to-year volatility in growth rates tend to have systematically higher growth rates. This relationship is clearly visualized in Figure 4.2, and is obviously not driven by outliers.

Table 4.1 Estimation results of Model I

Regressors	1984-2003	1979-2003	1954-2003
Intercept	6.014 (8.855)	5.771 (5.712)	5.792 (5.258)
Standard deviation	0.794 (5.140)	0.698 (3.178)	0.085 (0.111)
R^2	0.504	0.280	0.022
Standard deviation			
Mean	4.193	4.472	9.853
Minimum	2.098 (HLJ)	2.409 (HLJ)	7.072 (GX)
Maximum	8.476 (GD)	7.856 (GD)	12.912 (LN)

Notes: Numbers in parentheses are t-ratios. HLJ = Heilongjiang, GD = Guangdong, GX = Guangxi, and LN = Liaoning.

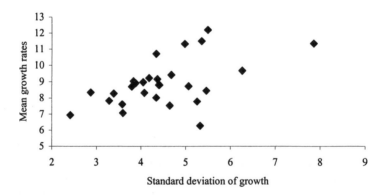

Figure 4.2 Relationship between mean and standard deviation of growth rate, 1979-2003

In models II and III, three control variables are introduced, that is, the ratio of capital formation over GRP, the ratio of government spending over GRP and logarithm of initial income. These variables are popular and robust ones used in the growth literature (Barro 1991, Levine and Renelt 1992). The model is estimated using an iterative maximum likelihood procedure in which the iteration stops when the estimated coefficients become stable. For models II and III, the reform era is the focus. The estimation results are presented in Tables 4.2 and 4.3.[3] Under the assumption of constant variance over time for each region (Model II), the relationship between volatility and growth is found to be positive and statistically significant. This relation holds even if three conditional variables are taken into consideration. According to Table 4.2, for every unit increase in the standard deviation, the rate of growth increases by about 0.4 units. To visualize this relation, the fitted mean rates of growth net of the impact of the control variables are plotted against the standard deviation in Figure 4.3 which shows clearly a positive linear relationship between the two variables.

Table 4.2 Estimation results of Model II

	Baseline model	Extended model
Constant	6.279 (9.294)*	8.159 (4.321)*
Standard deviation	0.443 (3.147)*	0.397 (2.312)**
Investment/output ratio		10.123 (6.652)*
Government/output ratio		-21.383 (-8.041)*
Log(initial income)		-1.027 (-1.788)***
Log likelihood	-2392.712	-2356.841
Standard deviation		
Mean	5.269	5.023
Minimum	2.767 (HLJ)	2.570 (HLJ)
Maximum	7.828 (GD)	7.656 (SC)

Notes: *, **and *** indicate significance at the level of 1%, 5% and 10% , respectively. HLJ = Heilongjiang, GD = Guangdong, and SC = Sichuan.

With the relaxation of the assumption of the constant variance over time, the relationship between volatility and growth is still found to be positive and statistically significant but the magnitude of the coefficient of standard deviation becomes small according to Table 4.3. With the inclusion of the control variables, the relationship is still significant and positive with the magnitude of the coefficient of standard deviation being even smaller. Table 4.3 illustrates that the average rate of growth increases by 0.239 units for every unit increase in volatility.

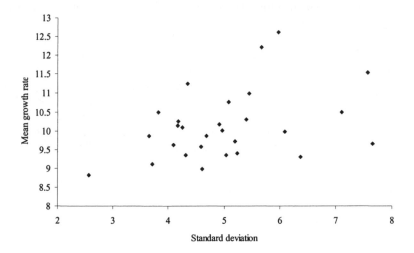

Note: The x-axis demonstrates the average growth rates net of the impact of the control variables. The latter is calculated using the results of model II presented in Table 4.2.

Figure 4.3 Relationship between growth rates and volatility

Table 4.3 Estimation results of Model III

	Baseline model	Extended model
Constant	7.283 (51.350)*	10.304 (129.066)*
Standard deviation	0.340 (4.582)*	0.239 (3271.943)*
Investment/output ratio		10.650 (25049.040)*
Government/output ratio		-21.018 (-15420.845)*
Log(initial income)		-1.533 (-72.274)*
Log likelihood	-1581.234	-1407.518

Note: All coefficients are significant at the level of 1%.

FURTHER ANALYSIS

The investigation in the preceding section can be extended further to cover several extra issues, that is, replacing the standard deviation by the variance of the rate of growth as used by some authors (Ramey and Ramey 1995), considering the relationship between innovation variance and growth, and exploring the impact of investment and government spending on volatility. These issues are in turn addressed in the following sections.

Rate and Variances of Growth

In the existing literature, the standard deviations of the error terms in models II and III are sometimes replaced by the variance of the error terms. The results are reported in Table 4.4 and they are very much the same as those in Table 4.2.[4] It is interesting to note that the most volatile economy is Guangdong which has for years been the frontrunner of economic reforms in China.

Table 4.4 Alternative Estimation Results of Model II

	Baseline model	Extended model
Constant	7.334 (9.631)*	9.272 (5.636)*
Standard deviation	0.042 (3.034)*	0.036 (2.043)**
Investment/output ratio		10.306 (6.800)*
Government/output ratio		-21.217 (-7.976)*
Log(initial income)		-1.106 (-1.937)***
Log likelihood	-2392.867	-2357.371
Variance		
Mean	29.288	26.612
Minimum	7.948 (HLJ)	6.810 (HLJ)
Maximum	61.009 (GD)	58.973 (SC)

Notes: *, **and *** indicate significance at the level of 1%, 5% and 10%, respectively. HLJ = Heilongjiang, GD = Guangdong, and SC = Sichuan.

Innovation Variance and Growth

So far the volatility of growth is defined using information about both predictable and unpredictable changes in growth. This section aims to examine the relationship between growth and the variance of innovations to a forecasting model for growth. The latter only relies on existing information, such as the logarithm of the initial income, the initial government spending over GRP and the initial investment-income ratio. In this exercise, some forecasting variables are also considered. These include a time trend, a time trend squared and the lagged rate of growth. Ramey and Ramey (1995) argued that this structure implies the existence of a unit root and a quadratic deterministic trend in per capita income. The estimation results are presented in Table 4.5.

Table 4.5 Relationship between innovation variance and growth

Variables	Model II	Model III
Constant	4.418 (2.071)**	7.702 (16.397)*
Standard deviation	0.353 (2.091)**	0.107 (10.064)*
Initial investment/output ratio	-1.930 (-1.090)	-1.278 (-5.668)*
Initial government/output ratio	-4.463 (-1.600)	-5.912 (-11.958)*
Log(initial income)	-0.250 (-0.442)	-1.007 (-5.218)*
Lagged growth rate	0.208 (6.063)*	0.178 (23.237)*
Time	0.322 (3.814)*	0.300 (64.626)*
Time-squared	-0.007 (-2.468)**	-0.006 (-39.054)*
Log likelihood	-2342.681	-1553.994
Standard deviation		
Mean	4.967	
Minimum	2.665 (HLJ)	
Maximum	7.940 (SC)	

Notes: * and ** indicate significance at the level of 1% and 5%, respectively. HLJ =
Heilongjiang and SC = Sichuan. In Model II constant variance over time for each
region is assumed. In Model III, the variance is assumed to vary over time and
across the regions, and region-specific autocorrelation is also considered.

It is found that, with or without the assumption of constant variance over
time, the relationship between growth and volatility is significantly positive.
With the assumption of constant variance over time, the rate of growth
increases by 0.353 units for every unit of increase in the standard deviation of
the rate of growth. This figure is substantially small (0.107) without the
assumption of the constant variance according to Table 4.5.

Investment and Volatility

Economic theories often link volatility to growth via investment. The
findings presented in Table 4.2 are however not very clear. The purpose of
this section is to provide further analysis about this issue. Table 4.6 reports
the main results. For the sake of saving space, only the coefficients of the
volatility variable are presented. According to Table 4.6, volatility and
growth are found to have a positive relationship in all cases. However, with
the inclusion of investment share variable, the magnitude of the coefficient
has halved, implying a possible link between volatility and investment shares.
This is confirmed by the results from the investment equations presented in
the second part of Table 4.6.

Table 4.6 Coefficients of volatility

	Coefficients (t-ratios)
Growth equations	
Including investment-output ratio	0.042 (4.910)*
Including initial investment-output ratio	0.110 (8.313)*
Excluding investment variables	0.092 (3.942)*
Investment equations	
Including control variables	0.0022 (23.755)*
Excluding control variables	0.0016 (18.809)*

Notes: In the "growth equations", the rate of growth is the dependent variable and the independent variables include an intercept, the standard deviation of the disturbance term, government spending over GRP, the logarithm of the initial income per capita, lagged growth rate, time trend and time trend squared. In the "investment equations", the ratio of investment over GRP is the dependent variable, the independent variables include an intercept, the standard deviation from the growth model with the investment-output ratio as a regressor, and the control variables include government spending over GRP, the logarithm of the initial income per capita. * indicates significance at the level of 1%. All models assume heteroscedasticity and group-specific autocorrelation.

Volatility is generally found to be positively related to investment shares in the Chinese case, implying that volatility may be linked to growth via investment. Mirman (1971) argued that, due to precautionary savings, higher volatility may lead to a higher savings rate and hence a higher investment rate. This explanation surely suits the Chinese case. Since economic reform program was initiated in the late 1970s, Chinese society has undergone dramatic changes. The abolition of the old socialist regime has created great uncertainties associated with education, housing, and the general welfare of all residents. These uncertainties have partly been responsible for the continuous rise of domestic savings in China as demonstrated in Figure 4.1.

Government Spending and Volatility

There are many potential sources of volatility. This section investigates government spending as a source of volatility. In the transitional economy of China, government spending has played an important role in stimulating economic growth when the economy is in recession, controlling aggregate demand when the economy is overheated and transferring resources for the purpose of reducing regional disparity. To examine the impact of government spending on volatility, we first estimate a forecasting equation for government spending and then investigate whether the variance of innovations in the growth equation is related to the squared forecast residuals of the government spending equation. The forecasting equation for government spending includes a constant, lagged government spending and GRP growth rate, the logarithm of the initial income per capita, a time trend and the squared time trend as the independent variables. The results are presented in Table 4.7.

Once again, growth and volatility are found to be related positively. Government spending volatility and growth volatility are negatively related according to Table 4.7. Thus, economic growth in Chinese regions is negatively affected by volatility in government spending. Ramey and Ramey (1995) drew the same conclusion using cross-country data. They further linked government-spending volatility to political instability. However, their explanation may not be applicable to China. In the transitional Chinese economy, though government is gradually withdrawing from business operations and focusing on institutional reconstructs, government spending has often been used as a temporary instrument for macroeconomic adjustment.

Table 4.7 Government spending and volatility

	Coefficients (t-ratios)
Growth equation	
Constant	5.211 (11.115)*
Standard deviation	0.116 (4.036)*
Investment/output ratio	0.732 (4.325)*
Log(initial income)	-0.685 (-3.773)*
Lagged growth rate	0.207 (17.606)*
Time	0.252 (16.899)*
Time-squared	-0.005 (-10.016)*
Log likelihood	-1580.086
Volatility equation	
Constant	9.537 (400.348)*
Squared residuals	-156.483 (-20.877)*
Log likelihood	-1441.621

Notes: The results from government spending equation are not reported due to space limitations. The saved residuals are used in the volatility equation.
     * indicates significance at the level of 1%. All models assume heteroscedasticity and group-specific autocorrelation.

CONCLUSION

Though there is a blossoming literature on economic growth in China, the relationship between growth and business cycle has rarely been investigated. This chapter presents some preliminary findings about the relationship between volatility and economic growth in China, and hence attempts to make a contribution to the understanding of the Chinese economy. Using historical data of Chinese regions, it is found that, during the period of economic reforms, volatility and growth are positively related. This relationship is true even if control variables are introduced.

The consensus view is that China's growth is largely driven by investment expansion (Woo 1998, Wu 2003, and Young 2003). For this reason, this chapter also examined whether volatility is related to growth via investment. It is found that investment shares over gross regional product are positively related to volatility. Thus, the impact of volatility on growth is generally reduced when investment share variables are incorporated into the models.

Furthermore, this chapter also investigated whether government spending affects volatility and hence economic growth. The empirical findings show that government spending volatility has a negative impact on output volatility. This may reflect the fact that, during the period of economic transformation in China, while a market-oriented system has not been in place, government spending has often been used as an instrument for macroeconomic control.

NOTES

1. See, for example, Naughton (1996), Woo (1998), Chow (2002) and Wu (2004).
2. The key variable on the right-hand side of the equations is the volatility variable which is generated endogenously. Thus, the conventional Granger-causality test approach cannot be employed. Equations (4.1), (4.2) and (4.3) imply that the causal direction goes from volatility to growth.
3. As 28 cross-sections are used, the sample is extended to cover the period of 1976-2003 or 28 years.
4. The results using the variance of the error terms for model III are similar to those reported in Table 4.3.

REFERENCES

Aizenman, J. and Marion, N., 1993. 'Policy uncertainty, persistence and growth', *Review of International Economics*, **1(2)**, 145-63.

Barro, R., 1991. 'Economic growth in a cross-section of countries', *Quarterly Journal of Economics*, **106 (2)**, 407-44.

Bean, C., 1990. 'Endogenous growth and the pro-cyclical behaviour of productivity', *European Economic Review*, **34**, 355-63.

Black, F., 1987. *Business cycles and equilibrium*, Cambridge, MA: Blackwell.

Blackburn, K., 1999. 'Can stabilization policy reduce long-run growth?', *Economic Journal*, **109(1)**, 67-77.

Caporale, T. and McKiernan, B., 1996. 'The relationship between output variability and growth: evidence from post-war UK data', *Scottish Journal of Political Economy*, **43(2)**, 229-36.

Chow, G. C., 2002. *China's Economic Transformation*, Malden, Mass.: Blackwell Publishers.

Dawson J. and Stephenson, F., 1997. 'The link between volatility and growth: evidence from the States', *Economic Letters*, **55**, 365-9.

Dawson J., DeJuan, J., Seater, J. and Stephenson, F., 2001. 'Economic information versus quality in cross-country data', *Canadian Journal of Economics*, **34**, 988-1009.

Dejuan, J. and Gurr, S., 2004. 'On the link between volatility and growth: evidence from Canadian provinces', *Applied Economics Letters*, **11**, 279-282.

Grier, K. and Tullock, G., 1989. 'An empirical analysis of cross-national economic growth, 1951-80', *Journal of Monetary Economics*, **24**, 259-76.

Hamilton, J. D., 1989. 'A new approach to the economic analysis of nonstationary time series and the business cycle', *Econometrica*, **57(2)**, 357-84.

Kneller, R. and Young, G., 2001. 'Business cycle volatility, uncertainty and long-run growth', *The Manchester School*, **69(5)**, 534-52.

Kormendi, R. C. and Meguire, P. G., 1985. 'Macroeconomic determinants of growth: cross-country evidence', *Journal of Monetary Economics*, **16**, 141-63.

Lensink, R., Bo, H. and Sterken, E., 1999. 'Does uncertainty affect economic growth? An economic analysis', *Weltwirtschaftliches Archiv*, **135(3)**, 379-96.

Levine, R. and Renelt, D., 1992. 'A sensitivity analysis of cross-country growth regressions', *American Economic Review*, **82(4)**, 942-63.

Lucas, R., 1987. *Models of Business Cycles*, Oxford: Blackwell.

Martin, P. and Rogers, C. A., 2000. 'Long-term and short-term economic instability', *European Economic Review*, **44**, 359-81.

Mirman, L., 1971. 'Uncertainty and optimal consumption decisions', *Econometrica*, **39(1)**, 179-85.

National Bureau of Statistics of China, 2001. *Statistical Yearbook of China 2000*, Beijing: National Statistics Press.

National Bureau of Statistics of China, 2004. *Statistical Yearbook of China 2004*, Beijing: National Statistics Press.

Naughton, B., 1996. *Growing out of the Plan: Chinese Economic Reform 1978-1993*, Cambridge and New York: Cambridge University Press.

Pindyck, R. S., 1991. 'Irreversibility, uncertainty and investment', *Journal of Economic Literature*, **29(3)**, 1110-48.

Rafferty, M., 2004. 'Growth-business cycle interaction: a look at the OECD', *International Advances in Economic Research*, **10(3)**, 191-201.

Ramey, G. and Ramey, V., 1995. 'Cross-country evidence on the link between volatility and growth', *American Economic Review*, **85**, 1138–51.

Saint-Paul, G., 1993. 'Productivity growth and the structure of the business cycle', *European Economic Review*, **37**, 861-90.

Sandmo, A. A., 1970. 'The effect of uncertainty on saving', *Review of Economic Studies*, **37**, 353-60.

Woo, W. T., 1998. 'Chinese economic growth: sources and prospects', in M. Fouquin and F. Lemoine (eds.), *The Chinese Economy*, Economica Ltd, Paris.

Wu, Y., 2003. 'Has productivity contributed to China's growth?', *Pacific Economic Review*, **8 (1)**, 15-30.

Wu, Y., 2004. *China's Economic Growth: a Miracle with Chinese Characteristics*, London and New York: RoutledgeCurzon Press Limited.

Young, A., 2003. 'Gold into Base Metals: Productivity Growth in the People's Republic of China during the Reform Period', *Journal of Political Economy*, **111(6)**, 1220-1261.

Zarnowitz, V. and Moore, G., 1986. 'Major changes in cyclical behaviour', in Gordon R. J. (ed), *The American Business Cycle: Continuity and Change*, Chicago: University of Chicago Press, 519-72.

5. Growth Prospect during 2005-2020

Shantong Li, Yongzhi Hou, Yunzhong Liu and Jianwu He

After more than two decades of rapid economic development since the beginning of reform in 1978, the Chinese economy has entered a new and dynamic period of development. During this period, China will have opportunities for economic development; however the government must be mindful of economic and social tensions. If China can seize these opportunities to take action to preempt problems arising from development and maintain rapid economic growth, its economic strength and its overall national strength will move to a new high and the living standard of its people will rise to a new level.

The development of the Chinese economy in the future will face a changing internal and external environment as well as various opportunities and challenges. Due to the interaction of these uncertain factors, the pace of economic development will be uncertain. Selecting different development strategies will lead to different development results. This chapter uses scenario analysis to simulate the prospect of China's economic development during the 11th Five-Year Plan and beyond.

First, we tried to give a baseline scenario in light of the unique features of the development and structure of the Chinese economy. Based on past and present development features, the baseline scenario analyzes development trends, from which possible scenarios will be derived. In addition to the baseline scenario, we designed two additional scenarios. One is a coordinated development scenario, in which the economy, society, resources and the environment will develop in a coordinated manner, in keeping with the requirements of the scientific concept of development and through industrial restructuring and efficiency improvement. The other is a "risk" scenario, which will give more consideration to the possible risks that might be encountered in the future.

The model used by this research is the DRCCGE2004 version of the dynamic recursion China CGE model developed by the Development Research Center of the State Council. The time span for the simulation ranges from 2005 to 2020.

SCENARIO DESIGN

First of all, this chapter hypothesized some external factors and simulated various scenarios of China's economic growth and structural changes from 2000 to 2020 in light of the unique features of the growth and structure of the Chinese economy and development trends (see Table 5.1). In simulating various scenarios, we also hypothesized the growth trends of population and labour, the process of urbanization, the growth rate of government consumption and the total factor productivity (TFP).[1] What we need to emphasize is that we also designed the preference of technological advance, which means that the advance of productivity is not neutral to different sectors. In the simulation, the share parameters for the production function (including the coefficient of intermediary inputs) are all updated so as to reflect the preference of technological changes in inputs.

The baseline scenario forecasts that the Chinese economy will continue its past development trend, the labour force will continue to grow at a fast pace, human resources accumulation and technological advance will likely bring about an incremental effect of scale, system reforms will deepen further, the reform of the financial system, the trade system, the investment system and the state-owned enterprises will promote a more rational and effective allocation of the factors between different sectors and different regions. The interaction of all these factors will help maintain TFP growth during the 2005-2020 period at the level of the past 25 years. That means the average annual growth rate will be between 2.0 per cent and 2.5 per cent. Urbanization and industrialization will move forward rapidly. Urbanization will continue to move forward rapidly at an average annual rate of 1.1 per cent, expected to reach about 49 per cent by the end of the 11th Five-Year Plan and about 60 per cent by 2020. Technological advance in the future will continue to have a certain preference.[2] The savings behavior of the Chinese people will unlikely change dramatically during the 11th Five-Year Plan but the savings rate will drop slightly after 2010. The WTO-related tariff concessions and other commitments will be fulfilled and the impact arising from WTO accession will continue.

The Fourth Plenary Session of the 16th Party Central Committee put forward the scientific concept of human-oriented, all-round, coordinated and sustainable development so as to better push forward economic and social development. This will be a basic guideline for China's development in the future. In keeping with this concept of development, we designed a coordinated development scenario. This scenario is based on a rapid and smooth progress in the reform of various systems, the stronger roles of the market in resource allocation, the vigorous advance in restructuring, and the progress in changing the mode of economic growth. On the basis of the basic scenario, we further hypothesized that the industrial structure would be further upgraded, and the reform of the systems and rules would promote rapid development of the service industry (especially the producer services) and eventually help optimize and upgrade the whole industrial structure. In the meantime, further market-oriented reforms would reduce distortions in the prices of various resources (including energy), rationalize the allocation of resources and increase the efficiency of resource and energy utilization at the micro level. Therefore, we hypothesized that the preference of technological advance and the changes in the rate of intermediary inputs would further favor the coordinated development of all industries on the basis of the baseline scenario. In particular, the intermediary use of the service industry and the high-tech industries by various sectors would be faster and push up the added value of the high-tech industries. On the basis of the baseline scenario, the TFP growth rate of the service industry would be one percentage point higher each year during the 2005-2010 period and 0.5 percentage points higher each year during the 2010-2020 period. On the basis of the basic scenario, the efficiency of energy utilization would be 0.2-0.5 percentage points higher and the movement of agricultural labour to non-farm industries would be accelerated.

In consideration of all the uncertain factors that may confront future development, we also simulated a "risk" scenario. This scenario addresses some main challenges and risks to China's economic development in the future. (1) The reforms of the banking system and the state-owned enterprises fail to move forward as expected and the development of the capital market is slow, which will make it difficult to avoid inefficient capital use in the early years of this century and perhaps beyond. (2) The urban facilities that are in relatively short supply will constitute constraints to labour flow and urbanization. The obstacles confronting system reforms will slow down such reforms, and rural-out migration will be slow. (3) Ageing population and higher rates of support will lead to a decline in savings rate (investment rate). (4) Increased trade frictions will have a negative impact on import and export levels. These factors will affect China's future TFP growth rate to a certain degree. With regard to these factors, we presumed in the "risk" scenario that the TFP growth rate would be lower than the average level of the past 25 years, at an average annual growth rate of 1.5-2.0 per cent, that labour flow would be slower and personal savings rate would be lower than in the baseline scenario.

PROSPECT ANALYSIS FOR 2005-2020

Based on the above hypotheses, we worked out the simulation results for the three scenarios by employing the DRCCGE2004 model.

Table 5.1 Scenario designs for the analysis of the prospect of China's economic growth

Scenario types	Scenario design
	Common assumptions of all scenarios:
	1. The changing trend of total population is exogenous, and we directly cite the prediction data of CPIC (China Population Information Center) as the total population.
	2. The growth of total labour and the supply change of agricultural land are exogenous.
	3. Take into account the commitments related to accession to WTO, such as tariff reduction.
	4. All tax rates but those related to exports and imports are kept unchanged; all transfers are exogenous.
	5. The imbalance of international balance of payments will be gradually reduced until its balance during the year 2005-2010, and this balance will be kept during the year 2010-2020.
	6. The growth rate of government consumption is exogenous.
Baseline scenario	*Related assumptions of baseline scenario are as follows:*
	1. Agricultural labour is rapidly shifted into non-agricultural industries.
	2. Technological progress is deflective and the change of intermediate input rate is exogenous.
	3. TFP is exogenous, assuming that the growth rate of TFP during the year 2005-2020 will be kept at the average level over the past 25 years, ranging from 2.0% to 2.5%.

Coordinated-development scenario	*Related assumptions of coordinated-development scenario are as follows:*
	1. Compared with the baseline scenario, the deflection of technological progress and the change of intermediate input rate are more oriented to coordinated development of all industries, which is mainly embodied by higher growth rate of intermediate inputs of service and high-tech sectors used by all sectors, and rising value-added rate in high-tech industries.
	2. Based on the baseline scenario, the annual growth rate of TFP in service sectors is one percent higher than that of the previous year during the year 2005-2010, and 0.5 percent higher during the year 2010-2020.
	3. Based on the baseline scenario, the energy utilization efficiency is improved by 0.2-0.5 percent.
	4. Agricultural labour is rapidly shifted into non-agricultural industries.
"Risk" scenario	*Related assumptions of "risk" scenario are as follows:*
	1. The shifting speed of labour is relatively slower compared with the baseline scenario.
	2. Household's propensity to save is lower than that of the baseline scenario.
	3. The growth rate of government consumption is a little bit higher than that of the baseline scenario.
	4. TFP is exogenous, assuming that the growth rate of TFP during the year 2005-2020 will be lower than that of the average level over the past 25 years, and be kept at the level of 1.5%-2.0%.

Baseline Scenario

Table 5.2 shows projected economic growth during the 2000-2020 period for the baseline scenario. In light of the current trend of economic growth, the economic growth rate during the 10th Five-Year Plan is estimated to be 8.7 per cent. The baseline scenario indicates that the GDP growth rate will be 8.1 during the 11th Five-Year Plan, slightly lower than during the 10th Five-Year Plan and that the economic growth rate will be 7.5 per cent and 6.8 per cent respectively for the 2010-2015 and 2015-2020 periods. Overall, the economic growth in the first 20 years of this century will still be relatively high, at an average annual growth rate of 7.8 per cent.

Table 5.2 Economic growth and its sources for 2000-2020 (baseline scenario)

Year	GDP growth (%)	Sources of growth (%)		
		Labour	Capital	TFP
2000-2005	8.8	0.5	6.4	1.9
2005-2010	8.1	0.4	5.6	2.1
2010-2015	7.5	0.2	5.0	2.3
2015-2020	6.8	0.0	4.5	2.3
2000-2020	7.8	0.3	5.4	2.1
2005-2020	7.4	0.2	5.0	2.2

In terms of the sources of economic growth, rapid capital accumulation remains the main driving force for China's rapid economic growth for 2000-2020. Although the contribution of capital input to GDP growth is progressively declining, it will continue to be as high as 65-70 per cent until 2020. The rapid capital accumulation is attributable to the high rate of domestic savings (high rate of investment) and the fast-growing foreign direct investment. It is expected that the high savings rate and high investment rate will continue during the 11th Five-Year Plan. As the changes in the age structure of the population will result in a higher rate of support, as the social security system will continue to improve and as the government's financial policy changes, the savings rate (investment rate) will decline somewhat, to about 35 per cent in 2020. Compared to capital, the contribution of the quantitative growth of labour will be very small. This is mainly determined by the changes in the age structure of China's population. The working-age population will continue to grow till 2010 and the contribution of labour growth to GDP will stay at about 5 per cent. With changes in the age structure of the population after 2010, labour growth will slow down and its contribution to GDP will also be declining. By 2020, the contribution of quantitative labour input to economic growth will be close to zero. Rapid TFP growth will become another leading push for China's sustained and rapid economic growth and its contribution will be increasingly important.

China is still in the period of industrialization, and rapid changes in industrial structure are an important feature of this period. The simulation results indicate that the shares of the primary, secondary and tertiary industries will be 10.7, 54.1 and 35.2 per cent respectively, at the end of the 11th Five-Year Plan. These will change to 7.1, 52.5 and 40.4 per cent, respectively, by the year 2020.[3] The importance of primary industry will persistently decline during the 11th Five-Year Plan and through to 2020. The importance of secondary industry will continue to rise during the 11th Five-Year Plan, which will be mainly manifested in the expansion of the energy sector arising from increasing demand for energy and capital goods used as intermediary inputs in projects resulting from the high rate of investment. In a sense, this is also a continuation of the features of the evolution of the industrial structure in recent years. In addition, the abolition of the multi-fiber agreement (MFA) for the WTO transitional period will stimulate an expansion of the textile and clothing sector. Compared with 2010, the secondary industry's proportionate contribution to GDP will decline slightly in 2020, mainly manifested in the declining significance of the mining and low-tech industries. As energy demand further expands, the relative importance of the energy sector will rise further. Because of the preference of technological advance for the intermediary demand, the proportions of electronic communications and other high-tech sectors will rise further. As the personal consumption demand for the service industry will constantly rise and as rapid industrial development spurs demand for productive service industries, the proportion of the service industry as a whole will rise slightly during the 11th Five-Year Plan and through to 2020.

Along with the adjustment of the industrial structure, the employment structure will also undergo drastic adjustment. The main manifestation is that rural out-migration will be fast during the 11th Five-Year Plan and through to 2020. The employment proportion of the primary industry will drop to 41.0 per cent by the end of the 11th Five-Year Plan and further to 34.2 per cent by 2020. That will be nearly 15 percentage points lower than the 2000 level. The proportion of secondary industry will rise slightly during the 11th Five-Year Plan, thanks to the rapid development of the textile and clothing industries. During the 2010-2020 period, however, the employment proportion of the secondary industry will fall slightly due to the lower GDP proportion of the secondary industry and the higher capital/labour ratio. Compared with the secondary industry, the service industry has a stronger capacity for labour absorption, whose employment proportion will reach 43.4 per cent by 2020.

Due to the impact of WTO accession and the upgrading of the industrial structure, the structure of trade will also change slightly. As the WTO transition period will end during the 11th Five-Year Plan, the reduced tariffs on farm products and the introduction of the tariff quota system will reduce the proportion of exports from the agricultural sector and increase that of its imports. The reduced tariffs on industrial goods and the abolition of the MFA against China will increase the importance of exports from the textile and clothing industries. In the meantime, the export competitiveness of the capital- and technology-intensive industries will be stronger thanks to the fast rise in the capital/labour ratio and in human capital.[4] Therefore, electronic communications and other products will see their export proportions rise further. In the long run, the relative scarcity of land and other resources and the continuous rise in the prices of farm products will persistently increase costs in the textile and clothing sectors (and those sectors directly related to farm products), and reduce the quantity of exports. By 2020, electronic communications, textiles, clothing, chemical and electric equipment will be the leading export sectors.

Coordinated Development Scenario

Table 5.3 shows the state of economic growth during the 2000-2020 period in the coordinated development scenario. For all periods, the economic growth rate in the coordinated development scenario will be higher than in the baseline scenario. The GDP growth rate will be 0.4 percentage points higher than in the baseline scenario during the 11th five-year plan, expected to reach 8.5 per cent. The rate is expected to be 8.2 per cent and 7.6 per cent for the 2010-2015 period and the 2015-2020 period.

Table 5.3 Economic growth and its sources for 2000-2020 (coordinated development scenario)

Year	GDP growth (%)	Sources of growth (%)		
		Labour	Capital	TFP
2000-2005	8.8	0.5	6.4	1.8
2005-2010	8.5	0.4	5.6	2.5
2010-2015	8.2	0.2	5.1	2.9
2015-2020	7.6	0.0	4.7	2.9
2000-2020	8.2	0.3	5.4	2.5
2005-2020	8.1	0.2	5.1	2.8

In terms of the sources of economic growth, rapid capital accumulation will still be the main driving force for China's rapid economic growth in this scenario. But the contribution of capital to economic growth will be smaller than in the baseline scenario. Conversely, the contribution of TFP will be higher than in the baseline scenario. This, in a sense, conforms more to the requirements of sustainable development, because on the one hand capital accumulation cannot maintain a sustained rapid growth for a long time due to various constraints and on the other, the rate of marginal income for capital will decline due to the deepening of capital.

In the coordinated development scenario, the service industry will undergo rapid development mostly due to the reform of its rules and systems and will play an increasingly important role in production and in boosting industrial competitiveness. This in turn will provide more development opportunities for the service industry, especially the modern service industry that serves production. For this reason, the efficiency of the service sectors will rise faster, rapidly increasing the proportion of the service industry in the whole economy. The primary, secondary and tertiary industries will account for 10.5, 52.5 and 37.0 per cent of GDP respectively at the end of the 11th Five-Year Plan and 6.4, 49.9 and 43.6 per cent respectively by the year 2020. The service sector's proportion of GDP in 2020 will be three percentage points higher than in the baseline scenario. With the deepening of marketization, the situation in which the current prices of resources (energy) fail to reflect their rarity will change and the price system will be more rational. As a result, the efficiency of resource (energy) utilization will be higher and the development of the energy-consuming and polluting sectors will face restrictions. These factors will make the development of the energy sector and the energy-consuming and polluting sectors become slower than in the baseline scenario. Meanwhile, the development of some high-tech industries such as electronic communications will be faster than in the baseline scenario.

In order to reflect the impact of economic development on the environment in the above two scenarios, we simulated the discharge of four major pollutants, namely SO_2, NOx, TSS and smog, in different scenarios. Table 5.4 shows the changes in pollutant discharges for the coordinated development scenario in comparison to the baseline scenario, which indicate that the discharge of all four major pollutants will be lower in the coordinated development scenario. In particular, the discharge of SO_2 and NOx will post greater changes. These two pollutants are mainly related to energy inputs. With the adjustment of the industrial structure and the enhancement of energy utilization efficiency, the discharge of these two pollutants in 2020 will be more than ten per cent lower than in the baseline scenario. Overall, the coordinated development scenario will see faster economic growth and lesser environmental pollution when compared with the baseline scenario.

Risk Scenario

Table 5.5 shows projected economic growth in the risk scenario from 2000 to 2020. During the 11th five-year plan, the GDP growth rate will be 7.5 per cent or 0.6 percentage points lower than in the baseline scenario. The economic growth rate is expected to be 5.8 and 4.8 per cent respectively for the 2010-2015 and 2015-2020 periods. The economic growth rate in the risk scenario will all be tangibly lower than in the baseline scenario. This is a fairly pessimistic scenario.

CONCLUSIONS

From the analysis of the above scenarios we can conclude that the economy will maintain rapid growth during the 11th Five-Year Plan at an average annual growth rate of about eight per cent. At 2000 constant prices, the aggregate GDP at the end of 11th Five-Year Plan will reach 2.4 trillion US dollars, which will be larger than that of Germany in 2000. The per capita GDP will be about 1700 US dollars.[5] Compared with the 11th Five-Year Plan period, the economic growth during the 2010-2020 period will be slightly slower, with an average annual growth rate of about seven per cent. By 2020, the aggregate GDP will be about 4.8 trillion US dollars, surpassing that of Japan in 2000. The per capita GDP will be about 3200 US dollars.[6]

Table 5.4 Pollutant discharge in coordinated development scenario

	2010	2020
NO2	-4.5	-11.1
NOx	-3.4	-12.9
TSS	-2.5	-6.6
Smog	-5.5	-8.3

*Notes:*The numbers indicate the percentage changes in pollutant discharge in the coordinated development scenario when compared with the baseline scenario.

Table 5.5 Sources of economic growth, 2000-2020 (risk scenario)

Year	GDP growth (%)	Sources of growth (%)		
		Labour	Capital	TFP
2000-2005	8.7	0.5	6.4	1.8
2005-2010	7.5	0.4	5.5	1.6
2010-2015	5.8	0.2	4.2	1.4
2015-2020	4.8	0.0	3.3	1.5
2000-2020	6.7	0.3	4.8	1.6
2005-2020	6.0	0.2	4.3	1.5

The most important driving force of rapid economic growth during the 11th Five-Year Plan and the 2010-2020 period will continue to be rapid capital accumulation, whose contribution rate will be 63.5 per cent in the coordinated development scenario, 67.4 per cent in the baseline scenario and 72.1 per cent in the risk scenario. At the same time, the model simulation results also indicate that the contribution to economic growth by TFP growth arising from urbanization, human capital investment, economic restructuring and technological innovation will be increasingly great. This contribution rate during the 2015-2020 period will be 10-15 percentage points higher than during the 10th Five-Year Plan. TFP growth will be a key to a sustained and rapid economic growth in the future.

The industrial structure will continue to be adjusted and become more rational thanks to deepening industrialization and urbanization during the 11th Five-Year Plan and the 2010-2020 period. The main changes in industrial structure during the 11th Five-Year Plan will be that the primary industry GDP share will continue to decline in contrast to the shares of secondary and tertiary industries which will rise slightly. At the end of the 11th Five-Year Plan, the contribution to GDP of the primary, secondary and tertiary industries are forecast to be 10.8, 54.2 and 35.1 per cent, respectively. During the 2010-2020 period, the main structural changes will be higher efficiency and an increase in the relative importance of the service industry. The proportions of the primary, secondary and tertiary industries will be 7.3, 52.5 and 40.2 per cent, respectively.

The simulation results indicate that if the national economy can post a coordinated and sustainable development, the damage of economic growth to the environment will be much smaller. In 2020, for example, the discharge of the four major pollutants in the coordinated development scenario will be 7-13 per cent lower than in the baseline scenario.

What is noteworthy is that in the next 10-15 years, China still faces a possible slowdown in its economic growth. For example, the negative impact of trade frictions on trade flows, the lower rate of savings, the slower rate of capital accumulation and the higher system costs arising from system contradictions could reduce China's economic growth rate to about 6 per cent.

NOTES

1. TFP is mainly set through model dynamics on the basis of TFP growth rate over the past two decades or so.
2. The preference of technological advance and the changes in the rate of intermediary inputs are mainly set with reference to the change trends reflected in China's input and output sheet 1987-2000 and the change trends of the relevant parameters of the United States.
3. The proportions of industrial structure we mentioned here are worked out on the basis of the existing statistical standards and parameters and the proportions of industrial structure of the base year as reflected in the 2000 input and output sheet.
4. According to WTO agreement, the MFA will be completely abolished in 2005.
5. According to the World Bank data, the countries with a per capita GDP of 1660-2000 dollars in 2000 were Russia (1660 dollars), Romania (1670 dollars), Jordan (1680 dollars),

Guatemala (1690 dollars), Macedonia (1710 dollars), Salvador (1990 dollars) and Thailand (2010 dollars).

6. According to the World Bank data, the countries with a per capita GDP of about 3200 dollars in 2000 were Turkey (3090 dollars), Panama (3260 dollars), Botswana (3300 dollars), Malaysia (3380 dollars), Estonia (3410 dollars) and Brazil (3570 dollars).

PART II

Urban Economy, Migration and Labour Market

6. Performance of City Economies

Yuk-shing Cheng and Sung-ko Li

INTRODUCTION[1]

China has been undergoing a rapid process of urbanization since the launch of economic reform in 1978. From this process has emerged a complicated city system. Chinese cities are assigned an administrative status based on their position in the hierarchy of the government: provincial level, deputy-provincial level, prefecture level or county level (Chung and Lam 2004).

A recent debate in the Chinese literature is whether the administrative status of a city has substantial impact on its performance. The underlying argument is based on the fact that different levels of governments have different powers and thus could have different ability in the mobilization of resources and different preferences in the choice of technology. One of the major elements is the budgetary power. In recent years, county-level governments have complained that their supervising prefecture-level government has centralized most of the fiscal revenues collected in their jurisdiction. County-level governments thus have little resources for promoting economic development. Without much investment in infrastructural projects, for instance, they cannot attract industrial investments from outside (Dai 2000). Recently, there have been calls for reforming this city system. One of the proposals is to weaken or even abandon the prefectures so that counties can be put under the direct jurisdiction of the provincial governments. Experiments have already been launched in some provinces (Wang 2005).

However, there is no rigorous empirical study that shows how bad the current system is. If the prefecture-level city can utilize the resources more efficiently than the county-level cities, the proposal to abandon the prefectures might not be a good one. In this chapter, we investigate the issue from the perspective of technical efficiency. A city has a higher technical efficiency if it can produce the same level of output with a smaller amount of inputs. Although a higher level government has bigger administrative power to mobilize resources, it is not clear whether the resources can be used efficiently. It is thus interesting to examine whether cities of higher administrative levels perform better than those of lower levels in terms of technical efficiency.

A comparison of the technical efficiencies of different Chinese cities can be done by estimating a production frontier and then calculating the distance of each city from the frontier (or the ratio of the observed output to the frontier output). A subtlety however is whether we should assume all different cities have the same technology (i.e. represented by the same production function). If we believe that prefectures and counties, for instance, are very different city economies, assuming that they can be represented by the same production function can lead to misleading results. If we estimate a production frontier for each kind of city, then the comparison of technical efficiency will become more complicated. In this chapter, we utilize a recently developed method to estimate the metafrontier of production units that can overcome this problem. Using this method, we can compare technical efficiencies of different groups of production units even if each group utilizes a distinct technology.

The rest of this chapter will be organized as follows. It first introduces the concepts related to the metafrontier and how technical efficiencies can be measured from different kinds of production frontiers. It then explains the specific empirical model to be used in our study and describes the treatments of the data. This is followed by discussion of the empirical results.

A METAFRONTIER MODEL

The idea of a metafrontier originates from the concept of meta-production function, which was first introduced by Hayami (1969) and Hayami and Ruttan (1970, 1985). The meta-production function was referred to as the envelope of the production function of individual units (countries in their studies). Lau and Yotopoulos (1989) consider the concept as "theoretically attractive" and "empirically attractive".[2] Later, several studies use the concept of a metafrontier by incorporating technical inefficiency into production (see Battese and Rao (2002) for a literature review). Recently, Battese, Rao and O'Donnell (2004) proposed procedures for estimating a deterministic metafrontier that is based on stochastic production functions.

To introduce the idea of a metafrontier, suppose we have a sample of production units, which theoretically have access to a common technology and thus face a common production frontier. Suppose further that the production units can be classified into different groups based on some external factors. The output of each group of production units in practice is constrained by these external factors and thus can never reach the common production frontier. Under this situation, one can model different groups of production units by group frontiers. The common theoretical frontier can then be represented by a metafrontier that envelops the group frontiers. The relationship between the group frontiers and the metafrontier is illustrated in Figure 6.1, which shows a simplified case of one input (x) and one output (y). With two different kinds of frontiers, we can define the technical efficiency of each unit in a useful way. One natural measure is the technical efficiency of each city with respect to the metafrontier. It can be decomposed into two components. The first one is the technological gap between the group frontier and the metafrontier. The second one is the technical efficiency with respect to the group frontier. Suppose we have an observation A, producing y_a with input x_a. Its technical efficiency with respect to the group frontier is y_a/y_g, whereas its technical efficiency with respect to the metafrontier is y_a/y_m. The technological gap ratio, which measures the distance between the outputs at the group frontier and metafrontier, is y_g/y_m.

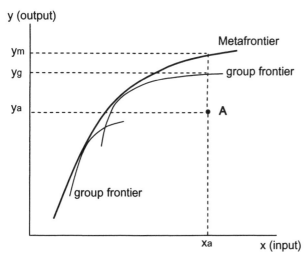

Figure 6.1 Metafrontier and technical efficiency

Battese, Rao and O'Donnell (2004) suggest that we can estimate the stochastic production frontier for each group of production units in empirical applications. Suppose there are R groups of units and N_j units in the *j*th group, the model can be specified as

$$Y_{it(j)} = f(\mathbf{x}_{it(j)}, \boldsymbol{\beta}_{(j)})e^{V_{it(j)} - U_{it(j)}}, i = 1,2,...,N_j, \ t = 1,2,...,T, \ j = 1,2,...,R, \quad (6.1)$$

where $Y_{it(j)}$ denotes the output for the *i*th unit in the *t*th time period for the *j*th group, $\mathbf{x}_{it(j)}$ a vector of values or functions of the inputs used correspondingly, $\boldsymbol{\beta}_{(j)}$ the parameter vector associated with the *x*- variables. The $V_{it(j)}$s are assumed to be independently and identically distributed (i.i.d.)

as $N(0,\sigma^2_{v(j)})$ random variables, independent of $U_{it(j)}$s, which are defined by the truncation of the $N(\mu_{it(j)},\sigma^2_{(j)})$ - distributions, where the $\mu_{it(j)}$ s are defined by some appropriate inefficiency model. For simplicity, suppose we have the following function,

$$Y_{it} = f(\mathbf{x}_{it},\boldsymbol{\beta}_{(j)})e^{V_{it(j)}-U_{it(j)}} \equiv e^{\mathbf{x}_{it}\boldsymbol{\beta}_{(j)}+V_{it(j)}-U_{it(j)}} \tag{6.2}$$

The metafrontier production model for the whole sample of units can be expressed by

$$Y^*_{it} \equiv f(\mathbf{x}_{it},\boldsymbol{\beta}^*) = e^{\mathbf{x}_{it}\boldsymbol{\beta}^*}, i = 1,2,...,N = \sum_{j=1}^{R} N_j;\ t = 1,2,...,T, \tag{6.3}$$

where β^* denotes the vector of parameters for the metafrontier function such that

$$\mathbf{x}_{it}\boldsymbol{\beta}^* \geq \mathbf{x}_{it}\boldsymbol{\beta}_{(j)} \tag{6.4}$$

This constraint guarantees that, for a given amount of inputs, the output at the metafrontier is no less than the output at the deterministic function of the group frontier. Battese, Rao and O'Donnell (2004) suggest that we can estimate the stochastic production function for each group of production units to find out $\boldsymbol{\beta}_{(j)}$ first and then use programming method to find out the $\boldsymbol{\beta}^*$. One possible criteria to derive $\boldsymbol{\beta}^*$ is the minimum sum of absolute deviations. This can be done by solving the following optimization problem:

$$\min L \equiv \sum_{t=1}^{T} \sum_{i=1}^{N} |\mathrm{Inf}(\mathbf{x}_{it},\boldsymbol{\beta}^*) - \mathrm{Inf}(\mathbf{x}_{it},\hat{\boldsymbol{\beta}}_{(j)})| \tag{6.5}$$

$$\text{s.t. } \mathrm{Inf}(\mathbf{x}_{it},\boldsymbol{\beta}^*) \geq \mathrm{Inf}(\mathbf{x}_{it},\hat{\boldsymbol{\beta}}_{(j)}) \tag{6.6}$$

where $\hat{\boldsymbol{\beta}}_{(j)}$ denotes the estimated parameters in the stochastic frontier. If the production function $f(\mathbf{x}_{it},\boldsymbol{\beta}^*)$ is assumed to be log-linear in the parameters (as it is in the following application), the problem in equation (6.5) and (6.6) is equivalent to solving the linear programming problem:

$$\min L \equiv \sum_{t=1}^{T} \sum_{i=1}^{N} (\mathbf{x}_{it}\boldsymbol{\beta}^* - \mathbf{x}_{it}\hat{\boldsymbol{\beta}}_{(j)}) \tag{6.7}$$

$$\text{s.t. } \mathbf{x}_{it}\boldsymbol{\beta}^{*} \geq \mathbf{x}_{it}\hat{\boldsymbol{\beta}}_{(j)} \qquad (6.8)$$

In this framework, various measures of technical efficiencies can be defined accordingly. To facilitate further discussion, we can rewrite equation (6.2) as:

$$Y_{it} = e^{-U_{it(j)}} \times \frac{e^{\mathbf{x}_{it}\boldsymbol{\beta}_{(j)}}}{e^{\mathbf{x}_{it}\boldsymbol{\beta}^{*}}} \times e^{\mathbf{x}_{it}\boldsymbol{\beta}^{*}+V_{it(j)}} \qquad (6.9)$$

Note that the first term on the right-hand side is technical efficiency of the *i*th unit in the *j*th group relative to the stochastic frontier for the *j*th group. This can be easily seen from the following equation:

$$TE_{it} = \frac{Y_{it}}{e^{\mathbf{x}_{it}\boldsymbol{\beta}_{(j)}+V_{it(j)}}} = e^{-U_{it(j)}} \qquad (6.10)$$

The second term on the right-hand side of equation (6.9) is the technology gap ratio (TGR):

$$TGR_{it} = \frac{e^{\mathbf{x}_{it}\boldsymbol{\beta}_{(j)}}}{e^{\mathbf{x}_{it}\boldsymbol{\beta}^{*}}} \qquad (6.11)$$

Lastly, we can compute the technical efficiency of the unit relative to the metafrontier as:

$$TE_{it}^{*} = \frac{Y_{it}}{e^{\mathbf{x}_{it}\boldsymbol{\beta}^{*}+V_{it(j)}}} \qquad (6.12)$$

Note that the following relation between the above three terms is obvious

$$TE_{it}^{*} = TE_{it} \times TGR_{it} \qquad (6.13)$$

EMPIRICAL ESTIMATIONS AND DATA ISSUES

We have chosen the model of Battesse and Coelli (1995) for estimating the stochastic production frontier for China's urban system. The model has the merit that the determinants of the inefficiency can be estimated together with the frontier function by a maximum likelihood method. Since we are going to employ cross sectional data, we skip the time subscript. The model, in translog form, can be specified as:

$$\ln(Y_i) = \beta_0 + \beta_L \ln L + \beta_K \ln K + \beta_{LL} (\ln L)^2 + \beta_{kk} (\ln K)^2 + \beta_{LK} (\ln L \ln K) + V_i + U_i$$
$$(6.14)$$

The errors of the model consist of two components. The term V_i are random variables which are assumed to be i.i.d. $N(0,\sigma_v^2)$, and independent of the U_i which are non-negative random variables assumed to be independently distributed as truncations at zero of the $N(m_i,\sigma_u^2)$ distribution. Here $m_{it} = z_i \delta$, where z_i is a $p\times1$ vector of variables which may influence the technical inefficiency of a firm; and δ is a $1\times p$ vector of parameters to be estimated. Battese and Coelli (1995) utilize the parameterization of Battese and Corra (1977) to replace σ_v^2 and σ_u^2 with $\sigma^2 = \sigma_v^2 + \sigma_u^2$ and $\gamma = \sigma_u^2/(\sigma_v^2 + \sigma_u^2)$. The log-likelihood function of this model is presented in the appendix in Battese and Coelli (1993). The estimations can be done with the computer program Frontier 4.1 (see Coelli 1996). Furthermore, we have chosen regional dummies as the determinants of the inefficiency (that is, z_i). Following Li and Hou (2003), we classified Chinese cities into eight regions (see Table 6.1).

Table 6.1 Classification of regions

	Region	Provinces
1	Northeastern	Liaoning, Jilin, Heilongjiang
2	North coastal	Beijing, Tianjin, Hebei, Shantong
3	East coastal	Shanghai, Jiangsu, Zhejiang
4	South coastal	Fujian, Guangdong, Hainan
5	Middle Yellow River	Shanxi, Inner Mongolia, Henan and Shaanxi
6	Middle Yangzi River	Anhui, Jiangxi, Hubei, Hunan
7	Southwestern	Guangxi, Sichuan, Guizhou, Yunnan
8	Northwestern	Gansu, Qinghai, Ningxia, Xinjiang

More precisely, in the estimation of the stochastic frontier, we specify the inefficiency model as follows:

$$m_i = \delta_0 + \sum_{i=1}^{7} \delta_i D_i \qquad (6.15)$$

where D_i is the dummy for the ith region listed above.

This chapter uses city-level data of 2002 for estimation. The output is GDP and inputs are capital and labour. To construct the capital data, we assume that there is a steady growth rate of investment so that we can infer the capital stock K in 2002. The relationship between investment and capital stock can be expressed by $K = I_{2002}/(g^* + \delta)$, where I_{2002} is the investment in 2002, g^* the steady growth rate of investment and δ the depreciation rate. The real growth rate of the investment in fixed assets during 1996-2002 is used as a proxy for the steady growth rate of investment.[3] The depreciation rate is assumed to be 10 per cent. The necessary data are available in *Statistical Yearbook of Chinese Cities*, from 1997 to 2003.

However, it is important to note that there have been administrative reforms that change the boundaries and administrative levels of the cities. For some cities, where it is impossible to find the actual investment growth or any reasonable proxy, we have to delete the observations.[4] Eventually, our data set for estimation includes 213 cities at prefecture level and 295 cities at county level, that is, a total of 508 observation points. Table 6.2 presents the summary statistics of our data set.

Table 6.2 Summary statistics of the data set (figures of 2002)

	213 Prefectures			295 Counties		
	GDP (Rmb billion)	Labour (1000)	Capital (Rmb billion)	GDP (Rmb billion)	Labour (1000)	Capital (Rmb billion)
Mean	14.64	153.59	19.38	7.16	52.50	4.27
S.D.	16.89	123.03	21.09	6.19	58.23	4.76
Max	117.59	729.10	144.73	41.00	519.20	41.34
Min	1.51	17.30	1.38	0.30	3.91	0.23

EMPIRICAL RESULTS

As noted above, our intention is to investigate the performance of the cities at different administrative levels (prefecture and county). We start by assuming that there are two different production technologies, one for the group of county-level cities and one for the group of cities at prefecture level. Then we test whether they indeed have different technologies. After confirming that they have different frontiers, a metafrontier is constructed. Analysis of technical efficiencies can then be conducted.

Frontier Estimation

Table 6.3 reports the estimation results for various stochastic production frontiers. The first two are respectively for the 213 prefecture-level cities and 295 county-level cities. In the third frontier, we pool the whole sample of 508 cities together for estimation, which is equivalent to assuming the two groups of cities share the same technology. A likelihood ratio (LR) test of the null hypothesis that the group frontiers are the same is performed.[5] The value of the LR statistic is 162.78, which is highly significant. Thus the result suggests that the two groups of cities utilize different technologies.

Table 6.3 Estimation of stochastic production frontiers

Variable	Coefficient	213 prefectures		295 counties		508 cities	
Constant	β_0	18.455	(1.544)	9.336	(4.163)	12.844	(2.489)
lnK	β_2	-1.473	(0.472)	0.004	(0.739)	-0.049	(0.491)
$(lnL)^2$	β_3	0.014	(0.093)	-0.177	(0.038)	-0.110	(0.034)
$(lnK)^2$	β_4	0.070	(0.042)	0.002	(0.034)	-0.011	(0.024)
$lnLxlnK$	β_5	-0.015	(0.150)	0.076	(0.061)	0.150	(0.042)
Constant	δ_0	0.457	(0.162)	1.275	(0.236)	1.065	(0.114)
D_1	δ_1	0.019	(0.135)	-0.774	(0.205)	-0.423	(0.122)
D_2	δ_2	-0.318	(0.214)	-1.901	(0.965)	-0.973	(0.218)
D_3	δ_3	-1.857	(0.684)	-2.228	(1.637)	-2.833	(0.297)
D_4	δ_4	-0.707	(0.407)	-0.994	(0.254)	-0.667	(0.137)
D_5	δ_5	0.143	(0.142)	-0.291	(0.189)	-0.081	(0.119)
D_6	δ_6	-0.271	(0.234)	-0.602	(0.201)	-0.398	(0.121)
D_7	δ_7	-0.382	(0.209)	-0.388	(0.192)	-0.329	(0.115)
γ		0.122	(0.044)	0.270	(0.043)	0.219	(0.018)
σ^2		0.239	(0.166)	0.581	(0.144)	0.211	(0.107)
Log-likelihood		-62.05		-179.14		-322.59	
LR test of the one-sided error		61.53		124.61		177.46	

Note: Figures in the parentheses are the standard errors.

Next, we solve the linear programming problem expressed in equations (6.7) and (6.8). The following metafrontier has been obtained:

$$\ln(Y_i) = 10.4053 + 0.2292 \ln L + 0.0100 \ln K - 0.1009(\ln L)^2 + 0.0017(\ln K)^2 + 0.0751(\ln L \ln K)$$
(6.16)

Technical Efficiency Estimates

With the estimated group frontiers and metafrontier, we can compute the technical efficiencies. Table 6.4 reports the summary statistics of each of the two groups of cities. It can be seen that TE (technical efficiency relative to the respective group frontier) of the prefecture-level cities averages 0.777, much higher than the average TE of the county-level cities. However, the standard deviation of the TE of the prefecture-level cities is only 0.142, much smaller than the 0.215 of the county-level cities. This indicates that the performance of Chinese prefectures differed less and they produced at output level closer to their group frontier than the county-level cities did.

Table 6.4 Technical efficiency of Chinese cities (summary statistics)

	213 prefectures			295 counties		
	TE	TGR	TE*	TE	TGR	TE*
Mean	0.777	0.512	0.397	0.625	0.969	0.607
S.D.	0.142	0.118	0.113	0.215	0.059	0.216
Max	1.000	1.000	0.779	0.930	1.000	0.929
Min	0.496	0.387	0.196	0.179	0.628	0.176

Note: TE: technical efficient relative to the group frontier; TGR: technical gap ratio; TE*: technical efficiency relative to the metafrontier.

However, there is a big difference in the TGR (technological gap ratio) of the two groups, with prefecture-level cities having an average much lower than that of the county-level cities (being 0.512 and 0.969 respectively). In a sense, the low average value of the prefecture-level cities implies they have a big technological gap with the metafrontier. This means that even if the prefecture-level cities can improve their technical efficiency up to their best performer (i.e. producing at the group frontier), they are still far behind the maximum possible output of China's city economies. Put simply, the prefectures appear to be systematically producing less output than they ought to be, a phenomenon that should arouse concerns.

Taking both factors together, the performance of the county-level cities is better than the prefecture-level cities. This can be seen from the value of TE* (technical efficiency of a city relative to the metafrontier): that of the county-level cities is 0.607 while that of prefectures is only 0.397.

Regional Patterns of Technical Efficiencies

One may be interested in the relative performance of the cities in different regions. In Table 6.5, we have computed the regional means of various indicators. In the lower part of the table, we follow the conventional (and also the official) classification method to divide China into three broad regions, eastern (coastal), central and western. The performance of cities in the three regions followed a flying-geese pattern, with cities in the eastern region having the best performance, followed by cities in the central and western regions respectively. Note that the TE* of the counties is higher than that of the prefectures in all the three regions.

Table 6.5 Technical efficiency of Chinese cities (regional means)

		213 prefectures			295 counties		
		TE	TGR	TE*	TE	TGR	TE*
	8-region classification						
1	Northeastern	0.631	0.523	0.332	0.600	0.966	0.579
2	North coastal	0.830	0.555	0.462	0.853	0.976	0.832
3	East coastal	0.982	0.526	0.516	0.883	0.986	0.871
4	South coastal	0.929	0.501	0.466	0.668	0.968	0.648
5	Middle Yellow River	0.560	0.535	0.300	0.398	0.957	0.380
6	Middle Yangzi River	0.808	0.490	0.396	0.515	0.952	0.492
7	Southwestern	0.854	0.467	0.398	0.438	0.974	0.426
8	Northwestern	0.639	0.521	0.330	0.298	0.957	0.283
	3-region classification						
1	Eastern	0.845	0.533	0.448	0.808	0.977	0.790
2	Central	0.724	0.508	0.365	0.508	0.963	0.489
3	Western	0.738	0.483	0.354	0.390	0.959	0.374

In the upper part of table, we follow the classification method used in the above stochastic frontier estimation and divide China into the eight regions. One can see that county-level cities have a higher TE* than prefecture-level cities in all the eight regions except for the northwestern region. The relative performance of the regions seems to be reasonable, with east coastal, south coastal and north coastal staying at the top three places in both prefecture-level and county-level cities.

However, one noticeable pattern is that the TGR of the county-level cities are all very high (above 0.95) in the eight regions, indicating that no particular region has a big technological gap with the metafrontier for countries. In contrast, prefecture-level cities in all eight regions have a value of TGR around 0.5, indicating that they all have a big technological gap with the metafrontier.

CONCLUSIONS

This chapter investigates the relative performance of Chinese cities at two different administrative levels, utilizing a recently developed quantitative method. We estimate the stochastic production frontiers for the two kinds of cities from which a metafrontier function is derived. Our preliminary results suggest that the prefecture-level cities have performed systematically worse than the county-level cities in terms of technical efficiency. Under the current system, prefecture-level cities have bigger power to mobilize resources, but it turns out that they are not utilizing the resources efficiently. Our result lends support to the argument that the existing administrative system of cities should be reshuffled.

NOTES

1. The work described in this chapter is partially supported by a grant from the Research Grants Council of Hong Kong Special Administrative Region, China (Project No. HKBU2010/02H).
2. According to Lau and Yotopoulos (1989), the concept is "theoretically attractive because it is based on the simple but appealing hypothesis that all producers (countries) have potential access to the same technology but each may choose to operate on a different part of it depending on specific circumstances". They are "empirically attractive because it justifies the pooling of data from different countries to estimate the common underlying production function".
3. In the case of Chongqing, we use the average annual growth rate of 1997-2002 instead because it was established as a provincial level city in 1997. There is no comparable data in 1996.
4. When inconsistent boundaries of the cities are found during 1996-2002, we try to use the investment growth of the whole prefectural region (i.e. including the prefecture-level city and all the counties under its jurisdiction). If the boundary of the prefectural region also changed, we delete the observation.
5. Specifically, the LR statistic is defined by $\lambda = -2\{\ln[L(H_0)/L(H_1)]\}$, where $\ln[L(H_0)$ is the value of the log-likelihood function for the stochastic frontier estimated by pooling all the data of the two groups together and $L(H1)$ is the sum of the values of the log-likelihood functions for the two group frontiers. The degrees of freedom for the Chi-square distribution involved are the number of restrictions imposed (16 in our case).

REFERENCES

Battese, George E. and Coelli, T. J., 1995. 'Frontier production functions, technical efficiency and panel data: with applications to Paddy farmers in India', *Empirical Economics*, **20**, 325-332.

Battese, George E. and Rao, D. D. P., 2002. 'Technology gap, efficiency, and a stochastic metafrontier function', *International Journal of Business and Economics*, **1**, 87-93.

Battese, George E., Rao, D. D. P. and O'Donnell, Christopher J., 2004. 'A metafrontier production function for estimation of technical efficiencies and technology gaps for firms operating under different technologies', *Journal of Productivity Analysis*, **21**, 91-103.

Battese, G. and T. Coelli, 1993. 'A stochastic frontier production function incorporating a model for technical inefficiency effects', Working Papers in *Econometrics and Statistics No.69*, University of New England, Australia.

Battese, G. E. and G. S. Corra, 1977. 'Estimation of a production frontier model: with application to the pastoral zone of eastern Australia', *Australian Journal of Agricultural Economics*, **21(3)**, 169-79.

Chung, J. H. and Lam, T. C., 2004. 'China's "city system" in flux: explaining post-Mao administrative changes', *China Quarterly*, **180**, 945-964.

Coelli, T. J., 1996. 'A guide to FRONTIER version 4.1: a computer program for stochastic frontier production and cost function estimation', *CEPA Working Paper 96/07*, Centre for Efficiency and Productivity Analysis, University of New England.

Dai, J., 2000. *China's City System*, Zhongguo Ditu Chubanshe.

Hayami, Y., 1969. 'Sources of agricultural productivity gap among selected counties', *American Journal of Agricultural Economics*, **51**, 564-575.

Hayami, Y. and Ruttan, V. W., 1970. 'Agricultural productivity differences among countries', *American Economic Review*, **60**, 895-911.

Hayami, Y. and Ruttan, V. W., 1985. *Agricultural Development: An International Perspective*, Baltimore: John Hopkins University Press.

Lau, L. J. and Yotopoulos, P. A., 1989. 'The Meta-production function approach of technical change in world agriculture', *Journal of Development Economics*, **31**, 241-269.

Li, S. and Hou, Y., 2003. 'An analysis of the regional socio-economic development of China', in *China Development Research: Selected Reports from the Development Research Centre of State Council*, Beijing: China Development Research Publisher, 244-259.

Wang, H., 2005. 'Implement province-control-county fiscal system, promote balanced socio-economic growth in counties', *Review of Economic Research*, **38**, 38-4.

7. Rural Migrants and Public Security

Ingrid Nielsen and Russell Smyth

INTRODUCTION[1]

From the founding of the People's Republic up until the start of economic reform China had a very low crime rate (Dutton 1997, Deng and Cordilia 1999). Between 1951 and 1965 the official crime rate dropped from 90 per 100,000 people to 30 per 100,000 people (Yu 1993, pp.43-44). Crime statistics were not collected from 1966 to 1971 at the height of the Cultural Revolution. From 1972 to 1976 the crime rate increased to 60 per 100,000 people (Yu 1993, pp.43-44). This latter increase has been blamed on the fact that the majority of young people had no school to attend or job to keep them occupied (Liang and Shapiro 1983), although crime rates were still low compared to the market reform period (Deng and Cordilia 1999). Since the beginning of the 1990s the official crime rate has hovered between 140 and 200 per 100,000 people most years, peaking at 215 per 100,000 people in 1991 (Guo 1996, p.3). The rate of serious crime has shown a marked increase between the late 1980s and mid 1990s. For example, between 1988 and 1995 homicides increased 71 per cent, assaults 171 per cent, robbery 351 per cent, serious theft 237 percent and larceny 72 per cent (Guo 1996, p.4). The sharp increase in the crime rate has fueled government and public concerns of a crime wave. As one commentator put it, "the government leadership considers China is currently experiencing a period of criminal 'high-tide'" (Ma 1995, p.247).

Nevertheless, despite the existence of official crime estimates, Silverman and Della-Giustina (2001) observed that such objective measures do not always bear in any substantial way upon community fear of crime. In fact, several studies have shown that the fear of personal crime is actually greater than its objective incidence (Borooah and Carcach 1997, Ito 1983). The frequent lack of correspondence between actual crime rates and the fear of crime has led to a strong research focus on the latter (Busselle 2003). While most existing research on fear of crime has been undertaken in the Anglo-American context (Ito 1983), the tendency for people to display a divergence between perceptions of objective crime rates and subjective crime vulnerability has been observed in China by Guo et al. (2001). These authors found that among residents of Guangzhou, recourse to "official crime statistics was almost irrelevant to people's crime estimates" (p.415). Yin (1985) made the point that in the Chinese context, few people make use of actual crime rate sources when assessing their community's vulnerability. This supported an earlier study by Tyler (1980) on the origins of crime-related judgments, which concluded that people are both willing and able to separate their beliefs about personal vulnerability to crime from objective rates of crime in their community.

Beginning with Becker (1968) and Ehrlich (1973), the economics of crime literature has focused most of its attention on explaining determinants of crime within a rational actor framework. There are several studies employing a 'supply of offences' function where the crime rate per capita is the dependent variable and explanatory variables include the probability of apprehension, severity of sentence and proxies for returns to legitimate and illegitimate earnings activities (see Cameron (1988) for a review). Economists have also examined the interaction between average crime rates and public spending on crime prevention across space and time as well as the substitutability between private and public spending on crime prevention (see e.g., Behrman and Craig 1987, Gyimah-Brempong 1989, Clotfelter 1977). Support for taking an economic approach to the study of perceptions of public safety comes from Pradhan and Ravallion (2003), who examined determinants of public safety in Brazil. Apart from that study, however, there has been no research in the economics literature on concern about public safety. This is true more generally for the determinants of public safety in transitional economies. It is important to begin to address this apparent gap in the literature because public perceptions of safety bear substantially upon both subjective quality of life and on further objective life quality measures, such as government spending on crime prevention and victimisation support. Presumably politicians also care about perceptions because how people perceive crime rates is important for political survival for politicians and/or their policies. This is true irrespective of whether perceptions of crime are an accurate reflection of crime rates.[2]

The current chapter adds to the scant literature on economic models of the determinants of public safety by drawing on a large survey of urban residents conducted in 2003 to examine the determinants of people's perceptions of public safety in Chinese cities. Public opinion polls have consistently shown that public safety is an important concern for people all over the world (Pradhan and Ravallion 2003) and public safety is a major issue in transitional economies such as China. A 1991 national survey of 15,000 people in China reported that two-thirds of respondents were seriously worried about the level of public safety (Research Institute of Ministry of Public Security 1991). As Situ and Liu (1996) have graphically described the fear of crime among residents in Guangzhou:

In Guangzhou, the residents' fear of victimisation has turned them into 'prisoners at home'. To prevent burglary, which is the number one type of crime in the city, they install iron bars to protect their windows and balconies (even those who live in the upper stories do this), replace their wooden doors by steel doors, install intercom systems at the entrance of their apartment buildings, and some even hire round-the-clock safety guards for their houses.

In this chapter we test the effect of both individual and neighbourhood effects on perceptions of current safety and perceived changes in public safety among the urban population in the two years prior to the survey. In the Chinese context much attention has been given to the perceived role of migrants in contributing to urban crime rates (Solinger 1999). Thus, we also examine the effect of attitudes to migrants on people's perceptions of crime rates. Because we find 'attitudes to migrants' to be an endogenous variable, we correct for endogeneity and report both corrected and uncorrected results.

The chapter is set out as follows. The next section discusses stereotypes of migrants in China. This is followed by an overview of the data, description of the empirical specification and discussion of the expected signs on the explanatory variables from an economic perspective. Then the empirical results are presented. Foreshadowing our main results, we find that the respondent's attitudes to migrants and whether he or she lives in the coastal region, plus the masculinity ratio, unemployment rate and expenditure on armed police in the locale in which the respondent resides are statistically significant predictors of perceptions of public safety, irrespective of how the dependent variable is defined. The final section suggests some avenues for future research.

ATTITUDES TO MIGRANTS AND PERCEPTIONS OF PUBLIC SAFETY IN CHINA

One of the central hypotheses that we test in this chapter is that urbanites' perceptions of public safety are influenced by their attitudes to migrants. It is estimated that 120-150 million peasant workers have relocated to China's cities (Pan 2002), with this number expected to increase to around 300 million by 2010 (Lague 2003). These rural to urban migrants are termed the 'floating population' (*liudong renkou*) because migrants' stays are typically temporary and follow work opportunities within and between locations. One result of the temporary nature of these migrants' stays in the city is that they tend to remain socially isolated from the indigenous urbanites, and relationships between the groups are, at best, strained. The predominant attitude towards the migrant population is one of suspicion (Roberts 2002). Chai and Chai (1997) noted that there is often outright hostility towards migrants and that this perception seems to have translated into the development of broad negative attitudes towards temporary migrants.

Another result of this massive migration phenomenon is the heterogenisation of China's cities. As Rountree and Land (1996) and Austin *et al.* (2002) observed, the social dynamics and demographic composition of urban centres affect residents' attitudes towards crime and their perceptions of public safety. China's urban centres have undergone substantial changes in demographic composition over the last few decades with the influx of the floating population being a major contributing factor. It is likely that these demographic changes may be important contributors to perceptions of compromised public safety in urban China, following Taylor and Covington's (1993) study, in which higher levels of fear were reported in environments that had undergone recent demographic change.

Migrants are often blamed for contributing to escalating crime rates in urban China. As Wang and Zuo (1999) have put it: "The stereotype of rural migrants is that they are uneducated, ignorant, dirty, and also have high propensities to be criminals" (p.278). Situ and Liu (1996) suggested that "new migrants constitute a large majority of the crime problem in the major Chinese cities" (p.295). Several studies have found that urban residents hold migrants responsible for a disproportionate amount of crime. A survey in the mid 1990s found that 74 per cent of Shanghai residents held migrants responsible for at least three of the following four problems: crime, transport, employment and environmental degradation (Solinger 1999, p.101). In the same survey, 81 per cent of respondents rated reduced safety of property as the most troubling effect of the presence of migrants in Shanghai, with 14 per cent of respondents terming it "serious". The main reason these people felt insecure was that they had personally experienced theft in the recent past (Solinger 1999, p.131). Another survey of residents also in the mid 1990s in Beijing, Guangzhou and Shanghai found that poor social order has become the "number one public enemy" and that respondents considered migrants to be the "root cause" of their insecurity and rising crime rates (Solinger 1999, p.131).

However, as Roberts (2001) noted "knowledgeable observers think migrants are scapegoats". Solinger (1999, p.102) stated "the ills associated with incipient markets: competitive labor markets, inflation, crowded transport vehicles .... and scarcer water and electricity, not surprisingly, became linked to migrants as well". Statistics for some specific localities suggest that migrants commit a disproportionate amount of crime in some big cities. According to official statistics, in Beijing 44 per cent of crimes solved by the police in 1995 were committed by transients (Xu 1995). In Guangzhou 80 per cent of burglaries in the mid 1990s were recorded by the police as being committed by transients and in Guangdong as a whole, 90 per cent of those charged with drug trafficking and prostitution were recorded as migrants (Chen and Luo 1995). Solinger (1999), however, has argued that the figures are often unreliable. Not all crimes attributable to migrants in the official statistics can necessarily be reliably attributed to migrants because, as Solinger (1999) has argued, authorities are often prejudiced against migrants and record crimes committed by urban vagrants as being committed by migrants.

Underpinning these stereotypes is the transformation of urban China into a hierarchical society, with well-defined and socially differentiated 'us' versus 'them' groups. Turner *et al.* (1987) term such discrete and hierarchically arranged social groups as 'in-groups' and 'out-groups'; an in-group being a more superior, or socially powerful group, and an out-group being a socially inferior, or less powerful, group. In urban China, the hierarchical arrangement of urban indigenous and migrant groups are good examples respectively of in- and out-groups that we argue are borne in part of the residential registration (*hukou*) system's clear social power differential favouring urbanites over rural migrants. One of social psychology's more reliable phenomena is the propensity of group members to favour their own over other-group members. This is referred to as in-group favouritism (Schaller 1992). In a study conducted by Malloy *et al.* (2004) among Chinese in-group and out-group samples, there was greater consensus in trait judgments within the in- and out-groups than there was between the in- and out-groups, indicating that the phenomenon of in-group favouritism extends to Chinese culture.

Apart from their structural origins within the *hukou* system, another explanation for the emergence of highly discrete in- and out-groups in urban China may be, as Roberts (1997, p.268) observed, the fact that "native place identity (*tongxiang*) is a critical component of personal identity in China". Roberts argued that the concept of ethnicity in China has long been defined in terms of birthplace - a differentiating tendency reinforced by the fact that Chinese Marxism encouraged urbanites to see themselves as the 'leading class', that is, as a veritable 'aristocracy of labour' from 1949. In part due to in-group favouritism, voluntary intergroup social contact between in-groups and out-groups tends to be limited. Prejudice towards same-group, and against other-group, members serves only to deepen in-group / out-group divides because, as Plous (2003, p.3) observed, "where prejudices lurk, stereotypes are seldom far behind". Stereotypes are frequently negative and this observation seems particularly apt in the context of urban China where, as Cheng and Selden (1994) pointed out, the term *mangliu,* which is used to describe the floating population, is a play on the word *liumang,* which means vagrant or hooligan.

The economic model of crime predicts that migrants would commit more crime because of the existence of labour market discrimination. Studies for the United States have consistently found that African Americans commit more crime and have higher incarceration rates. An important reason for this is the existence of segmented labour markets, which makes the marginal return to illegal earning activities, such as dealing drugs, much higher for African American males (Freeman 1996). In China, in urban areas the floating population and local urban residents participate in segmented labour markets. Several studies using datasets for the mid 1990s found that the

Chinese labour market is segmented between urban residents and rural migrants (Knight and Song 1999; Knight *et al.* 1999; Meng and Zhang 2001). More recently, Appleton *et al.* (2004) and Maurer-Fazio and Dinh (2004) examined labour market segmentation between continuously employed urban workers, urban workers who had been laid-off and reemployed and rural migrants. Both studies found evidence of labour market segmentation into these three categories with non-retrenched urban workers receiving a wage premium. A survey of migrants in Shanghai found a clear division between the floating population and local residents in terms of occupational composition, living conditions and income and benefits (Feng *et al.* 2002). There is also evidence of occupational stratification at the national level. According to 1990 census data, nationally only 3 per cent of all long-term migrant employees are in professional/cadre/clerical positions compared with 24 per cent for urban residents (Yang and Guo 1996).

It is common for the floating population to be forced to do jobs that the urban populace do not want (Yang and Guo 1996; Feng *et al.* 2002). These jobs are often so-called 'Three-D' jobs - jobs which are dirty, dangerous and demeaning - which are common in industries such as construction and mining for males and sanitation and textiles for females. A wealth of anecdotal evidence documented in Roberts (2001) and elsewhere supports this claim. In some cases occupational stratification has been institutionalised. While actual reports of migrants taking the jobs of urban residents are spasmodic, perceptions that migrants are taking jobs from the urban populace and pushing wages down is fuelling labour market tensions between the urban and migrant populations. This fear has influenced government policies with local officials viewing migrants as a burden on their cities (Solinger 1999; Guo and Iredale 2003). At one level this manifests itself in subtle forms of discrimination. For example, in Shanghai employers using migrant labour are required to contribute 50 renminbi to an unemployment fund for each migrant labourer they employ.[3] The proceeds from this fund are used exclusively to assist unemployed permanent urban workers (Feng *et al. 2*002). Some municipal governments have implemented regulations to protect urban labourers through reserving specific job categories for urban workers and making explicit suggestions that urban residents not be underpaid compared to outsiders. For instance, in the late 1990s, according to a report in the *Beijing Daily* (April 10, 1997), the Labour Bureau of one of Beijing's districts stipulated that at least 35 types of jobs should not be open to the floating population (cited in Wang and Zuo 1999). In other cases, municipal governments have adopted more direct action against migrant communities. Guo and Iredale (2003) reported that a number of 'migrant villages' in Beijing have been 'cleaned up' or 'demolished' since the late 1990s as migrant communities have been repatriated to the countryside.

DATA AND ANALYTICAL ISSUES

Since 2001, China Mainland Marketing Research Company (CMMRC) has conducted an annual survey of approximately 10000 urban residents, asking a range of questions relating to their perceptions of changes in living standards, changes in economic circumstances, expenditure on household items and background characteristics such as age, education, gender, income and occupation. CMMRC employs multi-stage stratified random sampling to ensure a representative sample in terms of age, gender and income. The respondents were interviewed in person in shopping districts of each city by a trained CMMRC interviewer. In each city there were four individuals conducting the survey in different shopping districts. All responses were checked for accuracy three times prior to being entered into the database; initially by a supervisor on location, then by a supervisor for the city and finally at the CMMRC offices in Beijing. All respondents who participated in the survey were aged 18 years or above and had always had an urban registration. Since January 2003 it has been possible for migrants in some cities to purchase an urban registration if certain conditions are met such as owning a house, having a stable job and/or investing a minimum amount in the city. There is no one in our sample in this category who was a migrant who purchased an urban registration.

This study employs data from the CMMRC survey, which was conducted in November 2003, to examine the determinants of people's perceptions of public safety. The 2003 survey contained information on 206 questions from 10716 respondents across 32 cities;[4] to which responses from 8127 or 8133 respondents contained usable data relating to the variables of interest to us depending on the specification. Data from the CMMRC survey was supplemented with data on the city in which the respondent lived. These latter data were obtained from China Statistical Yearbook, China Labour Statistical Yearbook, China Social Statistics and China Urban Statistical Yearbook.

We used the following specification to examine urbanites' perception of public safety:

$$PERCEPTION=f(X, Z, MIGRANT, \varepsilon) \qquad (7.1)$$

Here *PERCEPTION* is an ordinal variable measuring the respondent's perception of public safety; X is a vector of individual and household characteristics (age, gender, education, household income, household size, marital status, occupation, place of residence); Z is a vector of city characteristics (such as the masculinity ratio, population density, number of schools and expenditure on armed police); *MIGRANT* is a measure of the respondent's attitude to migrants and ε is the error term, reflecting unobserved random factors. In the survey conducted by CMMRC there were two questions asking about perceptions of public safety and we examined them in alternative specifications. In one specification the dependent variable measured the response to the question: 'Over the past two years what changes in public safety have you encountered in your living area?'. The options were 'considerable fall', 'slight fall', 'no change', 'some improvement' or 'significant improvement'. In the second specification the dependent variable measured the response to the question: 'Are you satisfied with your current living standards in terms of the level of public safety?'. The respondent answered on a five point scale ranging from one (extremely satisfied) up to five (extremely dissatisfied).

Table 7.1 provides a breakdown of the frequencies for both dependent variables. Overall, 63.2 per cent of respondents considered that there had been either 'some improvement' or 'significant improvement', 21.0 per cent of respondents considered there had been no change and 15.8 per cent of respondents said there had been either a 'slight fall' or 'considerable fall' in public safety in the two years prior to the survey. On the current level of satisfaction with public safety, 37.0 per cent expressed 'satisfaction' or 'extreme satisfaction', 35.2 per cent answered on the mid-point of the scale and 27.8 per cent of respondents expressed 'dissatisfaction' or 'extreme dissatisfaction'.

Table 7.1 Subjective assessments of public safety

'Over the past two years what changes in public safety have you encountered in your living area?'	
	%
Significant improvement	8.4
Some improvement	54.8
No change	21.0
Slight fall	13.5
Considerable fall	2.3
'Are you satisfied with your current living standards in terms of the level of public safety?'	
Extremely satisfied 1	5.3
2	31.7
3	35.2
4	19.5
Extremely dissatisfied 5	8.3

We used an ordered probit model to estimate equation 7.1, employing the two proxies for the dependent variable in alternative specifications. It is possible that the respondent's perception of migrants is an endogenous variable. This will be the case if the respondent's perception of migrants is based on the same human capital, job-related and personal factors that influence their perception of public safety. If this is the case, the error term (ε) will be correlated with *MIGRANT*, producing biased coefficients. In order to test whether *MIGRANT* was correlated with the error term we calculated the Hausman test. We used the respondent's level of satisfaction with transportation as the instrumental variable. There is much evidence that the influx of migrants into China's cities has placed severe pressure on the urban public transport system (Lee 1998). Migrants are often blamed by urban residents in China for clogging up transportation and contributing to traffic congestion (Solinger 1999, p.101). A survey by Ding and Stockman (1999) of 500 urban households in Shanghai in 1995 found that 90.8 per cent of respondents considered that migrants worsened traffic conditions and that 30.1 per cent of respondents thought that the effect of migrant presence in the city on traffic congestion was serious. A report by the Wuhan Economic Research Institute (2003, p.35) similarly found that urban "residents voiced the common complaint that migrants … are responsible for most of Wuhan's transport problems. For instance, residents blame migrants for most traffic infractions". Thus, it is reasonable to believe that people's satisfaction with transportation will be correlated with their perception of migrants, but not with their perception of public safety. The Hausman test suggested that *MIGRANT* was an endogenous variable in both versions of equation (7.1).[5] On this basis the estimation of equation (7.1) proceeded in two stages. In the first stage we estimated a reduced form probit regression for the endogenous variable, *MIGRANT*. In the second stage we estimated an ordered probit regression for *PERCEPTION* after substituting estimates for the endogenous variable *MIGRANT*, into equation (7.1).

The definition of each of the explanatory variables that we have employed to explain people's perception of public safety, together with either their mean values or, for the binary variables, the percentage of '1' responses, are given in Table 7.2. The mean age of respondents in the sample was 39 years, 50.2 per cent were female, 30.2 per cent were single and 26.0 per cent lived in one of the coastal provinces. The median household income of respondents was 2001-2250 RMB per month; 39.3 per cent had a three year higher education or above, 28.9 per cent had completed senior middle school and 20.9 per cent had a junior middle school education or less. On occupation, 35.6 per cent of respondents were in professional occupations, 31.3 per cent were manual, semi-skilled or technical workers, 15.9 per cent were retired and 8.8 per cent were unemployed.

Overall, with the exception of the education profile, the characteristics of the sample are fairly representative of the urban population as a whole. In 2001 the average household income was 1800 RMB and 40.7 per cent of people lived in one of the coastal provinces (SSB 2002, pp.94, 145). In 2002 49.9 percent of the urban population was female, the mean age of urban residents was 37 years and 25.2 per cent were single (SSB 2003a, pp.7, 38-40; SSB 2003b, p.67). The retirement age for blue collar workers in urban areas is 55 for women and 60 for men. In 2002 9.8 per cent of the urban population were aged 60 years or older and 14.4 per cent were aged 55 years or older (SSB 2003a). In order to reduce the surplus labour problem in state-

Table 7.2 Definition and descriptive statistics for the explanatory variables

Variable name	Variable description	Descriptive statistics
Gender	Binary variable where 0 = male and 1 = female	49.8% male
Age	Age in years	Mean age = 39.11 years ($\underline{SD}$ = 13.90 years) in a range of 18-100 years
Age^2	Age squared	Mean squared age = 1722.59 ($\underline{SD}$ = 1210.75) in a range of 324-10000
Household income	Average monthly household income of respondent (from 1-20 where 1 is 260 RMB or below and 20 is greater than 20,000 RMB)	Median = 9 (2000-2250 RMB)
Average income in the city	Average monthly income per capita in the city (RMB)	Mean average income = 1612.84 RMB ($\underline{SD}$ = 870.22 RMB) in a range of 5.00-3939.18
Marital status	Binary variable where 0 = not married and 1 = married	69.8% married
Size of household	Number of people living in the respondent's household	Mean = 3.21 ($\underline{SD}$ = 1.14) in a range of 1-13
Junior middle school	Binary variable equal to 1 if highest educational qualification is junior middle school or less, otherwise equal to 0	20.9% junior middle education or less
Senior middle school	Binary variable equal to 1 if highest educational qualification is senior middle school, otherwise equal to 0	28.3% senior middle education or less
Three year higher degree or above	Binary variable equal to 1 if highest educational qualification is a three year degree or above, otherwise equal to 0	39.3% three year degree or above

Senior professional occupation	Binary variable equal to 1 if a senior professional occupation, otherwise equal to 0	0.5% senior professional occupation
Middle professional occupation	Binary variable equal to 1 if a middle professional occupation, otherwise equal to 0	9.3% middle professional occupation
Lower professional occupation	Binary variable equal to 1 if a lower professional occupation, otherwise equal to 0	25.8% middle professional occupation
Technical occupation	Binary variable equal to 1 if a technical occupation, otherwise equal to 0	14.1% technical occupation
Semi-skilled occupation	Binary variable equal to 1 if a semi-skilled occupation, otherwise equal to 0	13.6% semi-skilled occupation
Manual occupation	Binary variable equal to 1 if a manual occupation, otherwise equal to 0	3.6% manual occupation
Unemployed	Binary variable equal to 1 if unemployed, otherwise equal to 0	8.8% unemployed
Retired	Binary variable equal to 1 if retired, otherwise equal to 0	15.9% retired
Coastal resident	Binary variable equal to 1 if a coastal resident, otherwise equal to 0	26.0% coastal residents
Attitudes to migrants in the city	Ordinal variable where 1 = most positive attitudes through 5 = least positive attitudes	Mean attitude score = 2.57 ($\underline{SD}$ = .89)
Floor space of buildings per capita in the city	Floor space of buildings completed in the city per capita (m^2/person)	Mean floor space = .79m^2 ($\underline{SD}$ = .50m^2) in a range of .06m^2 – 2.23m^2
Average change in selling price of houses in city	Average change in selling price indices of houses in the city (2000-2002) where preceding year = 100	Mean average change = 101.83 ($\underline{SD}$ = 1.48) in a range of 99.10 – 106.30
Average change in renting price in the city	Average change in renting price indices in the city (2000-2002) where preceding year = 100	Mean average change = 103.02 ($\underline{SD}$ = 7.59) in a range of 95.50 – 133.20
Unemployment rate in the city	Percentage registered unemployed in the city	Mean unemployment rate = 3.6% ($\underline{SD}$ = .91%) in a range of 1.40% to 4.90%

(continued overleaf)

(Table 7.2 continued)

Variable name	Variable description	Descriptive statistics
Masculinity ratio	Ratio of males to females in the city (departure from 100)	Mean males = 104.23 ($\underline{SD}$ = 3.55) in a range of 92.84 – 112.29
Expenditure on armed police per capita	RMB expenditure on armed police per capita in the city	Mean expenditure = 1.91RMB ($\underline{SD}$ = 1.53 RMB) in a range of 0.01 RMB – 6.04 RMB
Number of schools per 100,000 population	Number of schools per 100,000 population in the city	Mean number of schools = 17.53 ($\underline{SD}$ = 13.22) in a range on 4.25 – 68.54
Population density	Population density in the city (persons/km^2)	Mean density = 1535.43 persons/km^2 ($\underline{SD}$ = 815.51 persons/km^2) in a range of 147 – 4276 persons/km^2

owned enterprises, as part of an ongoing process of restructuring, some enterprises have introduced semi-retirement (*neitui*) at ages younger than the official retirement age, with semi-retired workers receiving 50-70 per cent of their position wage with no bonuses (Smyth *et al.* 2004). It is conceivable that some of the respondents in the sample who are designated as retired are semi-retired.

In 2002 among the urban population, 54.7 per cent completed junior middle school or less, 26.6 per cent had completed senior middle school, 4.4 per cent had a three year higher education and 0.3 per cent had a postgraduate degree (SSB 2003b, p.7). This means that in our sample, those with a junior middle school education or less are underrepresented and those with a tertiary degree are overrepresented relative to the urban population as a whole. One explanation for the education profile of our sample is that the survey was conducted in large cities where the educational level is much higher than in other areas. Previous studies which have interviewed respondents in large Chinese cities have also found better educated individuals to be disproportionately represented relative to the urban population as a whole. For example, in a survey of 500 households in Putuo District in Shanghai in 1995 conducted by Ding and Stockman (1999), 21 per cent of respondents had a three year higher education or above. In a survey of employees in manufacturing enterprises in three cities (Nanjing, Shanghai and Tianjin) in 1994-1995, Zhu (1997) found that 73.3 per cent of respondents had tertiary qualifications. This peculiarity with respect to educational level also seems to reflect those who typically answer surveys on the streets in China and respondents in street surveys more generally. In the 2002 survey administered by CMMRC, almost 40 per cent of respondents had a three year higher degree or above (CMMRC 2002). Holbrook *et al.* (2003) found that the educational levels of respondents are skewed and that respondents with a lower education level are generally reluctant to respond to surveys conducted in the street as they believe they may have more to lose. Studies comparing respondent education levels in various surveys have found fewer low-education respondents in telephone samples than in face-to-face samples (see Greenfield *et al.* 2000; Groves 1977). We now proceed to examine the rationale and expected signs for each of the explanatory variables.

Attitudes towards Migrants

In the CMMRC survey, the question asked: "Do you welcome migrants to live and work in your home city?" Responses were on a five point scale ranging from one (migrants are warmly welcomed) to five (migrants are particularly unwelcomed). Existing research suggests that race is a strong predictor of perceptions of public safety (Pain 2001). Results from extant studies suggest that fears frequently focus on other ethnic or minority groups. For example, in the United States, Tabb *et al.* (1984) found that working class whites believe that an influx of blacks into their neighbourhood increases crime rates and reduces housing values. Moreover, these fears are often based on stereotypes of particular ethnicities (Smith 1984; Lea and Young 1984). Using these studies as a guide, we expect that respondents who are fearful of migrants will have a lower perception of public safety. As the discussion in the proceeding section suggests, there are strong stereotypes around migrants and criminality in Chinese cities with migrants blamed for a disproportionate amount of crime in China's cities. Individuals who have a poor image of migrants are more likely to link increased migrant presence in China's cities to a perceived reduction in the level of urban public safety even if these fears are based on 'irrational prejudices'.

Individual and Household Characteristics

The expected sign on the coefficient for the household income of the respondent is *ex ante* unclear. On the one hand those with higher incomes should be better able to purchase private protection (Gavaria and Pages 2002) or, if public safety has properties of a local public good, mobilise local public action to prevent crime or move to a safer neighbourhood (Pradhan and Ravallion 2003). If this is the case, the rich should have better perceptions of public safety. On the other hand, though, those on higher incomes will be more desirable targets for potential offenders, which might make those on higher incomes less satisfied with public safety. This latter interpretation is consistent with the economic model of crime following Ehrlich (1973), which proxies returns to illegitimate earning activities using household income where household income is a measure of "the availability of thievable property" (Witt *et al.* 1999, p.391). The wealthy will face a trade-off in terms of how much they invest in private protection depending on the extent to which they are willing to bear some victimization risk. Gavaria and Pages (2002) developed a model that shows that the trade-offs the rich make will vary with different sorts of crime depending on whether the risk is random (such as muggings) or if the criminal has targeted the victim to maximise expected gains (such as burglaries).

The empirical evidence from existing studies for income is mixed. In two studies using data for the United States (Skogan and Maxfield 1981; Toseland 1982) as well as in a study employing Australian data (Borooah and Carcach 1997), it has been found that higher income individuals have less fear of crime. Pradhan and Ravallion (2003) also found that there was a positive, although small, income effect on the perceived current level of satisfaction with public safety in Brazil. Baba and Austin (1989) and Keil and Vito (1991), however, found that income levels had no significant impact on perceived levels of public safety. Meanwhile, Gavaria and Pages (2002) found a positive correlation between socioeconomic status and the probability of victimisation in Latin America. Their explanation was that their findings were being "driven by both the difficulties of the relatively wealthy in protecting themselves against street crime and the tendency of burglars and kidnappers to target wealthy victims" (Gavaria and Pages 2002, p.182). Hraba *et al.* (1998) found that wealth was positively related to perceived risk of crime in the Czech Republic, arguing that this reflected the fact that "the wealthy may feel vulnerable to crime, particularly property crime" (Hraba *et al.* 1998, p.239).

The expected sign on the coefficient of the respondent's education is *ex ante* unclear. While Hraba *et al.* (1998) found that in the Czech Republic, the more educated had a higher perceived risk of crime, several earlier studies found that concerns about public safety were stronger among people with lower levels of education (see e.g., Erskine 1974; Clemente and Kleinman 1977; Keil and Vito 1991). While the latter finding might simply reflect that the less educated live in less safe neighbourhoods, the former can be explained by Festinger's (1957) theory of cognitive dissonance. In the context of crime perception, Pradhan and Ravallion (2003) observed that cognitive dissonance often leads people to downplay the level of danger in their environment, since admitting to oneself that one lives in an unsafe environment is too psychologically provocative. To the extent that local crime rate knowledge is an indicator of education, this suggests that an individual's education might negatively influence his or her concern for public safety.

In addition to the respondent's education and income we include other individual and household characteristics for age, gender, marital status, size of the household and respondent's occupation to account for possible heterogeneity in preferences. There are several studies which suggest that older people have higher levels of fear of crime (see e.g., Skogan and Maxfield 1981) and lower levels of perceived safety (Baba and Austin 1989). This is in spite of the fact that most crime statistics indicate that older people are less likely to be the victims of crime, especially compared with teenagers and young adults. Warr (1984) has argued that the greater fear of crime among older people is attributable to their differential sensitivity to risk, despite their lower exposure. Others have suggested that higher levels of fear among the elderly might be partially due to social isolation (Sundeen and Matthieu 1976). The effect of age on perceptions of safety has, however, not been consistent. Clemente and Kleinman (1977) and Braungart *et al.* (1980), using data for the United States, and Keil *et al.* (1996) using data for Romania did not find significant age effects. For China, Curran and Cook (1993), citing data from the Ministry of Public Security, argued that those aged 16 to 28 years were more fearful of crime than those aged over the age of 28. Ferraro (1995) and LaGrange and Ferraro (1989) concluded that the effect of age on perceptions of public safety is non-linear. These authors found that perception of public safety is lower among younger people, is higher in middle age and is lower again in old age. To allow for the possible non-linear effect of age on perceptions of public safety, we include both the actual age and the squared value of the respondent's age as independent measures.

Most existing studies have found that women have a lower perception of public safety than men (see e.g., Borooah and Carcach 1997; Perkins and Taylor 1996). One explanation for this gender difference might be the positive relationship between fear and the potential for victimization (Taub *et al.* 1981). Women's fear of crime is fundamentally connected to their vulnerability to rape and sexual harassment (Ferraro 1995). Warr (1984) found that the possibility of rape is the primary fear of most women. We also interact the gender of the respondent with the masculinity ratio. If females are mainly fearful of sexual crime we expect that women living in cities with a higher masculinity ratio will have a lower perceived level of public safety.

Clark (1988) found that there is a direct negative relationship between burglary risk and the number of people in the home, while Mukherjee and Carach (1998) found that households comprised of a married couple are at less risk of burglary victimisation than single-person households. Following Mukherjee and Carach (1998), we expect married people to perceive public safety more favorably; and following Clark (1988), we expect perceptions of public safety to increase with larger numbers of people living in the household. In including a variable for occupation, we follow Keil *et al.* (1996), who included a measure of occupation in their study of perceptions of public safety in Romania. While there is no *a priori* expectation that the respondent's occupation will affect concerns over public safety one way or another, the rationale for including this variable is to see to what extent the traditional working class is concerned about public safety. Curran (1998) has expressed the view that rising crime rates and perceived fear of crime among the working population is threatening social stability and the course of market reforms in China. Thus, considering the effects of occupation on perceptions of public safety provides insights into whether fear of crime is an issue with which the government should be concerned in relation to urban workers, in addition to other grievances among the working class such as the growing problem of laid-off workers.

City Specific Characteristics

We include average income and the number of schools per 100,000 population in the city in which the respondent lives to investigate potential neighbourhood effects on perceptions of public safety. A stylised fact in the economics of crime literature is that crime tends to be spatially concentrated in low income areas (Pradhan and Ravallion 2003). One reason for this might be that in the Ehrlich (1973) supply of offences function the marginal return to illegitimate earning activities is higher for low income individuals. But, even though the marginal returns to crime are higher for low income individuals, this does not explain why, if criminals live in poorer neighbourhoods, they still do not commit crime in richer neighbourhoods where the marginal reward to crime is higher. Freeman *et al.* (1996) developed a model explaining the spatial concentration of crime in poor areas. Their model is based on a positive externality that criminals create for each other in equilibrium where the probability of detection is lowest in low income areas where the greatest number of criminals are concentrated, holding police resources constant.

We interact the respondent's household income with average income in the city. We expect that high income individuals in low income cities will have lower perceptions of public safety. Cullen and Levitt (1999) examined the effect of crime on urban flight, showing that in the United States, each additional reported crime leads on average to one fewer resident in that locale. Using an interaction term allows us to examine the extent to which public safety concerns encourage residential differentiation, such as "people flight", by non-poor people concerned about safety in low income areas.

The number of schools per 100,000 people is a measure of education as an external neighbourhood effect. We expect that individuals who live in cities with better educated populations will have better perceptions of public safety. One reason for this is that the economic approach to crime suggests that crime rates will be lower in cities with better educated populations. First, in the time allocation model of Ehrlich (1973) education reduces the amount of time available for criminal activities for those enrolled in schools. Second, education enhances human capital skills in legitimate earning activities more than illegitimate earning activities and increases the opportunity cost of crime (Wong 1995). Third, education acts to promote 'good citizenship' and as such generates positive externalities on social welfare reflected in greater respect for the property rights of others (Bodman and Maultby 1997). Another reason why individuals who live in cities with better educated populaces can be expected to have a better perception of public safety is through its effect on reducing cognitive dissonance. As Pradhan and Ravallion (2003, p.19) put it: "If own-education matters to concern for public-safety via its effect on knowledge about the true probabilities of crime, then one's neighbors' education could well have the same effect, assuming that education fosters different knowledge sets in different people, but that this knowledge is shared amongst concerned neighbours". We also interact the respondent's education with the number of schools in the city in which he or she lives. If education reduces cognitive dissonance and generates a positive externality, having better educated neighbours should accentuate the impact of concern for public safety on differences in own education (Pradhan and Ravallion 2003).

We include the floor space of buildings per capita and the average change in selling and rental price of housing as indicators of the attractiveness of the city to criminals. In addition, the average change in selling and rental prices of housing in the city will influence perceptions of public safety through demand for housing (Pradhan and Ravallion 2003). We include population density and a dummy variable for whether the respondent lives in a coastal province to examine the effect of city size on perceptions of public safety.

We expect that respondents living in cities in coastal provinces and living in more densely populated cities to have a lower perception of public safety.

One reason for expecting that respondents in cities in coastal provinces will have lower perceptions of public safety is that the market reforms have progressed further in the coastal provinces and this has resulted in higher levels of income inequality. Existing studies show that areas with higher income inequality tend to have higher crime rates (Witt *et al.* 1999) and lower perceived levels of public safety (Pradhan and Ravallion 2003). In this respect, it is arguable that there is a link between an increase in income inequality in China in the 1980s and 1990s, the massive increase in recorded crime rates and falling perceptions of public safety. Rising income levels mean that people who have benefited from reform are more concerned about crime now that they have property which can be stolen, and rising income inequality implies that there are also more people with less.

A second reason for expecting lower perceptions of public safety in cities in the coastal provinces and in the more densely populated cities is that these cities tend to be larger. Gavaria and Pages (2002) found a positive correlation between victimisation rates and city size, suggesting that perceptions of public safety can be expected to be lower in larger cities. This could be because (i) larger cities harbour a higher proportion of crime prone individuals; (ii) the marginal returns to crime are higher in larger cities because either large cities contain a higher proportion of wealthier victims or markets for second-hand goods are better developed or (iii) the probability of detecting crime in big cities is lower because there are diseconomies of scale in the production of arrests or larger cities invest less in law enforcement (Gavaria and Pages 2002).

Of the other city specific variables we expect that perceptions of public safety will be lower in cities with higher unemployment rates. The economic approach to crime suggests that unemployment will have a positive effect on crime rates both in a time allocation sense and because the marginal returns to crime for the unemployed will be higher. Existing studies for developed countries typically suggest that a one percentage point increase in unemployment results in a one per cent increase in property crime, although unemployment does not appear to influence violent crime (see Levitt 2004; Raphael and Winter-Ebmer 2001). We expect that perceptions of public safety will be lower in cities with higher masculinity ratios because most blue collar property crime is committed by males (Reilly and Witt 1996). We expect perceptions of public safety to be higher in cities which spend more on armed police per capita. Existing studies suggest that increased police presence deters crime through increasing the probability of apprehension (Witt *et al.* 1999; Di Tella and Schargrodsky 2004; Klick and Tabarrok 2004). The visibility of armed police can be expected to make people feel safer.

EMPIRICAL RESULTS

Table 7.3 presents the ordered probit results both uncorrected and corrected for endogeneity of perceptions of migrants where the dependent variable is 'Are you satisfied with your current living standards in terms of the level of public safety?', where respondents' answers were made on a five point scale ranging from one (extremely satisfied) to five (extremely dissatisfied). In the following discussion we focus only on the corrected results. Of the statistically significant variables with the expected signs, our first main finding is that respondents who view migrants as being unwelcome in their home city are less likely to be satisfied with current living standards in terms of public safety. We find that in cities which spend more on armed police per capita, respondents are more likely to be satisfied with current public safety. However, consistent with expectations, respondents living in cities in the coastal provinces or living in cities with a higher percentage of males are less likely to be satisfied with current public safety.

The coefficients on floor space of buildings per capita and average changes in the renting and selling prices of houses in the city are each statistically significant with a negative sign. This implies that as new buildings go up and rental and selling prices of houses increase people are more satisfied with current levels of public safety. In other words, in cities in which it is considered more desirable to live and work, reflected in higher demand for housing, people are also more likely to feel safer from crime.

The unemployment rate in the city is statistically significant with a negative sign.[6] We hypothesised that the unemployment rate in the city would have a positive sign given that the economic model suggests that higher unemployment will result in higher crime rates. We expected, based upon Ehrlich's (1973) time allocation model, that those who are unemployed would have more time to allocate to crime and have a lower opportunity cost of committing crime. An alternative perspective, however, on the crime-unemployment nexus, which is consistent with our results, is the 'opportunity perspective' which has been put forward in a series of articles by the criminologist Kenneth Land and his colleagues (see Cohen *et al.* 1980; Cantor and Land 1985, 2001). The opportunity perspective sees crime as a function of the supply of suitable targets for victimisation. This perspective suggests that crime will fall during times of high unemployment and thus people will feel more secure, because in times of economic downturn the circulation of people and the level of spending on new property is reduced, curtailing the amount of plunderable victim stock. Moreover, as the unemployment rate rises, more people will remain in their homes or close neigbourhood which builds social cohesion and improves their perception of public safety through reducing the incidence of property crime and curtailing the level of violent crime, most of which occurs outside the home.

Table 7.3 Ordered probit regression where the dependent variable is: 'Are you satisfied with your current living standards in terms of the level of public safety?'

Variable	Uncorrected		Corrected	
	Estimate	Wald	Estimate	Wald
Gender	.221	.077	.571	.517
Age	-.001	.042	.003	.155
Age²	.000	.001	-.000	.287
Household income	.000	.001	.001	.025
Average income in the city	.000	2.406	.000	4.233**
Marital status	.070	4.019**	.063	3.197***
Size of household	.018	2.829***	.017	2.440
Junior middle school	-.034	.210	-.045	.370
Senior middle school	.008	.012	.024	.118
Three year higher degree or above	.018	.070	.041	.364
Senior professional occupation	.025	.020	.009	.003
Middle professional occupation	.062	.930	.044	.468
Lower professional occupation	.036	.428	.021	.154
Technical occupation	.048	.664	.034	.326
Semi-skilled occupation	.025	.190	.019	.103
Manual occupation	-.173	4.743**	-.186	5.529**
Unemployed	-.090	1.886	-.072	1.204
Retired	-.000	.000	-.007	.010
Coastal resident	.079	2.061	.104	3.555***
Attitudes to migrants in the city	.144	114.829*	.038	161.674*

Floor space of buildings per capita in the city	-.106	4.788**	-.117	5.865**
Average change in selling price of houses in city	-.054	26.729*	-.052	24.833*
Average change in renting price in the city	-.020	61.368*	-.021	66.158*
Unemployment rate in the city	-.101	26.851*	-.100	26.344*
Masculinity ratio	.026	4.250**	.029	5.523**
Expenditure on armed police per capita	-.039	12.435*	-.042	14.649*
Number of schools per 100,000 population	.001	.103	.002	.352
Population density	-.000	21.712*	-.000	30.478*
Gender x masculinity ratio	-.002	.069	-.005	.461
Household income x average income in the city	-.000	5.309**	-.000	7.563***
Number of schools x junior middle education	.001	.040	.001	.170
Number of schools x senior middle education	-.000	.004	.000	.021
Number of schools x three year degree or higher	-.000	.017	-.002	.251
Threshold 1	-6.719	15.242*	-6.486	14.195*
Threshold 2	-5.431	9.966*	-5.918	9.122*
Threshold 3	-4.508	6.865**	-4.270	6.157**
Threshold 4	-3.660	4.526**	-3.418	3.946**
-2 Log Likelihood (Unrestricted)	23089.103		23120.988	
-2 Log Likelihood (Restricted)	22754.593		22739.575	
- 2LR Statistic (33 df)	334.511*		381.413*	
Nagelkerke Pseudo R^2	.043		.049	
Number of observations	8127		8127	

Notes: *, **and *** imply that the coefficient is statistically different from zero at the 1%, 5% and 10% level of significance, respectively. Wald statistics are calculated from heteroskedastic-consistent standard errors. A Hausman test using satisfaction with public transportation as the instrument suggests that attitudes towards migrants in the city be endogenous ($p < 0.0001$). Therefore, we report results both corrected and uncorrected for endogeneity of attitudes towards migrants. The reference category for occupations is people not in the labor market such as homemakers and students. The reference category for education is people with a polytechnic education.

Of the other variables which are statistically significant in Table 7.3, the coefficient on population density is zero to three decimal places, indicating that it has no practical effect on perceptions of public safety in the current sample. Marital status has an unexpected positive sign, but its confidence intervals at the 95 per cent level bound zero, so we cannot reliably predict whether the sign on this variable is positive or negative. The only occupation which is statistically significant is the coefficient on manual workers, which has a negative sign, suggesting that manual workers have a better perception of public safety than those not in the labour market, which was the reference category.

There is no evidence of an income effect in Table 7.3. The respondent's household income is statistically insignificant. While average income in the city and the term interacting household income and average income in the city are statistically significant, the coefficient on both terms is zero to three decimal places, indicating that neither has any practical effect on perceptions of public safety. Similarly, neither the respondent's education, the number of schools per 100,000 persons nor the terms interacting own education with the number of schools per 100,000 persons are statistically significant. This suggests that neither socioeconomic status (own-education and own-income) nor neighbourhood effects reflected in the education and average income of others in the city have any effect on the respondent's level of satisfaction with current public safety.

We find that neither age, gender, nor the size of the household has any statistically significant effect on perceptions of public safety. Note also that while the masculinity ratio is statistically significant, gender interacted with the masculinity ratio is statistically insignificant. This finding could reflect the fact that in urban China, criminological studies have found that property theft is the crime feared most by the populace (Situ and Liu 1996). Meanwhile existing studies for developed countries suggest that gender differences on public safety are most pronounced in relation to crime against the person and more specifically the female fear of being a victim of sexual crime.

Table 7.4 presents the ordered probit results both uncorrected and corrected for endogeneity of perceptions of migrants where the dependent variable is: 'Over the past two years what changes in public safety have you encountered in your living area?' Answers are on a five point scale ranging from one (significant improvement) to five (considerable fall). Focusing on the corrected results, in Table 7.4 there are several significant variables with coefficients that have the same sign as in Table 7.3. Of these variables, respondents who consider migrants are not welcome and respondents who live in one of the coastal provinces are more likely to have perceived a fall in public safety in their living area. The increase in the average rental and selling price of housing in the city has a positive effect on people's perceptions of changes in public safety, although floor space of buildings per capita ceases to be significant. Consistent with the results in Table 7.3, the unemployment rate in the city is statistically significant with a negative sign, giving further credence to the opportunity perspective. Respondents in cities which spend more on armed police are less likely to perceive a fall in public safety, while respondents in cities with a higher masculinity ratio are more likely to perceive a fall in public safety. Note though, that both gender and gender interacted with the masculinity ratio have a statistically insignificant effect on perceptions of changes in public safety. The population density variable is statistically significant, but it has no practical effect on perceptions of changes in public safety in the two years prior to the survey.

In terms of occupation, the coefficient on manual workers is statistically significant with a negative sign as in Table 7.3 and, in addition, a dummy variable for whether the respondent is unemployed is also statistically significant with a negative sign. The respondent's household income and the average income in the city are statistically insignificant. The respondent's income interacted with average income in the city is statistically significant, but the coefficient on this variable indicates that it has no practical effect on perceptions of public safety in the current sample. In contrast to Table 7.3, in Table 7.4, both age and age squared are statistically significant. The sign on the coefficient on age is positive suggesting that older respondents are more likely to perceive a fall in public safety, while the coefficient on age squared is zero to three decimal points, indicating that it has no practical effect in our sample.

Respondents with a senior middle school education are more likely to perceive a fall in public safety relative to those with a polytechnic education, while the other dummy variables for the respondent's education are statistically insignificant. The result for those with a senior middle school education is consistent with the argument that education reduces cognitive dissonance, although the fact that the other own education variables are statistically insignificant means that support for this explanation is qualified. When the number of schools per 100,000 people is interacted with junior middle school, the interaction term is statistically significant with a negative sign; however, its coefficient is quantitatively small. Schools interacted with senior middle school education is also statistically significant with a negative sign, but its confidence intervals at the 95 per cent level bound zero, so we cannot reliably predict whether it is positive or negative.

CONCLUSION

We have examined the determinants of perceptions of public safety in urban China using a large survey administered in 2003 which contains approximately 8,130 valid responses on questions of interest to us, supplemented with city specific variables likely to influence perceptions of public safety from the locale in which the respondent lived. We find strong

Table 7.4 Ordered probit regression where the dependent variable is: 'Over the past two years what changes in public safety have you encountered in your living area?'

Variable	Uncorrected		Corrected	
	Estimate	Wald	Estimate	Wald
Gender	.072	.008	.562	.465
Age	.011	2.596	.015	5.330**
Age²	-.000	2.743***	-.000	5.214**
Household income	.005	.528	.007	1.015
Average income in the city	.000	.647	.000	2.271
Marital status	.021	.345	.013	.138
Size of household	-.007	.356	-.009	.663
Junior middle school	.078	1.039	.052	.453
Senior middle school	.152	4.510**	.168	5.454**
Three year higher degree or above	.018	.070	.048	.470
Senior professional occupation	.131	.525	.114	.394
Middle professional occupation	-.016	.055	-.048	.516
Lower professional occupation	-.030	.288	-.058	1.049
Technical occupation	-.005	.007	-.035	.324
Semi-skilled occupation	-.056	.877	-.078	1.681
Manual occupation	-.145	3.157***	-.178	4.678**
Unemployed	-.149	4.762**	-.149	4.761**
Retired	.128	3.546***	.108	2.480
Coastal resident	.104	3.324***	.128	4.985**
Attitudes to migrants in the city	.142	104.849*	.130	600.872*

	Coef.	Wald	Coef.	Wald
Floor space of buildings per capita in the city	.018	.136	.005	.008
Average change in selling price of houses in city	-.040	13.554*	-.040	13.350*
Average change in renting price in the city	-.023	76.612*	-.025	87.065*
Unemployment rate in the city	-.105	27.423*	-.108	28.773*
Masculinity ratio	.023	3.108***	.029	5.163**
Expenditure on armed police per capita	-.074	42.515*	-.079	48.715*
Number of schools per 100,000 persons	.001	.213	.002	.434
Population density	-.000	7.044**	-.000	12.785*
Gender x masculinity ratio	-.000	.001	-.005	.360
Household income x average income in the city	-.000	5.614**	-.000	9.136**
Number of schools x junior middle education	-.007	4.377**	-.005	2.744*
Number of schools x senior middle education	-.005	2.606	-.005	2.648*
Number of schools x three year degree or higher	-.003	1.037	-.005	2.320
Threshold 1	-5.441	9.335*	-5.211	8.482*
Threshold 2	-3.718	4.361**	-3.437	3.691***
Threshold 3	-3.040	2.916***	-2.726	2.322
Threshold 4	-1.964	1.217	-1.596	.796
-2 Log Likelihood (Unrestricted)	20158.220		20185.946	
-2 Log Likelihood (Restricted)	19800.947		19319.997	
- 2LR Statistic (33 df)	357.272*		865.949*	
Nagelkerke Pseudo R^2	.047		.110	
Number of observations	8133		8133	

Notes: *, **and *** imply that the coefficient is statistically different from zero at the 1%, 5% and 10% level of significance, respectively. Wald statistics are calculated from heteroskedastic consistent standard errors. A Hausman test using satisfaction with public transportation as the instrument suggests that attitudes towards migrants in the city be endogenous (p < 0.0001). Therefore, we report results both corrected and uncorrected for endogeneity of attitudes towards migrants. The reference category for occupations is people not in the labor market such as homemakers and students. The reference category for education is people with a polytechnic education.

support for our central hypothesis that the individual's attitude to migrants affects his or her perception of public safety. However, in contrast to a similar recent study by Pradhan and Ravallion (2003) for Brazil, we find little evidence that own education, own income or neighbourhood effects have any effect on perceptions of public safety. Similarly, in general the individual's personal and household characteristics seem to have little role to play in influencing perceptions of public safety. This is true for the individual's age, gender, marital status, occupation and size of household, although being in a manual occupation seems to be important and age was statistically significant with the expected sign in the model examining perceptions of changes in public safety. Apart from whether the individual welcomes migrants, the factors which seem most important in explaining perceptions of public safety are city specific variables. These variables include the unemployment rate in the city, the masculinity ratio, expenditure on armed police, whether the individual lives in the coastal region as opposed to the central or western region and average changes in housing and rental prices in the city reflecting the demand for housing and the city's urban development.

One of the limitations of our study is that because we do not have the data we are unable to examine how desire for increased public safety affects current perceptions of public safety, which is an interesting issue examined by Pradhan and Ravallion (2003) with their Brazilian crime data. Pradhan and Ravallion (2003) found that the desire for increased public safety has a positive own-income effect, but a negative neighbourhood effect. If we had data on desire for increased public safety it would provide a richer framework for examining income and neighbourhood effects. This could be the basis for further research. A second limitation of our study, in common with most studies, is that we do not have data on perceptions of public safety disaggregated into different sorts of crimes. The limited evidence from criminological studies is that the determinants of perceptions of public safety differ for different sorts of crimes. One obvious difference, mentioned earlier in this chapter, is gender differences in perceptions of crime against the person and in particular fear of sexual assault. In light of our findings that gender is a statistically insignificant determinant of perceptions of public safety in our sample, this is a result which requires further investigation with more disaggregated perceptions data.

We have focused on how attitudes to migrants influence people's perceptions of public safety in China. We do not consider how people's perceptions of other central issues in China influence their perceptions of public safety. Examples would be their attitude to the pace of marketization and their views on corruption and their level of trust in the government and the police. Several studies for both China and other transitional countries have suggested that increased levels of organised and other forms of crime, including violent crime are associated with bureaucratic corruption and marketization (see e.g., Kwong 1997; Squires Meaney 1991; Glinkina *et al.* 2000; Radaev 2000). This can be expected to influence perceptions of public safety. Dammert and Malone (2002) found that Argentinean citizens had lower perceptions of public safety, despite lower levels of crime rates and victimisation relative to other Latin American countries, because of lower levels of public trust in the police and more experience with corruption. Future research could examine how attitudes to marketization and bureaucratic corruption influence people's perception of public safety using data for China or transitional economies in Central and Eastern Europe, including Russia, where organised crime is a major problem.

NOTES

1. This project was supported by a grant from the Monash Institute for the Study of Global Movements. We thank Joanna Nikopoulos and Xiaolei Qian for research assistance.
2. For example, in the United States, Mayor Giuliani's response to declining crime rates in New York City was to ask police to keep important data from the media (New York Times, 2005).
3. The renminbi (RMB) is the Chinese currency. In May 2005 US$1= 8.28 RMB.
4. The cities sampled were Beijing, Tianjin, Shijiazhuang, Taiyuan, Huhehaote, Shenyang, Changchun, Harbin, Shanghai, Nanjing, Hangzhou, Hefei, Fuzhou, Nanchang, Jinan, Zhenzhou, Wuhan, Changsha, Guangzhou, Nanning, Haikou, Chongqing, Chengdu, Guizhou, Kunming, Lasa, Xi'an, Lanzhou, Xining, Yinchuan, Wulumuqi and Xiamen.
5. We implemented the version of the Hausman test proposed by Davidson and MacKinnon (1989), which carries out the test by running an auxiliary regression. In the second stage, the coefficient on the first stage residuals for MIGRANT was significantly different from zero (p<0.0001) in both cases.
6. We use the official unemployment rate at the city level. It might be argued that the official unemployment rate underestimates the true unemployment rate once workers laid-off from state owned enterprises are considered. Thus, we also experimented with using the percentage of laid-off workers to on-post workers in state-owned enterprises, which is available at the provincial level and the results were quantitatively similar.

REFERENCES

Appleton, S., Knight, J., Song, L., and Xia, Q., 2004. 'Contrasting paradigms: segmentation and competitiveness in the formation of the Chinese labour market', *Journal of Chinese Economic and Business Studies*, **2**, 185-205.

Austin, D. M., Furr, L. and Spine, M., 2002. 'The effects of neighbourhood conditions on perceptions of safety', *Journal of Criminal Justice*, **30**, 417-427.

Baba, Y. and Austin, D. M., 1989. 'Neighbourhood environmental satisfaction, victimization and social participation as determinants of perceived neighbourhood safety', *Environment and Behavior*, **21**, 763-780.

Battese, G. and T. Coelli, 1993. 'A stochastic frontier production function incorporating a model for technical inefficiency effects', Working Papers in *Econometrics and Statistics No.69*, University of New England, Australia.

Becker, G., 1968. 'Crime and punishment: an economic approach', *Journal of Political Economy*, **76**, 1169-1271.

Behrman, J. R. and Craig, S. G., 1987. 'The distribution of public services: An exploration of local government preferences', *American Economic Review*, **77**, 37-49.

Bodman, P. and Maultby, C., 1997. 'Crime, punishment and deterrence in Australia: A further empirical investigation', *International Journal of Social Economics*, **24**, 884-901.

Borooah, V. K. and Carcach, C. A., 1997. 'Crime and fear, evidence from Australia', *British Journal of Criminology*, **37**, 635-656.

Braungart, M., Braungart, R. G., and Hoyer, W. J., 1980. 'Age, sex and social factors in fear of crime', *Sociological Focus*, **13**, 55-65.

Busselle, R., 2003. 'Television exposure, parents' precautionary warnings, and young adults' perceptions of crime', *Communication Research*, **30**, 530-556.

Cameron, S., 1988. 'The economics of crime deterrence: a survey of theory and evidence', *Kyklos*, **41**, 301-323.

Cantor, D. and Land, K., 1985. 'Unemployment and crime rates in post World War II United States: a theoretical and empirical analysis', *American Sociological Review*, **50**, 317-332.

Cantor, D. and Land, K., 2001. 'Unemployment and crime rate fluctuations: a comment on Greenberg', *Journal of Quantitative Criminology*, **17**, 329-342.

Chai, J. and Chai, B., 1997. 'China's floating population and its implications', *International Journal of Social Economics*, **24**, 1038-1052.

Chen, Y. and Luo, Y., 1995. 'Watch your doors and windows – burglary prevention is the focus', *Yangcheng Evening News*, February **28**, 5.

Cheng, T. and Seldon, M., 1994. 'The origins and social consequences of China's *hukou* system', *The China Quarterly*, **139**, 644-668.

China Mainland Marketing Research Company (CMMRC), 2002. *Urban Hotspots*, Beijing: China Mainland Marketing Company.

Clark, D., 1988. *An Analysis of Guardian Effectiveness in the Prevention of Residential Burglary*, Ph.D. Dissertation. State University of New York at Albany.

Clemente, F. and Kleinman, M. B., 1977. 'Fear of crime in the United States: A multivariate analysis', *Social Forces*, **56**, 519-531.

Clotfelter, C. T., 1977. 'Public services, private substitutes, and the demand for protection against crime', *American Economic Review*, **67**, 867-877.

Cohen, L. E., Felson, M. and Land, K. C., 1980. 'Property crime in the United States: a macrodynamic analysis, 1947-1977, with *ex ante* forecasts for the mid-1980s', *American Journal of Sociology*, **86**, 661-692.

Cullen, J. and Levitt, S., 1999. 'Crime, urban flight and consequences for cities', *Review of Economics and Statistics*, **81**, 159-169.

Curran, D., 1998. 'Economic reform, the floating population and crime', *Journal of Contemporary Criminal Justice*, **14**, 262-280.

Curran, D. and Cook, S., 1993. 'Growing fears, rising crime: Juveniles and China's justice system', *Crime and Delinquency*, **39**, 296-315.

Dammert, L. and Malone, M. F. T., 2002. 'Insecurity and fear in Argentina: The impact of trust in police and corruption on citizen perception of crime', *Desarrollo Economico-Revista de Ciencias Sociales*, **42**, 285-301.

Davidson, R. and MacKinnon, J., 1989. 'Testing for consistency using artificial regressions', *Econometric Theory*, **5**, 363-384.

Deng, X. and Cordilia, A., 1999. 'To get rich is glorious: Rising expectations, declining control and escalating crime in contemporary China', *International Journal of Offender Therapy and Comparative Criminology*, **43**, 211-229.

Di Tella, R. and Schargrodsky, E., 2004. 'Do police reduce crime? Estimates using the allocation of police forces after a terrorist attack', *American Economic Review*, **94**, 115-133.

Ding, J. and Stockman, N., 1999. 'The floating population and the integration of the city community: A survey of the attitudes of Shanghai residents to recent migrants', in Pieke, F. N. and Mallee, H. (eds.) *Internal and International Migration: Chinese Perspectives*, Richmond, UK: Curzon Press.

Dutton, M., 1997. 'The basic character of crime in contemporary China', *China Quarterly*, **149**, 160-177.

Ehrlich, I., 1973. 'Participation in illegitimate activities: a theoretical and empirical analysis', *Journal of Political Economy*, **38**, 521-565.

Erskine, H., 1974. 'The polls, fear of crime and violence', *Public Opinion Quarterly*, **38**, 131-145.

Feng, W., Zuo, X. and Ruan, D., 2002. 'Rural migrants in Shanghai: Living under the shadow of socialism', *International Migration Review*, **36**, 520-545.

Ferraro, K., 1995. *Fear of Crime: Interpreting Victimization Risk*, New York, NY: SUNY Press.

Festinger, L., 1957. *A Theory of Cognitive Dissonance*, Stanford, CA: Stanford University Press.

Freeman, R., 1996. 'Why do so many young American men commit crimes and what might we do about it?' *Journal of Economic Perspectives*, **10**, 25-42.

Freeman, S., Grogger, J. and Sonstelie, J., 1996. 'The spatial concentration of crime', *Journal of Urban Economics*, **40**, 216-231.

Gavaria, A. and Pages, C., 2002. 'Patterns of crime victimization in Latin American cities', *Journal of Development Economics*, **67**, 181-203.

Glinkina, S., Grigoriev, A. and Yakobidze, V., 2000. 'Crime and corruption', in Klein, L. and Power, M. (eds) *The New Russia: Transition Gone Awry*, Stanford: Stanford University Press.

Greenfield, T. K., Midanik, L. T. and Rogers, J. D., 2000. 'Effects of telephone versus face-to-face interview modes on reports of alcohol consumption', *Addiction*, **95**, 277-284.

Groves, R. M., 1977. 'An experimental comparison of national telephone and personal interview surveys', *Proceedings of the Section on Social Statistics: American Statistical Association*, 232-41. Washington DC: American Statistical Association.

Guo, F. and Iredale, R., 2003. 'Unemployment among the migrant population in Chinese cities: Case study of Beijing', *Proceedings of the Fifteenth Annual Conference of the Association for Chinese Economic Studies Australia (ACESA)*.

Guo, X., 1996. 'China: Social transformation and crime control', *Juvenile Delinquency Studies*, **171**, 2-7.

Guo, Z., Zhu, J. and Chen, H., 2001. 'Mediated reality bites: Comparing direct and indirect experience as sources of perceptions across two communities in China', *International Journal of Public Opinion Research*, **13**, 398-418.

Gyimah-Brempong, K., 1989. 'Production of public safety: are socioeconomic characteristics important factors?' *Journal of Applied Econometrics*, **4**, 57-71.

Holbrook, A., Green, M. and Krosnick, J., 2003. 'Telephone versus face-to-face interviewing of national probability samples with long questionnaires: comparisons of respondent satisficting and social desirability bias', *Public Opinion Quarterly*, **67**, 79-126.

Hraba, J., Bao, W. N., Lorenz, F. O. and Pechacova, Z., 1998. 'Perceived risk of crime in the Czech Republic', *Journal of Research in Crime and Delinquency*, **35**, 225-242.

Ito, K., 1983. 'Research on the fear of crime: Perceptions and realities of crime in Japan', *Crime and Delinquency*, **39**, 385-392.

Keil, T. J., Austin, D. M. and Andreescu, V., 1996. 'Concerns about neighbourhood safety in two Romanian cities: Copsa Mica and Buceresti', *East European Quarterly*, **30**, 97-114.

Keil, T. J. and Vito, G., 1991. 'Fear of crime and support for the death penalty', *Justice Quarterly*, **8**, 447-464.

Klick, J. and Tabarrok, A., 2004. 'Using terror alerts to estimate the effect of police on crime', *Paper presented at the Fourteenth Annual Meeting of the American Law and Economics Association*, Northwestern University, Chicago, May 2004.

Knight, J. and Song, L., 1999. 'Employment constraints and sub-optimality in Chinese enterprises', *Oxford Economic Papers*, **51**, 284-299.

Knight, J., Song, L. and Huaibin, J. 1999. 'Chinese rural migrants in urban enterprises: three perspectives', *Journal of Development Studies*, **35**, 73-104.

Kwong, J., 1997. *The Political Economy of Corruption in China*, Armonk: M.E. Sharpe.

LaGrange, R. L. and Ferraro, K. F., 1989. 'Assessing age and gender differences in perceived risk and fear of crime', *Criminology*, **27**, 697-717.

Lague, D., 2003. 'The human tide sweeps into cities', *Far Eastern Economic Review*, January **9**, 24-28.

Lea, J. and Young, J., 1984. *What's to be Done about Law and Order?* London: Penguin.

Lee, S., 1998. 'Higher earnings, bursting trains and exhausted bodies: The creation of traveling psychosis in post-reform China', *Social Science and Medicine*, **47**, 1247-1261.

Levitt, S., 2004. 'Understanding why crime fell in the 1990s: four factors that explain the decline and six that do not', *Journal of Economic Perspectives*, **18**, 163-190.

Liang, H. and Shapiro, J., 1983. *Son of the Revolution*, New York: Vintage Books.

Ma, Y., 1995. 'Crime in China: characteristics, causes and control strategies', *International Journal of Comparative and Applied Criminal Justice*, **19**, 247-256.

Malloy, T., Albright, L., Diaz-Loving, R., Dong, Q. and Lee, Y., 2004. 'Agreement in personality judgments within and between nonoverlapping social groups in collectivist cultures', *Personality and Social Psychology Bulletin*, **30**, 106-117.

Maurer-Fazio, M. and Dinh, N., 2004. 'Differential rewards to, and contributions of, education in urban China's segmented labour markets', *Pacific Economic Review*, **9**, 173-189.

Meng, X. and Zhang, J. 2001. 'The two-tier labour market in urban China: Occupational segregation and wage differentials between urban residents and rural residents', *Journal of Comparative Economics*, **29**, 485-504.

Mukherjee, S. and Carach, C., 1998. *Repeat Victimization in Australia*, Canberra: Australian Institute of Criminology.

New York Times, 2005. *New York Times Opinion Column*, available at http://www.nytimes.com/2005/05/10/opinion/10tierney.html?hp, May 10.

Pain, R., 2001, 'Gender, race, age and fear in the city', *Urban Studies*, **38**, 899-913.

Pan, P., 2002. 'Poisoned Back into Poverty: As China Embraces Capitalism, Hazards to Workers Rise', *Washington Post*, August 4, A01.

Perkins, D. and Taylor, R., 1996. 'Ecological assessments of community disorder: their relationship to fear of crime and theoretical implications', *American Journal of Community Psychology*, **24**, 63-107.

Plous, S. 2003. 'The psychology of prejudice, stereotyping, and discrimination: An overview', in Plous, S. (ed.) *Understanding Prejudice and Discrimination*, New York, NY: McGraw-Hill.

Pradhan, M. and Ravallion, M., 2003. 'Who wants safer streets? Explaining concern for public safety in Brazil', *Journal of Economic Psychology*, **24**, 17-33.

Radaev, V., 2000. 'Corruption and violence in Russian business in the late 1990s', in Ledeneva, A. and Kurkchiyan, M. (eds) *Economic crime in Russia*, London: Kluwer.

Raphael, S. and Winter-Ebmer, R., 2001. 'Identifying the effects of unemployment on crime', *Journal of Law and Economics*, **44**, 259-283.

Reilly, B. and Witt, R., 1996. 'Crime, deterrence and unemployment in England and Wales: an empirical analysis', *Bulletin of Economic Research*, **48**, 259-283.

Research Institute of the Ministry of Public Security, 1991. *Do You Feel Safe?* Beijing: Masses Press.

Roberts, K. D., 1997. 'China's 'tidal wave' of migrant labor: What can we learn from Mexican undocumented migration to the United States?' *International Migration Review*, **31**, 249-293.

Roberts, K. D., 2001. 'The determinants of job choice by rural labour migrants in Shanghai', *China Economic Review*, **12**, 15-39.

Roberts, K. D., 2002. 'Rural migrants in urban China: Willing workers, invisible residents', *Asia Pacific Business Review*, **8**, 141-158.

Rountree, P. and Land, K., 1996. 'Perceived risk versus fear of crime: Empirical evidence of conceptually distinct reactions in survey data', *Social Forces*, **74**, 1353-1376.

Schaller, M., 1992. 'In-group favoritism and statistical reasoning in social inference: Implications for formation and maintenance of group stereotypes', *Journal of Personality and Social Psychology*, **63**, 61-74.

Silverman, E. and Della-Giustina, J., 2001. 'Urban policing and the fear of crime', *Urban Studies*, **5-6**, 941-957.

Situ, Y. and Liu, W., 1996. 'Transient population, crime and solution: The Chinese experience', *International Journal of Offender Therapy and Comparative Criminology*, **40**, 293-299.

Skogan, W. G. and Maxfield, M. G., 1981. *Coping with crime*, Sage: Beverly Hills.

Smith, S. J., 1984. 'Negotiating ethnicity in an uncertain environment', *Ethnic and Racial Studies*, **7**, 360-373.

Smyth, R., Deng, X. and Wang, J., 2004. 'Restructuring state-owned big business in former planned economies: The case of China's shipbuilding industry', *New Zealand Journal of Asian Studies*, **6**, 100-129.

Solinger, D., 1999. *Contesting Citizenship in Urban China: Peasant Migrants, the State and the Logic of the Market*, Berkeley, CA: University of California Press.

Squires Meaney, C., 1991. 'Market reforms and disintegrative corruption in urban China', in Baum, R. (ed.) *Reform and Reaction in Post-Mao China: The Road to Tiananmen*, New York: Routledge.

State Statistical Bureau (SSB), 2002. *Statistical Yearbook of China*, Beijing: State Statistical Bureau.

State Statistical Bureau, 2003a. *China Population Statistical Yearbook*, Beijing: State Statistical Bureau.

State Statistical Bureau, 2003b. *China Population Statistical Yearbook*, Beijing: State Statistical Bureau.

Sundeen, R. and Matthieu, J. 1976. 'Crime and its consequences among the elderly in three urban communities', *Gerontologist*, **16**, 211-219.

Tabb, R. P. D., Taylor, D. G. and Dunham, J. D., 1984. *Patterns of neighbourhood change: Race and crime in urban America*, Chicago: University of Chicago Press.

Taub, R., Taylor, D. G. and Dunham, J. G., 1981. 'Neighbourhoods and safety', in Lewis, D. A. (ed.) *Reactions to crime*, Newbury Park, CA: Sage.

Taylor, R. and Covington, J., 1993. 'Community structural change and fear of crime', *Social Problems*, **40**, 374-395.

Toseland, R., 1982. 'Fear of crime: Who is most vulnerable?' *Journal of Criminal Justice*, **10**, 199-209.

Turner, J., Hogg, M., Oakes, P., Reicher, S. and Wetherell, M., 1987. *Rediscovering the social group: A self-categorization theory*, New York: Basil Blackwell.

Tyler, T. R., 1980. 'Impact of directly and indirectly experienced events', *Journal of Personality and Social Psychology*, **39**, 13-28.

Wang, F. and Zuo, X., 1999. 'Inside China's cities: institutional barriers and opportunities for urban migrants, *American Economic Review, Papers and Proceedings*, **89**, 276-280.

Warr, M., 1984. 'Fear of victimization: Why are women and the elderly more afraid?' *Social Science Quarterly*, **65**, 681-702.

Witt, R., Clarke, A. and Fielding, N., 1999. 'Crime and economic activity: a panel data approach', *British Journal of Criminology*, **39**, 391-400.

Wong, Y. C. R., 1995. 'An economic analysis of the crime rate in England and Wales, 1857-1992', *Economica*, **62**, 235-246.

Wuhan Economic Research Institute, 2003. *A lifetime of walking: Poverty and transportation in Wuhan*, Wuhan Economic Research Institute, Wuhan, China.

Xu, L., 1995. 'National conference on management of transient population held', *Legal Daily*, **July 9**, 1 (in Chinese).

Yang, Q. and Guo, F., 1996. 'Occupational attainment of rural to urban temporary economic migrants in China 1985-1990, *International Migration Review*, **30**, 771-787.

Yin, P., 1985. *Victimization and the aged*, Springfield Ill.: Charles C. Thomas.

Yu, L., 1993. *The study of the crime problem in contemporary China*, Beijing: Chinese University of Public Security Press.

Zhu, C. J., 1997. 'Human resource development in China during the transition to a new economic system', *Asia Pacific Journal of Human Resources*, **25**, 19-44.

8.   Job-matching Efficiency

Sheng Yu

The rapid economic transformation during the past two decades has brought dramatic changes in China's labour market. First, the flow of migrants has increased significantly as the restriction on rural-urban migration has been loosened over time. Second, employment in state-owned and collective enterprises declined sharply with state-owned enterprises (SOEs) reform gaining pace and the expansion of the urban private sector. Third, job creation has shifted from capital-intensive industries to labour-intensive industries as China's openness to trade increases. These three dramatic changes - migration changes, sectoral employment restructure and industrial employment shift - shook the basis of the lifetime employment system in China's labour market and introduced potential competition among workers, which promotes China's labour market reforms. As a consequence, a more market-oriented labour market is emerging in urban China.

Despite the progress made on labour market reforms, there currently exists a sizable surplus of labour in China's urban labour market making unemployment a potential threat to economic growth especially after the mid 1990s. By the end of 2003, the registered urban unemployment rate, as measured by the Ministry of Labour and Social Service (MOLSS), has climbed to a record high of 4.3 per cent.[1] The serious problem of unemployment in urban China accompanied by the incomplete social security system intensified income inequality and urban poverty, which caused a large amount of relevant social problems. This highlights the necessity for establishing modern institutions and active labour market policies to facilitate the matching between unemployed workers and job vacancies in the newly created marketplace. The working mechanism of the dynamic labour market in China defined by the aggregate matching function should first be specified.

The question, on how the job-matching process works in transitional economies and whether it exhibits a similar pattern with those in developed countries, has been subject to extensive research. For example, Munich, Svejnar and Terrel (1999) estimated the sectoral matching function of the Czech Republic and Slovakia with a standard time series method and analyzed worker-firm matching in transitional economies, while Profit and Sperlich (2004) applied the non-parametric additive method to explore the properties and development of the matching function in the Czech Republic and compared the result with that in western European countries.[2] However, few of the previous studies tried to measure the efficiency of job-matching processes in the labour market. Specifically, there has been no study undertaken to test for a causal relationship between economic transformation and changes in the efficiency of job-matching. This restricts academics and policy-makers from applying the search models to analyzing the more generalised employment problem in transitional economies.

With the stochastic frontier analysis, this chapter estimates the stochastic matching function with seven year and 26 provincial data and examines the efficiency of job-matching in both the temporal and spatial contexts in China's urban labour market. In particular, it explores the determinants of matching efficiency in response to economic transformation. Three main innovations are made: (1) the chapter estimates a Cobb-Douglas matching function by using Chinese data; (2) the chapter uses the stochastic frontier technique, which was originally devised for analyzing the production function, to specify the efficiency of job-matching in China; (3) the chapter examines the determinants, specific to economic transformation, behind the efficiency (or inefficiency) of job-matching.

I first review the related literature, especially the corner stones made to examine the matching function empirically. I then specify the theoretical framework for estimating the matching function and examining the efficiency of the job-matching process. This is followed by a description of the data collection and the empirical function for the stochastic efficiency analysis. Subsequently, I discuss the relationship between China's economic transformation and its impact on the dynamic employment determination. In the final section, I present the estimated results and detailed analysis. The section starts with discussion of the properties of the aggregate matching function in urban China. The changes in matching efficiency of employment frontier over time are then described. Finally, the impact of factors related to economic transformation, such as openness to trade, privatization and urbanization, on the matching efficiency of employment frontier in China's urban labour market is investigated.

LITERATURE REVIEW

In modern labour economics, the matching function has been widely used to describe the generation of employment in the labour market.[3] As a generalized device relating the flow of new hires to the stocks of unemployment and vacancies, the function generally can be defined as $M = m(U,V)$ where M is the number of jobs formed during a given interval, U is the number of unemployed workers looking for jobs and V is the number of vacant jobs. A large number of empirical studies, including Blanchard and

Diamond (1989, 1990), Burda and Wyplosz (1994), Bell (1997), Yashiv (2000), have been undertaken to examine the existence and stability of the function with the data from US or European countries from two perspectives.

First, they examined the functional form of the matching function. From Pissarides (1986) and Blanchard and Diamond (1989) to Anderson and Burgess (2000) and Yashiv (2000), labour economists have tried a large variety of function forms, such as the linear function, the log-linear CES function and the trans-log function, to estimate the matching relationship in the labour market. Despite their different consideration for choosing other variables, most of these studies tended to agree "the matching function converged on a Cobb-Douglas form with the flow of hires on the left-hand side and the stock of unemployment and vacancies on the right hand side (Peterongolo and Pissarides 2001, p.424)". This helps to simplify the discussion on the job-matching process in the labour market to two factor elasticities, measuring the extent of the externalities from unemployment and vacancies on employment creation, and a constant, measuring the efficiency of the job-matching process. Based on this empirical property of the matching function, this chapter directly applies the Cobb-Douglas specification to estimate the matching function in China's labour market.

Second, they examined the returns to scale of the matching function. Although constant returns to scale was widely accepted as a stylized fact in the estimated aggregate matching function with a log-linear approximation, both increasing and decreasing returns to scale were found in some estimated disaggregate matching functions (Peterongolo and Pissarides 2001). For example, Blanchard and Diamond (1989) and Coles and Smith (1996) found that the estimated matching function in US and British manufacturing sectors showed the trend of increasing returns to scale, while Burda and Wyplosz (1994) and Yashiv (2000) found the estimated matching functions in some European countries and Israel showed the trend of decreasing returns to scale. A possible explanation on such divergences from constant returns is that there exist some other variables, such as different institutional arrangements or individual labour market characteristics, influencing the job-matching process in a systematic way. This helps to extend the discussion on the matching function to be a useful tool for analyzing other determinants of job-matching in the labour market. Based on this empirical property of the matching function, this chapter discusses economic transformation and its impact on the efficiency of job-matching in China's urban labour market.

In addition to examining the form and returns to scale of the matching function in developed countries, some recent studies turned to explore the matching function and its properties in some East European transitional economies. For example, Munich, Svejnar and Terrel (1999) estimated the sectoral matching function in the Czech Republic and Slovakia with standard time series data and found decreasing returns to scale in the matching function, while Profit and Sperlich (2004) re-examined the matching technology in the Czech Republic during the transitional period with the nonparametric method and found that economic transformation in the Czech Republic might have negative effects on returns to scale in the matching function (at least locally). These studies generally not only elaborate on the empirical studies on the matching function especially in transitional economies but also make it possible to analyze the relationship between various labour market policies and job-matching process in the labour market.

Although the previous studies have provided a large amount of useful empirical information on the matching function in both developed economies and some specific transitional economies in East Europe, none of them tried to measure the efficiency of job-matching in transitional economies and specify how economic transformation can affect the matching efficiency due to the lack of a suitable method. To fill this gap, this chapter makes use of the similarity between the matching function and the production function, and borrows the stochastic frontier analysis, which was originally devised to assess production efficiencies of industrial sectors, to measure the efficiency of the job-matching process in China and examine its determinants due to economic transformation.

THE STOCHASTIC FRONTIER ANALYSIS AND MATCHING EFFICIENCY

The stochastic frontier analysis, employed by Coelli (1992), Coelli and Battese (1996), Kong *et al.* (1999), and Coelli, Sanzidur and Colin (2003), is devised to analyze the production function for measuring the technology efficiency of production. The core of the approach is to utilise "the specification (in the production function) which allows for a non-negative random component in the error term" (Kompas 2004, p.1633) to generate a measurement of technical efficiency or the ratio of actual to expected maximum output, given inputs and the existing technology. Applying this approach to analyze the matching function, one can measure the efficiency of job-matching in the labour market (a measurement of the labour market distortion level) given unemployment, vacancies.

Specifically, indexing the regional labour market by i and time period by t, the mathematical specification of the stochastic matching function for examining the efficiency of job-matching can be written as:

$$M_{it} = m(V_{it}, U_{it}; \beta)e^{v_{it} - u_{it}} \qquad (8.1)$$

where M_{it} represents new hires, which is the output of the aggregate matching function; V_{it} and U_{it} represent vacancies and unemployment, which are the inputs of the matching function; and β represents the matching coefficient, which is a vector of parameters to be estimated. The error term

v_{it} is assumed to be independently and identically distributed, $N(0, \sigma_v^2)$, which captures random variation in new hires due to factors beyond the control of the regional labour market, such as different labour market institutional arrangements. The error term u_{it} is non-negative and captures technical inefficiency in the aggregate matching function.

Following Battese and Coelli (1995), it is assumed that the error term is specific to individual regional labour markets and independently distributed as non-negative truncations of the distribution $N(\mu, \sigma_\mu^2)$. The efficiency distribution parameter can then be specified as

$$u_{it} = \delta_0 + z_{it}\delta + \omega_{it} \tag{8.2}$$

where ω_{it} is the residual with the distribution of $N(0, \sigma_\omega^2)$, z_{it} is a vector of specific factors that determine the efficiency of job-matching and δ is a vector of parameters to be estimated. Moreover, it is assumed that the factors specific to the regional labour market are related with the economic transformation, which include openness to trade, urbanization, and privatization and so on. Input variables, such as unemployment and vacancies, can be included in both equations (8.1) and (8.2), given that technical efficiency effects are stochastic (Battese and Coelli 1995).

With the above specification, the assumption of $u_{it} \geq 0$ in equation (8.1) guarantees that all observations either lie on, or are beneath, the stochastic matching frontier. Following Battese and Coelli (1993), variance terms are parameterised by replacing σ_v^2 and σ_u^2 with

$$\sigma^2 = \sigma_\varepsilon^2 + \sigma_\mu^2 \text{ and } \gamma = \frac{\sigma_\mu^2}{\sigma_\varepsilon^2 + \sigma_\mu^2} \tag{8.3}$$

The efficiency of job-matching in the i th regional labour market in the t th period can be defined as

$$ME_{it} = \frac{E(M_{it}|\mu_{it}, V_{it}, U_{it})}{E(M_{it}|\mu_{it} = 0, V_{it}, U_{it})} = e^{-u_{it}} \tag{8.4}$$

where E is the expectations operator. Thus, the measure of matching efficiency is based on the conditional expectation given by equation (8.4), provided the values of $\varepsilon_{it} - u_{it}$ evaluated at the maximum likelihood estimates of the parameters for the aggregate matching function, where the expected maximum value of M_{it} is conditional on $u_{it} = 0$ (Battese and Coelli, 1988).

The measure ME_{it} has a value between zero and one and the overall mean efficiency of job-matching is

$$ME = \left\{ \frac{1 - \phi[\sigma_u - (\mu / \sigma_u)]}{1 - \phi(\mu / \sigma_u)} \right\} e^{-\mu + (1/2)\sigma_u^2} \tag{8.5}$$

where $\phi(.)$ represents the density function for the standard normal variable.

The above discussion has specified the theoretical basis for using the stochastic frontier analysis to examine the efficiency of job-matching in China. Based on this model, the data collection and empirical specification of the model can thus be identified.

EMPIRICAL SPECIFICATION AND DATA DESCRIPTION

The chapter chooses the model of Battese and Coelli (1995) to estimate the stochastic matching function for China's urban labour market. The model has the merit that the determinants of the efficiency can be estimated together with the frontier function by maximum likelihood method. Two empirical functions of the model are specified as follows.

First, the empirical stochastic matching function can be written in log-linear Cobb-Douglas form with equation (8.1).

$$\ln M_{it} = \beta_0 + \beta_1 T + \beta_2 \ln V_{it} + \beta_3 \ln U_{it} + \beta_4 DM98 + \beta_5 DM99 + v_{it} - u_{it} \tag{8.6}$$

where M_{it} is the flow of new hires in labour market i during time period t, V_{it} is the stock of vacancies in labour market i during time period t, and U_{it} is the stock of unemployment in labour market i during time period t. Two dummy variables, $DM98$ and $DM99$, are used to capture the impact of abnormal years. A sound explanation for such a specification is that China's government interfered with the job-matching process by pushing the Employment Service Centre to solve the employment problem of "laid-off" workers in 1998 and 1999 which changed the structure of job-matching in the labour market. Meanwhile, the time trend is given by T, which captures the systematic change in matching technology over time.

Second, the empirical matching efficiency function can be written as the linear form with equation (8.2).

$$u_{it} = \delta_0 + \delta_1 OPEN + \delta_2 PRIV + \delta_3 URBN + \delta_4 HUMA + \varpi_{it} \tag{8.7}$$

where ϖ_{it} is an error term to account for random differences in the matching technical efficiency across region. *OPEN* represents the openness to trade in labour market i during time period t, *PRIV* represents the privatization process in labour market i during time period t, *URBN* represents the urbanization process in labour market i during time period t and *HUMA* represents the human capital in labour market i during time period t. Since the economic transformation in China is mainly promoted by three major reforms: openness to trade, privatization and urbanization, the impacts of economic transformation on the efficiency of job-matching and economic transformation are examined through analyzing these three reforms respectively. The coefficient of each reform in equation (8.7) captures its independent effects. In addition, the impact of human capital stock on the efficiency of job-matching in China is also specified.

With equations (8.6) and (8.7), the chapter uses the panel data to make the estimation. The observations are collected annually, from 26 provinces, including Beijing, Tianjin, Hebei, Shanxi, Inner-Mongolia, Liaoning, Jilin, Heilongjiang, Shanghai, Jiangsu, Zhejiang, Anhui, Jiangxi, Shandong, Henan, Hubei, Hunan, Guangdong, Guangxi, Sichuan, Guizhou, Yunnan, Shaanxi, Gansu, Qinghai, Ningxia and Xinjiang, over seven years, from 1997 to 2003. Two groups of data are specified respectively for estimating the stochastic matching function or for analyzing the efficiency of job-matching process.

The first group of data comes from the statistics of Careers Service Centre in China, which includes three series of data: unemployment, vacancy and new hires. Unemployment (input A) is defined as the number of total registered job seekers (including the unemployed workers, laid-off workers and other on-job seekers) during the year plus the "left-over" unemployment from last year's match (which is equal to the number of registered job seekers minus that of the placed registered job seekers). Vacancy (input B) is defined as the number of total registered job vacancies during the year plus the left-over job vacancies from last year's match (which is equal to the number of registered job vacancies minus that of the placed registered job vacancies). And new match (output) is defined as the number of placed job-seekers or job vacancies during the year. All data series are available in China Statistical Yearbook, issues 1998-2004.

Tables 8.1 and 8.2 show descriptive statistics on the data over time and across regions respectively. Two statements need to be made before the data could be used for making the estimation. First, although the Employment Service Centre is not the only medium to help match job seekers and job vacancies in China, it plays an important role in linking the flow of new hires with the stocks of unemployed persons. During the period 1996-2003, the annual new hires through the Employment Service Centre in China was 10.70 million on average, which accounted for 4.71 per cent of the total urban employment or around half of the total urban new hires. This makes the sample a reasonable representative of the dynamic labour market in China. Second, although the definitions of unemployment, vacancy and new hires are mildly different from those in the previous empirical studies, the data series are suitable for analyzing the matching function: (1) the data on job seekers and job vacancies are adjusted to account for the impact of the previous year's matching;[4] (2) the data on unemployment, vacancies and new hires come from the same statistical agency, which are more consistent for estimation. Meanwhile, since the statistical criteria are made by the National Bureau of Statistics and have not changed since 1995, the definition of new hires, job seekers and job vacancies should be consistent both across regions and over time.

The second group of data is part of China's macroeconomic statistics. Four variables are chosen to capture economic transformation and accumulation of human capital in China, which include the openness to trade index, the privatization index, the urbanization index and the human capital index. The openness to trade index is defined as the ratio of the total import and export value of each region over their total GDP, which measures the degree of openness in each province. The privatization index is defined as the ratio of the employment of non-state-owned enterprises over that of the whole economy in each region, which measures the extent that private-owned enterprises dominate the economy. The urbanization index is defined as the ratio of the urban population over the total population in each region, which measures the size and role of urban economy in the whole economy. The human capital index is defined as the ratio of population with college or higher-level education over the total population, which measures the education structure of labour force. All the data for calculating these four variables are available in *China Statistical Yearbook,* issues 1997-2004.

The estimations on the model can be done with the software FRONTIER 4.1 (Coelli 1996).[5] Hypothesis tests for the stochastic matching function and the matching efficiency model are made with generalized likelihood ratio (LR) tests (LR ratio = -24.98). The null hypotheses that the inefficiency of job-matching process is not systematic ($\gamma = 0$) and economic transformation indices do not influence the technical inefficiency of the matching function ($\delta_i = 0$ for all i) are both rejected (LR ratio = 17.82). This implies that the estimate of the matching function is fitful, and economic transformation has played an important role in affecting the efficiency of the job-matching process in China.

Table 8.1 Descriptive statistics of new hires, vacancies and unemployment: 1996-2003 (10,000 persons)

Year\Item	Number of employment service centre	Number of new hires	Standard error of new hires	Number of job seekers	Standard error of job seekers	Number of job vacancies	Standard error of job vacancies
1996		30.43	18.51	47.05	32.30	103.98	65.11
1997		27.83	16.52	50.92	36.01	101.73	68.30
1998		30.84	19.65	51.87	41.10	92.45	66.30
1999		33.72	26.58	59.82	63.61	93.16	79.70
2000	29,024	43.23	33.61	83.66	87.23	121.23	110.13
2001	26,158	47.23	38.42	99.76	104.83	136.08	122.47
2002	26,793	56.15	46.93	126.89	148.16	153.69	137.87
2003	31,109	30.43	18.51	47.05	32.30	103.98	65.11

Source: Author's own calculation.

Table 8.2 Descriptive statistics of new hires, vacancies and unemployment across regions (10,000 persons)

Year\Item	Average number of employment service centres	Number of new hires	Standard error of new hires	Number of job seekers	Standard error of job seekers	Number of job vacancies	Standard error of job vacancies
Beijing	406	29.02	2.59	84.51	25.72	113.82	29.62
Tianjin	173	34.20	27.40	36.35	16.90	163.63	55.41
Hebei	1,445	51.64	17.15	87.62	45.54	122.74	39.89
Shanxi	1,301	17.31	5.01	24.18	3.97	45.00	26.63
Inner Mongolia	856	20.37	5.11	29.15	9.80	49.10	11.10
Liaoning	1,416	63.15	20.11	97.54	39.43	182.95	35.68
Jilin	989	26.04	7.75	35.35	12.69	55.84	25.02
Heilongjiang	1,056	28.94	11.13	42.32	25.85	102.84	41.25
Shanghai	437	24.90	13.03	117.37	81.15	101.56	53.85
Jiangsu	1,964	63.78	20.49	118.29	52.54	170.88	48.41
Zhejiang	1,879	117.00	45.66	277.26	125.10	358.20	99.38
Anhui	1,882	32.14	14.72	49.65	28.04	88.50	23.96
Jiangxi	750	29.21	10.70	42.94	19.56	76.28	13.31

Shandong	1,340	73.12	28.08	130.12	66.27	180.35	55.22
Henan	1,215	59.51	10.36	79.37	23.22	168.98	30.24
Hubei	822	52.91	12.63	91.54	32.53	141.37	17.89
Hunan	825	33.47	5.67	80.86	14.85	143.74	25.41
Guangdong	1,525	91.38	62.18	287.34	209.58	358.11	165.12
Guangxi	338	27.58	6.05	40.96	10.68	69.80	16.55
Guizhou	712	9.42	1.56	16.13	5.29	29.52	13.07
Yunnan	1,356	24.39	3.40	35.16	8.30	40.88	12.30
Shaanxi	1,505	30.86	9.82	43.92	12.46	92.75	17.34
Gansu	563	14.46	4.74	21.16	10.45	31.71	8.55
Qinghai	274	24.23	6.97	25.33	8.94	30.33	9.48
Ningxia	222	6.00	2.75	9.94	5.35	19.01	5.53
Xinjiang	397	15.73	5.32	26.96	12.09	42.20	6.54

Source: Author's own calculation.

THE MATCHING EFFICIENCY OF CHINA'S LABOUR MARKET AND ITS DETERMINANTS

Table 8.3 (upper panel) shows the estimate of the stochastic matching function and the efficiency of job-matching in China's labour market with 26 provinces' data during the period 1997-2003. Given the assumption of a log-linear Cobb-Douglas matching function, the estimated matching efficiency of employment frontier in China is on average 80.19 per cent. That is, there exists some inefficiency of job-matching in China's labour market.

Table 8.3 The estimation results

	Coefficient	Standard error	T-ratio
The matching function (MLE)			
CONSTANT	89.91	191.10	0.47
TIME TREND	-26.60	57.91	-0.46
LN_VACANCY	0.38	0.05	7.44
LN_UNEMPLOYMENT	0.42	0.05	8.30
DUMMY_98	-0.12	0.07	-1.92
DUMMY_99	-0.02	0.06	-0.30
Matching inefficiency analysis			
Constant	-	-	
OPEN	2.03	0.97	2.09
PRIV	-6.52	3.32	-1.96
URBN	3.80	1.74	2.18
HUMA	-6.04	5.74	-1.05
Sigma-squared	0.41	0.19	2.13
Gamma	0.91	0.05	17.82
Average matching efficiency			
LR test of the one-sided error		-24.98	
Log likelihood function		84.10	

Source: Authors' own calculation.

First, the estimate on the Cobb-Douglas matching function, using the maximum likelihood estimation (MLE) method, shows that the relationship between flow of new hires and the stocks of vacancies and unemployment in

China is characterised with mild decreasing returns to scale. As is shown in Table 8.3 (upper panel), the estimated coefficients of unemployment and vacancies are 0.42 and 0.38 respectively, and both are statistically significant at one per cent level (t-ratios are 7.44 and 8.30). Moreover, the hypothesis test that the estimated matching function is constant or increasing returns to scale ($\beta_V + \beta_U \geq 1$) is rejected at five per cent level (Wald-test value is 2.75).

This implies that (1) the job-matching process in China's labour market is normal, since both the elasticities of new hires in response to unemployment and vacancies, with the log-linear Cobb-Douglas formed matching function, are positive and around 0.40-0.70 and 0.30-0.50 respectively (Peterongolo and Pissarides 2001); (2) decreasing returns to scale is one of the important characteristics of China's matching function, which suggests that there exists some inefficiency in the dynamic labour market. Thus, further analysis of the determinants of efficiency of job-matching, especially those related with economic transformation in China, should be made.

Second, the negative elasticities of specific-year dummy variables, and the insignificant time trend and constant show that the estimated matching function in China is unstable. As is shown in Table 8.3 (upper panel), the estimated coefficients in front of specific-year dummy variables, $DM98$ and $DM99$, are -0.12 and -0.02 respectively. Especially, the t-ratio for $DM98$ is -1.92, which means that the dummy $DM98$ is statistically significant at five per cent level. This implies that the matching relationship between the flow of new hires and the stocks of unemployment and vacancies in China is vulnerable to external shocks, especially government intervention. Meanwhile, the estimated coefficients of the logged time trend and the constant are insignificant (t-ratios are 0.47 and -0.46), which shows that the new hires in China are not increasing significantly over time given the vacancies and unemployment.[6] Both of the above phenomena provide some additional evidence for the existence of distortions in China's labour market.

Third, the average efficiency of job-matching in China, estimated with the log-linear Cobb-Douglas formed matching function, is increasing over time, which implies that China's labour market reform during the past decade made great progress and that the obstacles to job-matching had been reduced. Figure 8.1 shows the average efficiency of job-matching, its upper and lower bounds, and variance in China during the period 1997-2003. Despite a mild drawback after 2001, the average efficiency of job-matching in China's labour market had been increasing, from 74 per cent to 83 per cent. Furthermore, an analysis of the increase of average matching efficiency shows that decrease in the variation of matching efficiencies, in particular, the rapid increase of matching efficiency in the less efficient regional labour market (from 0.04 down to 0.01), is the main reason. This implies that China's labour market reform, with economic transformation, since the mid-1990s have been effective in improving the efficiency of job-matching between job seekers and job vacancies in the less efficient regional labour market.

Fourth, the efficiency of job-matching across regions in China shows a structural problem: large regional labour markets are usually equipped with low matching efficiency. Figure 8.2 (a) and (b) show the first ten and the last ten provincial labour market ranking with the efficiency of job-matching during the period 1997-2003, respectively. The provinces in the eastern region with the relatively large labour market, such as Shanghai, Tianjin, Beijing, and so on, have the lowest efficiency of job-matching, while their counterparts in the middle and western regions with the relatively small labour market, such as Qinghai, Henan, Yunnan and so on, have the highest efficiency of job-matching.[7] This shows that the larger the labour market is, the lower the matching efficiency of the employment frontier is in China. A possible explanation for this phenomenon is that China's labour market is experiencing rapid reform. Since there are many factors, such as rural to urban migration, unskilled and skilled labour, the need to be incorporated into the new marketplace, the larger the labour market is the more problems are encountered. This can also be used to explain the decreasing return to scale in the estimated matching function.

Table 8.3 (lower panel) shows the estimated results from the matching efficiency model, which specifies some determinants behind the efficiency of job-matching in China's labour market. Generally, the privatization and human capital accumulation tends to increase the efficiency of job-matching while openness to trade and urbanization tends to decrease the efficiency of job-matching in urban China (see Figure 8.3 for their relative effects).

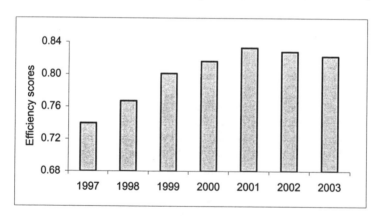

(a) The average efficiency of job-matching in China

Figure 8.1 The efficiency of job-matching

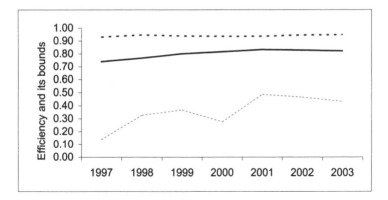

(b) The range of matching efficiency in China

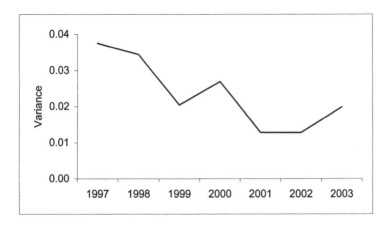

(c) The variance of matching efficiency of employment frontier

Source: Authors' own calculation.

Figure 8.1 The efficiency of job-matching (continued)

First, openness to trade is positively related with inefficiency of job-matching in China's labour market. Although it is widely argued that openness to trade may increase dynamic employment efficiency through changing the labour market institutional arrangement and reallocating workers across sectors in developing countries, it is not the case in China's labour market (Martin and Matusz 2001a). As is shown in Table 8.3 (lower part), the estimated coefficient of openness to trade is 2.03, which is positive and statistically significant at five per cent level (t-test is 2.09). This implies

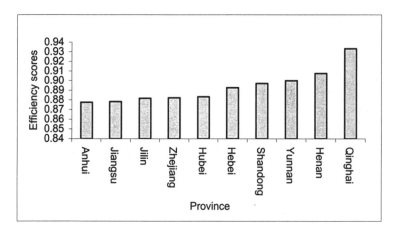

(a) The ten provinces with the highest matching efficiency

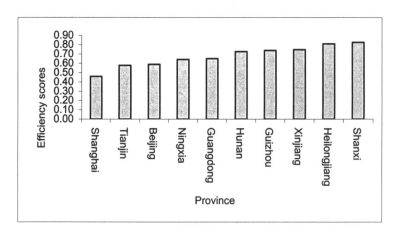

(b) The ten provinces with the lowest matching efficiency

Source: Authors' own calculation.

Figure 8.2 The top and bottom ten regions.

that openness to trade in China decreased the efficiency of job-matching during the period 1997-2003. A possible explanation is that although openness to trade helps to provide more job opportunities, it will take time to reallocate labour from the diminishing importable sectors to the booming exportable sectors. Reflected in the performance of labour market, the efficiency of job-matching is decreased by openness to trade.[8]

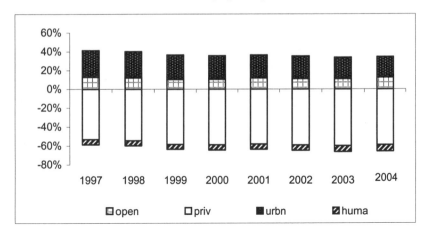

Source: Authors' own calculation.

Figure 8.3 Contribution of various factors to the efficiency of job-matching (per cent).

Second, privatization is negatively related with inefficiency of job-matching in China's labour market. Privatization of state-owned enterprises (SOEs) is an important component of economic transformation in China, which not only improves the production efficiency but also helps to promote labour market reform. With the more flexible arrangement, the privatised firms cancel the 'once-for-all' employer-employee relation in SOEs and restore the market oriented hiring and firing contract arrangements. This not only facilitates the employment placement channels, but also encourages the unemployed worker's active job seeking (Meng 2000). As is shown in Table 8.3 (lower part), the estimated coefficient of privatization is -6.52, which is negative and statistically significant at five per cent level (t-test is -1.96). This implies that privatization in China tends to reduce the labour market frictions due to institutional arrangement and to facilitate the matching between job seekers and job vacancies. Consequently, the efficiency of job-matching - the important measurement of the dynamic labour market efficiency - is increased. As Garnaut *et al.* (2005) argued, the rapid privatization and the growth *de novo* of private sector has transformed the structure of the labour market, which improved the labour market institutional arrangement and increased the efficiency of employment.

Third, urbanization is positively related with the efficiency of job-matching in China's labour market. Urbanization is one of the most important "causes and consequences" of China's industrialization and economic growth. It generally promotes the migration from rural to urban areas, which, generally, benefits both the rural and urban labour market in the long run (Meng 2000). However, due to the structural problems and various distortions in China's current labour market, urbanization in China, at least for the moment, tends to decrease the matching efficiency of the employment frontier. As is shown in Table 8.3 (lower part), the estimated elasticity to the matching inefficiency is 3.80, which is positive and statistically significant at five per cent level (t-test is 2.18). This implies that urbanization in China tends to reduce the efficiency of job-matching in China. A possible explanation is that although the rural-urban migration increases the urban labour supply, most of the new entrants are not qualified for the newly created urban jobs. This causes the segregation of the urban labour market, which undermines the efficiency of job-matching (Knight and Song 2003). As a consequence, the higher the level of unemployment and vacancies there is in the urban labour market, the lower the level of new hires.

Fourth, the accumulation of human capital is also an important factor in reducing the inefficiency of job-matching in China's labour market. Due to search theory, skilled labour usually has higher efficiency in job-matching than unskilled labour (Peterongolo and Pissarides 2001). Thus, as human capital is accumulated, the matching efficiency of the employment frontier tends to increase. As is shown in Table 8.3 (lower part), the estimated coefficient of human capital is -6.04, which is negative. This implies that the inefficiency of job-matching in China's labour market is partly due to a lack of skilled labour. Specifically, although China has made great progress in improving the quality of labour supply during the last two decades, the labour force of China on average is still less educated than labour forces of other developed and some developing countries.[9] By 2003, the number of qualified workers only accounted for 30 per cent of total employment. Therefore, it is still important to increase investment in education for unemployed workers to improve matching efficiency and increase employment.

CONCLUSION

This chapter adopts the stochastic frontier analysis to estimate the Cobb-Douglas matching function in urban China, using 7-year and 26-province panel data. The results show: first, the estimated matching function for urban China with the log-linear Cobb-Douglas form exhibits decreasing returns to scale; second, although there exists some inefficiency of job-matching in China's urban labour market, the inefficiency is decreasing over time; third, economic transformation has significant effects on the efficiency of job-matching: openness to trade and urbanization tend to decrease it while privatization and human capital accumulation tend to decrease the matching inefficiency. This provides a series of policy implications. It suggests that accelerating the privatization process and increasing investment in education for unemployed workers may help to improve the efficiency of labour markets in economic transition.

NOTES

1. Alternative measures show higher unemployment rates in recent years. For example, taking account of laid-off workers, the total for registered unemployment and *Xia Gang* (out of work) reached 5.5 per cent of the urban labour force by the end of 2002 (Brooks and Tao 2003).
2. Other empirical investigations of the aggregate matching function in transitional economics can be found in Boeri and Burda (1996), Burda and Profit (1996) for Czechs, and Berman (1997), Yashiv (2000) for Israel.
3. The function attracts public attention not only because "it enables the modelling of frictions in otherwise conventional models with a minimum of added complexity" but also because "it quantifies the labour market distortions without explicit reference to their sources" (Peterongolo and Pissarides 2001, p.390).
4. Usually, the registered job seekers, who cannot find job within 24 months, will be re-categorised into the pool of long-term unemployed and be left out of this market.
5. The estimation process contains three steps. The first step is to make OLS estimation. The second step is to use a grid search method to evaluate a likelihood function for values of γ

    (between 0 and 1) based on the OLS estimates of β_0 and σ^2. The third step is to use the

    maximum likelihood values selected in the grid search as the starting values in a quasi-Newton iterative procedure to achieve the global maximum estimate.
6. See Peterongolo and Pissarides (2001) for the estimations of the aggregate matching function in developed countries.
7. See China Statistical Yearbook 2004 for the exact definition of the eastern, middle and western regions.
8. See Magee's (1973) discussion on the welfare of openness to trade with the distorted factor market.
9. From 1996 to 2003, those in the labour force with less than a junior middle school education saw their numbers decrease by four per cent and the number of employed persons with higher education increased by one per cent.

REFERENCES

Anderson, P. M. and Burgess, S. M., 2000. 'Empirical matching functions: estimation and interpretation using state-level data', *Review of Economics and Statistics*, **82**, 93-102.

Battese, G. E. and Coelli, T. J., 1993. 'A stochastic frontier production function incorporating a model for TIE', *Working Papers in Econometrics and Applied Statistics*, **69**, 22, Department of Econometrics, University of New England, Armidale.

Battese, G. E. and Coelli, T. J., 1995. 'A model for technical inefficiency effects in a stochastic frontier production function for panel data', *Empirical Economics*, **20**, 325-332.

Bell, B. E., 1997. *A Comparative Analysis of the Aggregate Matching process in France, Great Britain and Spain*, Banco de Espana-Servicio de Estudios, Banco de Espana-Servicio de Estudios, 54-85.

Berman, E., 1997. 'Help wanted, job needed: estimates of a matching function from employment service data', *Journal of Labour Economics*, **15**, 252-291.

Blanchard, O. J. and P. Diamond, 1990. 'The aggregate matching function' in Diamond, P. (ed.) *Growth/Productivity/Unemployment: Essays to Celebrate Bob Solow's Birthday*, MIT press, 159-201.

Blanchard, O. J. and Diamond, P., 1989. 'The Beveridge curve', *Brookings Papers on Economic Activities*, 1, 1-60.

Boeri, T. and Burda, M. C., 1996. 'Central and eastern European labour markets: active labour market policies: job-matching and the Czech miracle', *European Economic Review*, **40**, 805-817.

Brooks, R. and Tao, R., 2003. 'China's Labour Market Performance and Challenges', *International Monetary Fund*, IMF Working Papers.

Burda, M. C. and Profit, S., 1996. 'Matching across space: evidence on mobility in the Czech republic', *Labour Economics*, **3**, 255-278.

Burda, M. and Wyplosz, C., 1994. 'Gross worker and job flows in Europe', *European Economic Review*, **38**, 1287-1315.

China Statistical Bureau, 2005. *China Statistical Yearbook 2004*, China Statistical Press.

Coelli, T. J., 1992. 'A computer program for frontier production function estimation: FRONTIER, Version 2.0', *Economics Letters*, **39**, 29-32.

Coelli, T. J., 1996. 'A guide to FRONTIER Version 4.1: A computer program for stochastic frontier production and cost function estimation', *CEPA Working Paper 96/07*, Centre for Efficiency and Productivity Analysis, Armidale, NSW.

Coelli, T. J. and Battese, G. E., 1996. 'Identification of factors that influence the technical inefficiency of Indian farmers', *Australian Journal of Agricultural Economics*, **40**, 19-44.

Coelli, T. J., Sanzidur, R. and Colin, T., 2003. 'A stochastic frontier approach to total factor productivity measurement in Bangladesh crop agriculture, 1961-1992', *Journal of International Development*, **15**, 321-333.

Coles, M. G. and Smith, E. 1996. 'Cross-section estimation of the matching functions: evidence from England and Wales', *Economica*, **63**, 589-597.

Garnaut, R., Song, L., Tenev, S. and Yang, Y., 2005. *China's Ownership Transformation: Process, Outcomes, Prospects*, IMF International Finance Corporation, The World Bank.

Knight, J. and Song, L., 2003. 'Chinese peasant choices: migration, rural industry or farming', *Oxford Development Studies*, **31**, 123-147.

Kompas, T., 2004. 'Technical efficiency effects of input controls: evidence from Australia's banana prawn fishery', *Applied Economics*, **36**, 1631-1641.

Kong, X., Mark, R. E. and Wan, G. H., 1999. 'Technical efficiency, technological change and total factor productivity growth in Chinese state-owned enterprises in the early 1990s', *Asian Economic Journal*, **13**, 267-281.

Magee, S. P., 1973, 'Factor market distortions, production, and trade: a survey', *Oxford Economic Papers*, **25**, 1-43.

Martin, S. and Matusz, S., 2001a. 'Globalization, employment, and income: analyzing the adjustment process', *Research Paper 2001/04*, Globalisation and Labour Markets Programme: Leverhulme Centre.

Meng, X., 2000. *Labour Market Reform in China*, Cambridge University Press.

Munich, D., Svejnar, J. and Terrel, K., 1999. 'Worker-Firm matching and unemployment in transition to a market economy: (why) were the Czechs more successful than others?' *Working Paper 107*, Davidson Institute, U. Michigan Business School.

Peterongolo, B. and Pissarides, C. A., 2001. 'Looking into the black box: a survey of the matching function', *Journal of Economic Literature*, **39**, 390-431.

Pissarides, C. A., 1986. 'Unemployment and vacancies in Britain', *Economic policy*, **3**, 676-690.

Profit, S. and Sperlich, S., 2004. 'Non-uniformity of job-matching in a transition economy - a nonparametric analysis for the Czech Republic', *Applied Economics*, **36**, 695-714.

Yashiv, E., 2000. 'The determinants of equilibrium unemployment', *American Economic Review*, **90**, 1297-1322.

PART III

Banking, Exchange Rates and Globalization

9. Banking Reform and Macroeconomic Management

Michael Thorpe

INTRODUCTION

The Chinese financial system can be characterized as "over-banked". The four large state-owned commercial banks are largely responsible for deposit gathering and on-lending of China's massive pool of household savings. Business funding is dominated by bank lending, with equity and debt markets poorly developed in China. The financial system is "repressed", with caps maintained on artificially low interest rates and directed credit allocation, historically to the large, inefficient state-owned enterprise (SOE) sector. Foreign banks, to date, have played only a small role in local currency business and in dealings with Chinese household and corporations. One result of this approach has been an inefficient and low profitability banking sector beset with high levels of non-performing loans (NPLs). Capital controls, which had been planned to be liberalized in the late 1990s, have been kept relatively tight to help protect the fragile financial system and provide time for restructuring. There is also an urgency to this due to the full national treatment to be offered to foreign banks in 2007 under China's WTO accession agreement.

Although extensive regulatory and prudential reforms have been cautiously instituted, along with moves to manage the NPL problem and commercialize the finance sector with greater involvement of the private sector and foreign institutions, there are pressing issues related to management of the macroeconomic policy environment that need to be addressed. The question of establishing the necessary conditions for conducting effective monetary policy and allowing market determined interest rates looms large. As well, the interaction of strong inflows of foreign direct investment (FDI) and a growing trade surplus with capital controls has seen a massive build-up in China's levels of foreign reserves over the past few years. This has raised the issue of China's exchange rate policy and the extent and impact of an undervalued *Renminbi* (RMB). Pressure from foreign governments, primarily the United States, along with sizeable speculative capital inflows (despite the controls in place) has also influenced this debate on China's currency policy.

In assessing the relative merits of China's exchange rate policy, liberalizing the capital account and introducing a more market based interest rate regime, cognisance must be made of the constraints of the so-called policy "trilemma" facing policy makers generally. It is not possible to simultaneously conduct an independent monetary policy, maintain an open capital account and maintain a stable exchange rate. Only two of the three choices are possible. In seeking to develop its financial sector and integrate the economy more into the global marketplace, the Chinese government has recognised the need for changes in these policy areas, but the trade-offs along with questions of timing and sequencing of reforms must be carefully addressed.

The following section of this chapter reviews the macroeconomic policy framework and institutional arrangements which have shaped the current economic macroeconomic environment. This is followed by a section outlining the current macroeconomic situation in China and the implications this presents for changes to policy. Policy options with respect to management of the exchange rate, liberalizing the capital account and deregulating interest rates are then discussed in light of the current situation in China.

MACROECONOMIC INSTITUTIONAL ARRANGEMENTS AND POLICY FRAMEWORK

Since the opening up of the Chinese economy in 1979, the evolution of macroeconomic policy has been shaped by the institutional features and political realities facing policy makers. In turn, the economic environment that has emerged constrains and influences the nature and extent of policy changes that are needed in an increasingly globalized economy.

The macroeconomic environment in China is characterized by an officially closed capital account and what can be characterized as a repressed financial system - a system of directed bank credit, domestic credit controls, restrictions on borrowing and lending abroad and foreign bank entry, and regulated interest rates (McKinnon 1991, Heffernan 2005). In July 2005 China scrapped the 11 year old peg of its currency to the US dollar. The RMB is now linked to a basket of currencies, the central parities of which are set at the end of each day. Daily movements are limited to within a 0.3 percentage range of its opening level. The central rate against the US dollar was re-valued 2.1 per cent at the time of the change.

While this financial repression has been aimed at limiting volatility and offering protection to a weak banking sector, in such situations the role of the financial system is greatly impaired, with savings decisions of investors distorted and allocation of capital tending to be inefficient with low quality investments widespread. Controlled interest rates make it difficult to price loans to reflect risk and have been a disadvantage to small and medium enterprises (SMEs) and new firms in the private sector with the SOEs in China favoured by the directed credit policy.

In China the result of such policies can be seen in an "overbanked" economy, a reliance on an immature bank-based capital market with weakly developed equity and debt markets, the establishment of a sizeable informal market as a source of funds and high levels of bad debts in the banking system. By most measures the banking system in China is quite large, with the banks playing a significant role in intermediation reflecting a very high domestic savings rate, the lack of alternative assets for local investors and capital account restrictions which further limit investment opportunities (Prasad 2004).[1]

China's banking system collects the bulk of China's huge pool of domestic savings, equivalent to around 40 per cent of GDP (Asian Development Bank 2004).[2] In the mid-1990s, about 85 per cent of the total financial assets of households was held in bank deposits (Huang 2003). By 2004 the figure was still 77 per cent which can be compared to a level of 26 per cent in the US. The share of households in total savings is 70 per cent, with about half of China's population having bank accounts.

China has bank lending currently equal to around 140 per cent of GDP, more than twice the levels which are observed in most industrial countries, as a result of official lending policies and what has been a lack of accountability and regulation generally in the financial system (Lee 2004). The figure a decade earlier was 88 per cent (Chong 2004).

The big four state-owned commercial banks in China control about 70 per cent of bank deposits and make about 70 per cent of loans, accounting for 60 per cent of corporate financing in China, all of which tends to be done on a bilateral loan basis (Mellor 2004; de Terra 2004). The SOEs account for 80 per cent of outstanding loans while producing just one third of output (The Economist 2004a).[3] This has resulted in the proliferation of informal and illegal banking activities and created great difficulty for private companies in China to access credit.[4] In the first quarter of 2005, bank lending (although down slightly overall) accounted for 99 per cent of business financing, reflecting a slump in an already moribund stock market and a reduction in offerings of government construction bonds.

Extensive reforms have been instituted in recent years to address many of the failings in the financial system. An important step has been a new regulatory regime for bank lending, a shift from a funds constraint to what is viewed as a capital constraint. Traditionally the banks have simply collected deposits and made (directed) loans. The main constraint was to ensure loans did not exceed a prudent proportion of deposits (around 75 per cent). This encouraged the development of a large scale deposit gathering network, a relationship-driven push for deposits and rapid growth of loans, with little attention to loan quality or profitability of asset growth. The result over the 1980s and 1990s was periodic boom-bust credit cycles and economic overheating. The new regulations, from March 2004, require banks to meet a target of eight per cent of total capital adequacy and four per cent of core capital adequacy by January 2007. These moves will remove a bias in lending towards the state sector.

A worrying result of the concentration of lending to the SOEs has been the burgeoning NPLs of the bank sector, particularly the commercial banks. Estimates vary, although there is agreement that levels have come down due to a mix of measures, including a shift of bad assets from banks to specially created asset management companies (AMCs), recapitalization of balance sheets by government and through an expansion of new lending.[5] Officially the level at the end of 2004 was given as 13.2 per cent overall (and 15.6 per cent for the commercial banks), although Standard and Poor's suggest a level of 35 per cent, excluding loans transferred to the AMCs and those which are still part of public sector holdings (The Economist 2005a, Mellor 2004). This latter figure translates to around 45 per cent of GDP, significant when compared to the bail-out of the S&Ls in the US which was equivalent to four per cent of GDP and the level of NPLs in Thailand in 1997 of 25 per cent (Kuo and Subler 2004).

Given the restrictions on their activities, the banks in China currently rely to an inordinate degree on net interest income from their borrowing and lending activities. This has been put as high as 90 per cent of total income (Liping 2001). Even though the big four are ranked in the top 40 banks in the world (based on assets), they are not in the top 700 in terms of return on assets. Profitability is a problem not only because of the lack of income options, but also because of the cost structure of the banking system.

Funds raised through the stock market corporate bond issuances are relatively small in China. Lending in 2003 was equivalent to about 26 per cent of GDP, compared to one per cent and 0.3 per cent of GDP raised on the stock market and via bonds respectively (Prasad 2004). At the start of 2004 the capitalization of the stock market was around 37 per cent (Lee 2004). Access to the domestic bond market in China is restricted and bureaucratic. Corporate bond issues in 2003 were only around 45.2 billion RMB, compared to 8.9 billion in 2000 (de Terra 2004). In 2004 the Chinese government bond market was worth around US$500 billion equivalent, compared to an estimated US Treasury market of US$8000 billion.[6]

Interest rate regulation and directed lending policies have resulted in increasing amounts of loans flowing out of the bank sector to the private loans market to meet the needs of SMEs and private enterprises (and more recently to the property market, fuelling a speculative bubble). While there are no precise measures available for the size of China's informal market, some reports suggest that in some cities it is larger than the formal banking system. The China Daily in late 2004 reported that informal lending in Wenzhou, Zhejiang province, had reached 670 billion, increasing 23 per cent over a 12 month period. One estimate suggests that around 0.8 to 1.2 per cent of GDP was diverted to the underground capital markets over a period of two months in 2004.[7] Based on these figures, the national market would be equal to at least 20-30 per cent of GDP.[8] The diversion of funds from the banks undermines attempts by authorities to control lending in the absence of an effective monetary policy framework.

An over-riding concern for authorities in China is the health and stability of the banking sector, with the result that financial market reform is proceeding cautiously, notwithstanding the growing need for alternative channels of capital (to bank financing) to be developed. In the current environment authorities are seeking to curb bank credit to restrain overinvestment in some sectors of the economy, manage the current (and potentially growing) NPL problem and create a sound financial system able to cope with the unfettered entry of foreign banks in 2007 under China's WTO accession agreement.[9] These concerns go to the heart of the major macroeconomic policy issues facing China.

As discussed below, a compounding issue for macroeconomic management is the interaction of efforts to maintain a stable exchange rate with strong export growth and significant capital inflows. A build-up in reserves has accentuated the problem of liquidity management, and raised concerns as to the extent of currency misalignment and an optimal exchange rate policy. A related policy matter is China's continued tight control on capital account transactions, despite recent, limited moves to free up capital flows. There is concern, for example, that greater freedom could, in the present climate, exacerbate currency pressures. Conversely, there is a view that the full national treatment of foreign banks in the context of liberalizing interest rates and/or an opening up of the capital account could precipitate a major crisis for domestic banks through a dramatic loss of funds.

The following section briefly reviews the current macroeconomic situation in China, highlighting those areas which are important in considering China's resolution of its macroeconomic policy "trilemma" (Taylor 2004). It is not possible to simultaneously conduct an independent monetary policy, have an open capital account and maintain a stable exchange rate. Only two of the three choices are possible. China's position is also viewed in the context of its external relations, particularly with the US. In view of the policy constraints, options with respect to the exchange rate, interest rate deregulation and the capital account are then assessed, with attention to the matter of timing and sequencing of policy changes.

CHINA'S CURRENT MACROECONOMIC ENVIRONMENT

There was little capital inflow into China until the mid 1980s. Bank lending was the largest share of inflows over the 1980s although FDI was slowly growing in importance to its current dominant position (Thorpe 2004). With regard to external debt, there has been little sovereign borrowing overseas until recently and SOEs have been discouraged from this market. While the external debt to GDP ratio has been stable for some time at around 15 per cent, the share that is short term has risen dramatically over the past few years. Currently it is around 45 per cent which does suggest some need for monitoring, although this figure reflects sizeable levels of trade credits (Prasad and Wei 2005).[10]

The long-standing pegged exchange rate (notwithstanding the recent policy shift) in concert with restrictions on capital outflows has meant that over the last several years, as a result of the surge inward of foreign direct investment and a growing trade surplus, the Peoples Bank of China (PBOC) has had to buy up significant amounts of foreign currency in exchange for local currency (Table 9.1).[11] This has been exacerbated by a significant rise in speculative capital inflows (despite tight restrictions). As a result, since 2001 foreign exchange reserves have ballooned (Hu 2004). Currently they stand at around 40 per cent of GDP, second only to Japan.[12] While an earlier rise over 1994-1997 reflected FDI inflows, there was a decline in the rate of increase up to 2000 following the Asian crisis. The recent spurt reflects continuing FDI flows, an export boom and significant levels of speculative capital inflow - notwithstanding the capital controls in place (Ryan 2004).[13] About half of the increase in international reserves in 2003 can be accounted for by non-FDI capital inflows (Prasad and Wei 2005). Reserves are rising at the equivalent of US$ 17 billion a month (The Economist 2005b). Around two thirds of China's reserves are held in US dollars, especially Treasury bonds.[14] Given that China's share of trade with the US, Japan and the EU is 36.5, 28.6 and 37.4 per cent respectively, the US dollar would seem to be currently overweighted in China's reserves. US treasury bonds also earn around a relatively low two per cent. As discussed below, moves by China to diversify the composition of its reserves would have implications for the US economy.

The increase in inflows of short-term capital has stemmed from investors taking advantage of relatively high interest rates in China and speculating on a revaluation. Capital controls on inflows have been circumvented in numerous ways including under-invoicing of export contracts, over-invoicing of import contracts, offshore borrowing by Chinese firms and households (including accessing of foreign currency credit cards of foreign banks), transfer pricing, leads and lags in settling contracts, varying terms on short term trade credits, savings remittances and tourist expenditures.[15] Foreign banks have also been motivated to borrow offshore and lend to FIEs, mostly

Table 9.1 Key macroeconomic indicators–China

	1999	2000	2001	2002	2003	2004
FX reserves (US$ billion)	154.7	165.6	212.2	286.4	403.3	609.9
Budget balance (% GDP)	-2.5	-3.1	-4.4	-3.0	-2.9	
External debt (% GDP)	15.3	13.5	14.5	13.5	13.7	14.2
	(10%)*					(45.6)*
CPI (%)	-1.4	0.3	0.5	-0.8	1.2	3.9
GDP growth		7.5	7.5	8.3	9.3	9.5
M2 growth					20.0	14.6
Credit growth			9.6	22.5	28.8	21.0**
Current account balance (% GDP)					3.2	4.2
Trade growth		32.0	7.5	22.0	37.1	36.0***
FDI (net inflows, US$ billion)		40.7	46.8	52.7	53.5	61.5

Notes: * Per cent of total external debt which is short-term.
      ** First four months.
      *** Estimated figure.

Sources: IFS Financial Statistics, World Bank, Prasad and Wei (2005).

in RMB. To help curb this inflow, foreign banks are now subject to quotas on this borrowing, squeezing their source of funds and increasing their costs as they are forced to borrow domestically (www.chinaonline 2004). Overall, such flows might be expected to continue if expectations do not change and if current interest rate differentials remain. Thus the pressure on the authorities is likely to continue to build, requiring an effective circuit breaker regarding exchange rate policy.

The surge in reserves has pumped money into the domestic economy, although the PBOC has sterilized the inflow to some extent by borrowing from the banking system. In 2004 authorities drained two thirds of the increase in reserves via sterilization. With more than one trillion RMB worth of bonds outstanding in China, sterilization may be reaching its limits as commercial banks, who are the main buyers of government bonds, become reluctant to remain active in the market. Sterilization also has a fiscal cost in that the rate of return on domestic (sterilization) instruments is less than that earned on foreign reserve holdings. However controls on capital outflows (to alternative assets) and interest rate controls have served to facilitate sterilization and contain the cost.[16]

The resultant leakage into the economy helped fuel a rapid growth in money supply and subsequent credit expansion over 2003 and 2004.[17] Growth of 40 per cent in fixed asset investment during 2003 caused overheating in some areas, with excessive lending blamed for soaring real estate prices and excess capacity in aluminium, cement, automobile and steel plants. As well, rapid expansion in production, especially by Chinese firms supplying the domestic market, has generated an accumulating surplus of manufactured goods leading to fears in some quarters of a future deflation. Supply gluts are a particular concern, seen as a potential trigger for severe financial crisis. This has been driven not only by the ease of access to loanable funds but by poor lending decisions. Power generation, meanwhile has been running up against capacity constraints, with the investment boom causing shortages. Overinvestment has also clogged transport links and driven up raw material prices. Rapid expansion in automotive sector, steel, aluminium and construction materials has led to serious overcapacity, with growth in some areas being choked by energy shortages. A general inefficiency in energy, land and capital usage resulted along with soaring raw material prices. Inflation also started to rise in mid 2004 as soaring costs fed into the prices of many consumer goods.

Commencing in 2004, the government instituted a range of policies to curb overinvestment which had raised fears of inflation and concerns of a speculative bubble in real estate. The PBOC raised bank capital adequacy ratios and applied administrative lending controls to fast growing areas while publicly calling on banks to push more loans towards coal production, power generation and transport projects (Dolven 2004; Lee 2004; Wonacott and Wu 2004).[18]

This situation brings into sharp focus the difficulties for policy makers. The boom in China to mid 2004 has been led by investment, resulting in strong growth in supply and also demand, but not a balanced outcome. Rather than "overheating" per se, the problem is overinvestment. Meanwhile the government is also seeking to switch public spending away from areas stimulating demand towards support for reform in other areas of the public sector including social security, science and technology and wage support.

The use of targeted credit and administrative (quantitative) controls appears to be a preferred policy approach, albeit with some limited market measures, in the absence of a flexible exchange rate and a liberalized interest rate regime. Some mortgage rates and rates on car loans, for example, were raised in May of 2004 by banks, and price caps have been imposed by authorities in some inflationary sectors, along with curbs on lending to key overheating sectors (Chung and Wu 2004). Measures to rein in steel prices have included government moves to scrap rebates on some steel exports, restricting access to imported raw materials for some producers and imposition of tighter land controls. Government control throughout the whole production and distribution process for energy has exacerbated problems (Ng 2005). Other measures aimed at controlling credit expansion include allowing exporters to retain foreign exchange earnings, giving Chinese institutions greater freedom to invest abroad and removing some export subsidies and import restrictions.

The approaches taken reflect the lack of sophistication in the Chinese authority's ability to manage the financial system at present and a preference for direct controls. China has limited experience with the use of monetary policy. Interest rates had been fixed for nine years (until the adjustment in October 2004) and so the extent to which the economy responds to interest rate changes is still somewhat uncertain.

The Chinese decision to increase interest rates in October 2004 saw a rise in lending rates of 27 basis points on loans with a one year maturity to 5.58 per cent while deposit yields rose to 2.25 per cent from 1.98 per cent. Banks also now have more flexibility in pricing loans with a longer maturity than one year. While lending rates are restricted to no less than 0.9 times the official rate, the cap on lending at more than 1.7 times the official rate has been scrapped. In the past banks were charging about nine per cent compared to interest rates of 15-20 per cent prevailing in China's informal lending market. The changes give lenders more freedom to fix loan rates and to take lending risk into greater account.[19] This decision to raise interest rates suggests that the government recognises the need to change the cost of capital, not just fine tune access to lending through controls. The fact, however, that interest rate adjustments to date have been limited reflects a continued caution regarding the use of market prices in place of administrative guidance to control credit.

POLICY OPTIONS

External Pressures

In 2004 the US ran a current account deficit of US$666 billion equivalent to 5.6 per cent of GDP, an increase of 25.5 per cent on the previous year. The corresponding deficit on the trade account was just over US$600 billion. In contrast to the late 1990s when the deficit was driven primarily by private capital inflows, the funding is now dominated by foreign central banks buying US Treasury paper.[20] Amid concerns as to the sustainability of expanding US debt levels, increased focus on rising unemployment at home and China's power-house economic progress, there is a growing protectionist sentiment in the US directed at China. This response is being driven by political as well as domestic economic concerns. The ending of WTO quota restrictions on clothing and textiles at the beginning of 2005 which saw a surge in Chinese exports in these products provided a lightning rod for influential US (and EU) interest groups. While negotiation regarding the re-imposition of some agreed level of quotas is being undertaken in respect of that particular issue, increasing pressure was also brought to bear on China to revalue the (then pegged) RMB to remove what was viewed as an "unfair" trade advantage. The question of China's exchange rate policy is discussed in more detail below, but several points can be made in regard to this matter in assessing US-China trade relations.

While the US-China trade imbalance in China's favour was US$162 billion in 2004 (about 27 per cent of the US total), overall China had a trade surplus of only US$32 billion for the period, running significant deficits with other countries (reflecting the strong import of intermediate goods, including capital equipment and components).[21] While China's export growth has been very strong, China's share of the imports of the US and EU tends to be relatively small (Table 9.2). Moreover, around 50 per cent of China's exports are undertaken by the so-called foreign invested enterprises (FIEs) (Thorpe 2004). In 2003 China accounted for 21 per cent of the growth in US exports, while for Germany and Japan the figures were 28 and 32 per cent respectively (Mellor 2004). About half of China's imports are employed in further processing and over 40 per cent of China's exports embody imports (Prasad 2004). Any revaluation of the RMB would mean a relatively muted rise in export prices because of their high import content.[22]

The US is at present compensated for its rising import and debt levels through increased investment (and profits) in China and also benefits from China's financing of its current account (and budget) deficit which keeps interest rates low, and consumer spending up. The US government, however, does need to stimulate growth elsewhere in the economy and reduce reliance on overseas savings. The US dollar needs to depreciate, but will a yuan appreciation achieve this, and to the extent necessary? Krugman (2005)

Table 9.2 China's market share in major export markets (per cent of each country's imports)

Year	US	EU	Japan
1970	0.0	0.6	1.4
1980	0.5	0.7	3.1
1990	3.2	2.0	5.1
1995	6.3	3.8	10.7
2000	8.6	6.2	14.5
2002	11.1	7.5	18.3
2003	12.5	8.9	18.5

Source: IMF database.

Table 9.3 Relative importance of China's international trade (per cent of GDP)

	Trade in Goods	Exports*	Imports*
1999	36.4	22.3	19.2
2002	48.8	28.9	25.9
2003	60.1	34.3	31.8

Notes: * Goods and Services.
Source: World Bank (2005)

argues that any significant revaluation by China would, in fact, generate short term pain in the US, with rising interest rates, a fall in consumer spending and property prices and reduced employment in construction. The longer term benefit will be the improved competitiveness of the US economy. A revaluation by China would also ease some pressure on its overheated economy, lowering the bill for imported oil and other raw materials, and reduce the push for protectionist responses among its trading partners. In fact, the recent changes to currency arrangements in China have apparently muted criticism from outside, despite the very limited size of adjustment to date. To the extent that China eventually allows more flexibility in its exchange rate, other Asian economies will have greater room to manoeuvre in revaluing their exchange rates, moves that have been resisted in order to avoid loss of global market share to China.

However, given China's overall share of US trade of around 10 per cent of US total trade, a revaluation by China of, say, 10 per cent would reduce the dollar's trade-weighted value by only one per cent (The Economist 2005b). If it were matched by a similar rise in all other Asian currencies, then the dollar's trade-weighted index would fall by 3.7 per cent. This is small compared with the US dollar's decline of 16 per cent since early 2002, let alone with what would be needed to cut America's current account deficit to a sustainable level. A report by HSBC has estimated that the dollar needs to fall by a further 30 per cent to reduce the US current account deficit to two to three per cent of GDP.

How China chooses to manage its macroeconomic policy options is an important element in dealing with the issue of global imbalances. However the US can not expect adjustment in a bilateral exchange rate to provide the solution to what are, to a large extent, domestic fiscal problems linked to the savings and investment patterns in the US and China.

The Macroeconomic Policy Constraint

Financial sector reform involves substituting market oriented, indirect government policy instruments and prudential regulation in place of direct price, allocative and operational controls of financial institutions. The matter of reform of the macroeconomic environment is therefore crucial. This raises the issue of financial liberalization which addresses questions related to exchange rate policy, capital account restrictions and the ability of authorities to conduct monetary policy in a deregulated interest rate environment.

The current reforms and restructuring under way in the finance sector in China are being undertaken in an environment of interest rate controls, a closed capital account and a tightly managed exchange rate. Impacting the reform process are pressures both from within and internationally for changes in all these areas. It is not possible, however, to simultaneously maintain an independent monetary policy, free capital flows and a stable currency - the so-called "trilemma" for policy regimes. Only two of the three choices are possible. Any policy adjustments must also be cognisant of the state of the banking industry and the need to ensure financial stability.

The remedy for distortions in financial markets is the elimination of interest rate controls and the encouragement of market-based credit allocation. In a globalized economy, it has become harder, however, to maintain stability in exchange rates and conduct an independent monetary policy directed to domestic objectives. A country's interest rate will tend to follow closely that of the partner to which it has pegged its currency because of the impact of capital flows in an integrated capital market (even with significant reserves held by the central bank). A country could choose to maintain an independent monetary policy in these circumstances only under conditions of tight capital controls, which means foregoing the benefits of integration. Monetary independence can be maintained with a liberalized capital account, but only with a flexible exchange rate. Global capital market integration also carries some inherent risks for a country. International shocks are readily transmitted and capital movements can be destabilizing for a country's exchange rate environment and financial system.

As has been discussed above, given that the capital account in China is somewhat porous in terms of inflows, and given the inward FDI and trade surplus, the resulting build up of foreign exchange reserves has meant that control of the money supply has been limited in the absence of market determined interest rates.

If China were to free up the capital account while seeking to maintain a stable and regulated exchange rate, effective management of monetary policy would be constrained. A more flexible float in such circumstances would allow for greater interest rate independence. Questions remain, however, regarding the policy objectives China wishes to pursue and the timing and sequencing of policy shifts involved in achieving these ends. The resolution of the "trilemma" remains a critical issue for China as it continues banking and finance sector reforms.

What are the benefits and risks for China from integrating more fully with global capital markets? What are the relative merits of a managed as opposed to a more flexible exchange rate regime? How can China shake off the financial repression which has been a central feature of macroeconomic management to date? These issues are considered in the following sections of the chapter.

Exchange Rate Policy

Some reports have suggested that China (and other Asian countries) have maintained undervalued currencies in conjunction with capital controls to keep exports competitive and fuel growth (The Economist 2004a).[23] While it is widely accepted that the Chinese currency is currently undervalued there are conflicting views (The Economist 2004b; The Economist 2005a; Prasad and Wei 2005). It should be noted that while the central rate of the RMB was adjusted up against the US dollar by 2.1 per cent at the introduction of the new regime in July 2005, the rate has been maintained at this parity since then (as at 30 August). Academic analysts and market analysts disagree as to the extent of any identified undervaluation of the RMB. Estimates have ranged from 25-30 per cent down to only slight misalignment. Moreover, there is no consensus on the policy prescription for China in adjusting its exchange rate arrangements.

Two results of undervaluation tend to be either a large multilateral trade surplus and/or high inflation. China's overall trade balance is relatively modest, exaggerated if anything by over and under-invoicing on exports and imports respectively. Inflation, particularly in certain sectors of the economy, has become a concern. This reflects a multitude of factors including a lax banking system fostering strong credit growth (not necessarily allocated efficiently) and infrastructure bottlenecks stemming from uneven growth, in part due to continuing government controls in many areas. A revaluation could help to curb the rapid growth in money supply and ease cost pressures coming from imports. It would also enable a more independent monetary policy to be pursued. The fact that the US would view an adjustment favourably would provide political benefit to China, even if not addressing the real issues of US and global imbalances. However the political cost of conforming to US demands on the issue is apparent and real.

It is not likely that a weak currency is in China's long term domestic interest because of its inflationary pressures and the threat that it does bring of retaliatory protectionism. An undervalued exchange rate also discourages investment in the non-traded sector of the economy and taxes domestic consumption. Childs (2005) has suggested that a significantly overvalued currency in China leaves the economy exposed to further overheating. Some estimates have put the fall in China's real trade-weighted exchange rate (adjusted for inflation differences with other countries) at 13 per cent over the period 2001 to early 2005 although this should be viewed in context of developments prior to this time (The Economist 2005a). Between 1994 and 2001, the real exchange rate rose 30 per cent, dragged up by a rising US dollar. During the 1997 Asian crisis China chose not to follow the actions of most its neighbouring economies and devalue its currency, despite pressure from its traded goods sector.

Any significant revaluation will also bring with it domestic costs. It would hurt exporters and import competing sectors such as agriculture, an area already under competitive stress, as well as holders of US dollar assets. In particular, it would erode the value of the recent sizeable US dollar capitalizations of key banks in China (Holland and Lague 2004). A revaluation has also been strongly argued against in terms of its likely adverse impact on regional neighbours which run trade surpluses with China (Holland 2004). However, these countries also compete in third markets with China and would gain from greater exchange rate flexibility in response to adjustments by China.

Several options for China in managing its exchange rate have been canvassed (The Economist 2005a). China has tended to follow the least disruptive of these options in its recent policy shift. The currency is linked to a basket of currencies, with the scope for daily movements of 0.3 per cent. To date, the rate has been kept stable. A suggested alternative was for a one-off significant revaluation, coupled with a float or managed peg to the US dollar. As discussed above, what constitutes significant varies according to market perceptions. The concern is that a small move is unlikely to temper speculative fervour and could lead to a loss of confidence by the market in the ability of authorities to effectively manage the currency. The impact of recent changes remains to be seen. Future policy responses will be guided by institutional and market developments.

The slower pace of reform currently being pursued will permit the foreign exchange market to deepen and there is likely to be less volatility. Karacadag *et al.* (2004) outline how the majority of exits from a fixed to a flexible exchange rate have been accompanied by crises and provide strategies for an orderly transition. Institutional and policy frameworks matter, as does the matter of timing and sequencing of policy changes. It is necessary to build the management capacity of key players in the foreign exchange market along with better market information flows to facilitate rate formation and the development of risk hedging instruments.[24]

Monetary authorities will also need to develop an alternative nominal anchor, such as inflation targeting, as it progressively frees up the exchange rate. In China this would require suitable institutional capacity and macroeconomic management tools, including deregulation of interest rates. This brings again to the fore the question of the "trilemma" trade-off. As discussed below, the timing of capital account liberalization in conjunction with exchange rate and interest rate policy adjustments is a major issue.

Capital Account Liberalization

Theory proposes that international financial capital flows should provide for a more efficient allocation of capital, including a greater diversification of asset holdings for investors. Inflows should encourage improved economic growth performance by augmenting domestic savings, lowering the cost of capital, assisting technology transfer and facilitating the development of local institutions (Prasad and Wei 2005). Integration of global capital markets allows inter-temporal trade, with lenders foregoing resources and consumption today to get more in the future and borrowers prepared to pay more later for a more immediate access to resources. Capital inflow should therefore facilitate consumption smoothing over time, offsetting output fluctuations, although to the extent that inflows are asymmetric, drying up in less favourable times, this may not always be the case.

Transparency, prudential controls and regulations, a stable macro economy and a supportive institutional environment are all critical factors in ensuring the benefits from capital liberalization are achieved (Taylor 2004). China's access to FDI has allowed more of the upside benefits while other capital controls have compensated for the poorly performing domestic finance sector and problems with SOEs (Huang 2003). This has also allowed for continued restrictions on "debt" from overseas which can create difficulties in such circumstances. From China's view point, a healthy banking and financial sector, a strong legal framework and regulatory environment would allow more latitude in easing capital controls. Capital controls serve to prevent speculative attacks. Excessive capital flows can cause currency and asset price volatility or, as witnessed in China (where controls have been porous and not all-encompassing), loss of control of monetary conditions. Over-borrowing can occur when credit controls are eased, resulting in asset bubbles and longer term debt-servicing problems. In the context of China this would be exacerbated by the lack of alternative investment opportunities domestically, the inability of banks to adequately assess credit risk and inadequate prudential and regulatory controls. Speculative inflow has already been seen to be fuelling inflation in property and real estate markets.

Controls also serve to keep funds within the domestic system, discouraging systemic crises as funds leaving one bank must go to another. In the extreme, a loss of confidence in institutions, precipitated by the opportunity to move funds offshore, could lead to a run on the banking system.[25] This is important given China's need to build-up its banking and financial system. An opening of the capital account allowing firms (and households) to hold foreign assets could be expected over the longer term to see significant outflows as investors seek to diversify savings into foreign assets. If interest rates were to also be deregulated, then any freeing of the capital account would require allowing more exchange rate flexibility.

Interest Rate Deregulation

As discussed above, the government in China continues to limit the role of the market in determining interest rates, relying on administrative controls to influence the expansion (and direction) of credit in the economy. In the current environment, rates would rise if there were to be more market flexibility. This would reduce the profit margins of banks (as presently operating) and harm healthy sectors of the economy (Chan 2004). Banks' margins on existing loans could be squeezed (if adjustments are not possible) and losses would be sustained on the holdings of long term government debt. Borrowers from less developed regions in China may be particularly disadvantaged at a time when improvements are being realised. To the extent that speculation continues regarding the value of the RMB, rising interest rates could accelerate capital inflows putting more pressure on the currency and creating an opportunity for further credit growth. The threat of NPLs could be expected to rise as a result of these influences noted above. With the government running a large budget deficit - public debt is currently around 30 per cent of GDP - any rise in rates would adversely affect the public sector already in need of tax reform to finance expenditures.[26] While there is currently no problem in servicing this debt, there is the possibility of financial crisis if the economy were to deteriorate. The downside to this, however, would be the risk of slowing the economy and exacerbating unemployment and social problems. Fiscal policy in China tends to be an ineffective tool, constrained as it is by socio-political factors.

If rates are liberalized, banks face the problem of gathering and assessing information on firms in pricing for risk in the markets. Deregulation is no guarantee of efficient capital allocation. Where there is uncertainty about rates and credit and lack of experience, imperfect screening can result, with highly productive customers excluded if information regarding the risk characteristics of individual firms is missing or not widely available (i.e. adverse selection). In fact, funding may be encouraged to high risk activities if interest rates are high, with good investors leaving the market (Villanueva and Mirakhor 1990). Borrowers may be encouraged to choose riskier projects with higher associated returns (i.e. moral hazard). To address these problems, balance sheets of companies need to be made transparent (Fry 1988). Stringent bank supervision is also needed, along with effective bankruptcy laws.

Well developed equity and bond markets in China can improve the allocative efficiency of capital through exercising fiscal discipline on firms and helping the generation and transmission of information flows in the marketplace. A decreased dependence on bank credit will reduce the vulnerability to interest rate shocks and the widening of capital markets will assist the development of risk management markets generally. Informal credit markets will also need to be brought under tighter supervision.

Such measures, along with a stable macroeconomic environment, need to be in place before interest rates can be completely liberalized. In the meantime, some regulation of rates by authorities may need to be temporarily maintained. However, the entry of foreign banks in 2007 is likely to lead to greater pressure for reform efforts in the area of interest rates.

Timing and Sequencing Issues

The early literature on financial development suggested that financial liberalization should be undertaken rapidly and at the same time as reforms in fiscal and trade policies. Later work has introduced the concept of sequencing of reform, suggesting that financial sector adjustment should follow last (McKinnon 1991). Moreover, domestic financial reforms should precede the opening up to global capital flows.

The experiences of Mexico (1994) and Thailand (1997) highlight the risk of liberalizing the capital account before allowing greater exchange rate flexibility. The Asian crisis, for example, was typified by a collapse of (an overvalued) exchange rate, exacerbated by capital outflow, leading to a collapse of the domestic financial system causing a shortage of working capital and an output contraction. While the situation in China can be viewed in many respects as being quite different, there are dangers. Overseas capital inflow is mainly direct investment, capital account transactions are (relatively) tightly controlled, the exchange rate is considered to be undervalued rather than overvalued and there are substantial foreign exchange reserves. However, this is a static view and ignores the possible effects of further inevitable liberalization.

If greater exchange rate flexibility is permitted, then the issue of capital account liberalization becomes more of a focus. Any move to ease capital controls should occur later rather than sooner to avoid any likelihood of destabilizing capital flight and a consequent banking crisis as domestic investors shift funds abroad. An open capital account leaves a country vulnerable to domestic and global investor sentiment, particularly if economic fundamentals are weak and financial markets are poorly developed and poorly regulated (Kose, Prasad and Terrones 2003).[27]

There is also the matter of whether interest rate liberalization should precede liberalization of the capital account. As discussed above, deregulation of interest rates requires a stable macroeconomic environment and a strong supporting institutional framework, including capital markets, legal and accounting frameworks, regulatory financial sector controls and the ability of banks to effectively assess credit risk. It may be necessary to maintain some interest rate controls for a while, even after capital controls have been eased. Stallings (2003) concludes that a crisis could result if efforts in this area are mismanaged. He considers a situation where interest rates are liberalized in conjunction with the ending of directed credit, banks are privatized and where proper prudential regulation and supervision is not in place. This could result in strong growth in credit, cronyism and excessive risk-taking in lending practices and inadequate provisioning for potential losses.[28] This is likely to be particularly problematic in an expansionary macroeconomic environment where capital controls are eased. An unsustainable "bubble economy" would result and as firms became overextended and were unable to service loan commitments, both the real and the financial sectors would face a systemic crisis in the face of collapsing asset prices.

CONCLUSION

China is faced with policy questions in respect of the choice of a suitable exchange rate regime, the (ongoing) liberalizing of its capital account and removing the financial repression that has shaped the banking and finance sector of the economy. The current macroeconomic environment and institutional arrangements have been shaped by past decisions and these, in turn, constrain and influence the nature and extent of necessary ongoing reform. As well, there are external factors impacting decision making, including China's trade and commercial relationships with its global partners and the unfettered entry of foreign banks into China in 2007.

China needs to allow for a more market based allocation of financial sector resources, particularly in regard to the domestic banking sector and equity and debt markets. Opening up the capital account to a much greater degree than at present can aid in this process. However, China needs to ensure that the domestic financial system is healthy enough and competitive enough to cope with the changes that will be introduced. This requires ensuring not only that the bad debts of the banks are effectively dealt with, but also that suitable domestic institutional and regulatory supports are in place.

One outcome of recent developments has been a growing awareness of the need to address what is seen as an undervalued currency. China has opted for a move to a tightly managed currency regime. Further policy adjustments in this area need to be considered in conjunction with possible changes to the capital account and to the introduction of more market oriented interest rates in the context of the current economic and institutional environment. Along with the extent of policy changes, the timing and sequencing of reforms need to be carefully considered to ensure that the financial system does not experience major difficulties.

NOTES

1. The level of intermediation by Chinese banks, as measured by M2/GDP, is amongst the highest in the world (Bonin and Huang 2002). The ratio was 1.9 at the end of 2004 (Prasad and Wei 2005). The high propensity of Chinese households to save which has underpinned the rapid growth of the Chinese banking system over the last decade reflects not only the lack of choices for investors, but also the periodic indexation of time deposit rates and a general labour market uncertainty linked to a trust in the stability of what is effectively a government-backed banking system.
2. China's savings more than doubled from 1997 to 2002 (Standard and Poor's 2004).
3. China has almost no companies with foreign currency debts.
4. The difficulty in accessing bank finance has led to firms seeking alternative funding avenues, a particularly important one being foreign partners (Thorpe 2004).
5. The extent to which new lending has sown the seeds for increased NPLs in the future remains a concern.
6. In a well functioning financial market, the bond and equity markets impose fiscal discipline on firms and provide an alternative source of funds. Secondary trading in equity markets also helps information flows. The bond market provides a range of instruments to meet varying liquidity needs of companies and government.
7. Underground banks pay around 7 to 10 per cent on deposits and charge around 10 to 20 per cent on loans.
8. Large outflows of bank deposits to the informal sector have also resulted from the existence of negative interest rates. For example, prior to the policy shift on rates in October 2004, deposits yielded 1.7 per cent compared to an inflation rate at the time of around 5.3 per cent.
9. An integral part of moves to improve the health of the banking system has been the introduction of greater regulatory and prudential controls and ongoing efforts to encourage foreign partnerships in local banks and the public listing of several major commercial banks in Hong Kong, commencing in late 2005.
10. The external debt picture also needs to be viewed in the context of any revaluation of the RMB, which would have a beneficial valuation effect.
11. China's trade surplus in 2004 was around US$40 billion. On services trade, China had a deficit for the year of US$11 billion (WTO 2005).
12. The eight major central banks in East Asia have amassed around US$ 2.3 trillion in foreign exchange reserves.
13. The fact that flows are not larger is perhaps indicative that capital controls on inflows are, in fact, relatively effective (Prasad and Wei 2005). FDI outflows are still small although they have increased in recent years due to government support. These are primarily linked to raw material supply and upstream products for importing and processing.
14. China's US Treasuries holdings reached US$191.1 billion at the end of 2004, an increase of US$4.4 billion from a month earlier, according to data released in January 2005 by the US Treasury Department. This represented a third of the total US$542.44 billion holdings in China's foreign exchange reserves at the time (Diyi 2005). The country's actual holding of US government debt is higher because its central bank has other investments through the Asian Development Bank and other institutions, which makes it difficult to arrive at an accurate number for the total value of US Treasuries China holds.

15. Early collection of export receipts and increased use of trade credit for imports are consistent with an expected revaluation.

16. The government has also used the reserves to shore up the balance sheets of the major banks in recent years. This could become more important if the level of NPLs rises.

17. In 2003 the money supply rose by 20 per cent with bank lending up by 21 per cent on year earlier figures, with much of this going to low quality investment (Holland 2004). Over the first quarter of 2004 lending by the commercial banks grew at an annual rate of around 21 per cent (with money supply growing at 19.2 per cent), feeding a growth in fixed asset investment of 43 per cent.

18. In April 2004, the PBOC announced that most banks will be required to hold reserves equal to at least 7.5 per cent of outstanding loans and other capital commitments (a rise of 0.5 per cent). For some weaker banks the level was set at eight per cent.

19. In the fourth quarter of 2004, the proportion of loans with interest rates lower than the benchmark rate was 23.23 per cent, up 2.43 percentage points from the previous quarter. Loans with interest rates higher than the benchmark rate accounted for 52.21 per cent, up 2.11 percentage points from the third quarter. Only 24.56 per cent of loans were made at the benchmark rate, down 4.54 percentage points.

20. The eight major central banks in East Asia currently hold around US$ 2.3 trillion in foreign exchange reserves.

21. China's current account surplus for the year was US$72 billion.

22. For example, the Chinese value-added (in parts and labour) in a mobile phone exported to America might be only 15 per cent of its price. So a 10 per cent revaluation would raise its price in dollars by only 1.5 per cent (The Economist 2005b).

23. Historically, this can be viewed as similar to policies adopted by Japan and Europe following the Second World War.

24. China has expanded foreign exchange trading by authorising eight new foreign currency pairs. Beginning in May 2005, seven foreign currencies will be paired against the US dollar along with trading in a Euro-Yen pair. The RMB will continue to be traded only against the US dollar, Hong Kong dollar, the Yen and the Euro. Such a move is in line with China's gradualist approach, recognising that a more effective foreign exchange market is a pre-condition for effective exchange rate reform in China.

25. A proper understanding of bank failures calls for an understanding of the policy and economic environment, the institutional framework, banking practices, the quality of supervision and the structure of incentives in place.

26. Government expenditure on capital construction was 13 per cent in 1978, but had fallen to three per cent by 1993 (Gao and Schaffer 1998). As the economy was liberalized, loans to SOEs through the banking system began to replace budgetary appropriations as the main source of fixed capital expenditure (for roads, utilities and the like) up to 1997. However, following the Asian crisis the PBOC responded by seeking to maintain economic momentum through increasing expenditure on infrastructure, financed through the issuing of bonds. The budget deficit in 2003 was 2.9 per cent of GDP (The Economist 2004a). The government also continues to finance SOE reform and rural migration.

27. Fischer (2003) takes a more sanguine view on the need to delay capital controls.

28. If these developments were linked to any liberalizing of the capital account while maintaining a fixed exchange rate, it would lend itself to currency misalignment (overvaluation) and disruptive capital flows.

REFERENCES

Asian Development Bank, 2004. *Annual Report*, Asian Development Bank, Manila.

Bonin, J. and Huang, Y., 2002. 'China's opening up of the banking system: implications for domestic banks', Ch 5 in Song, L. (ed.), *Dilemma of China's*

Growth in the Twenty First Century, Asia Pacific Press, Australian National University.

Chan, C., 2004. 'Borrowing curbs carry bad-loan risk', *South China Morning Post*, May 8, B3.

Childs, B., 2005. 'OECD warns of wider global economic gaps', *International Herald Tribune*, May 25, 17.

Chong, F., 2004. 'Banks to break China's fall in a soft landing', *The Australian*, June 16, 29.

Chung, O. and Wu, Z., 2004. 'Guessing game on timing of rate rise', *The Standard*, May 11, A1.

de Terra, N., 2004. 'Why don't you grow up?' *The Banker*, October, 52-53.

Diyi, C. R. 2005. *First Financial and Economic News*, 20 January.

Dolven, B., 2004. 'Smoke signals', *The Far Eastern Economic Review*, May 13, 46.

Fischer, S., 2003. *Review of World Economics*, **139**, 1, 1-37.

Fry, M. J., 1988. *Money and Banking in Economic Development*, John Hopkins University Press.

Gao, S. and Schaffer, M. E., 1998. 'Financial discipline in the enterprise sector in transition economies: How does China compare?' *Working Paper*, February, Centre for Economic Reform and Transformation, Heriot-Watt University.

Heffernan, S., 2005. *Modern Banking*, John Wiley and Sons Ltd.

Holland, T., 2004. 'An incredible balancing act', *The Far Eastern Economic Review*, 18 March, 46-49.

Holland, T. and Lague, D., 2004. 'Wasteful transfusion', *The Economist*, January 22, 26.

Hu, B., 2004. 'Foreign banks to win most from mainland growth', *South China Morning Post*, May 8, B3.

Huang Y., 2003. 'Transforming the banking sector', Ch 5 in Garnaut, R. and Song, L., *China: New Engine of World Growth*, Asia Pacific Press.

Karacadag C., Duttagupta R., Fernandez G. and Ishii S., 2004. 'From fixed to float: fear no more', *Finance and Development*, December, 20-23, 20-23.

Kose, M., Prasad, E. and Terrones, M., 2003. 'Financial integration and macroeconomic volatility', *IMF Staff Papers*, **50**, 119-42.

Kuo, K. and Subler, J., 2004. 'Capital changes in the wind', *China Economic Review*, August, 16-19.

Krugman, P., 2005. 'The Chinese connection', *International Herald Tribune*, May 21/22, 6.

Lee, L., 2004. 'Food slows rate of inflation in China', *The Australian Financial Review*, 16 March, 13.

Liping, H., 2001. 'The Banking and Securities Sector', in Holbig, H. and Ash, R. (eds), *China's Accession to the World Trade Organisation, National and International Perspectives,* Routledge

McKinnon, R., 1991. *Money and Capital Development*, Washington D.C., Brookings Institution.

Mellor, W., 2004. 'China's quest for fiscal maturity', *International Herald Tribune*, July 29.

Ng, E., 2005. 'China must loosen grip on power', *South China Morning Post*, October 6, B2.

Prasad, E. (ed.), 2004. 'China's growth and integration into the world economy', *Occasional Paper 232*, International Monetary Fund, Washington.

Prasad, E. and Wei, S. J., 2005. 'The Chinese approach to capital flows: patterns and possible explanations', *IMF Working Paper* WP/05, April, IMF, Washington.

Ryan, C., 2004. 'Banking on China to ease the strain', *The Australian*, 13-14 November, 27-28.

Stallings, B., 2003. 'The role of the financial sector in creating growth and stability', Ch 13 in Jan Teunissen (ed.), *China's Role in Asia and the World Economy*, Fondad, The Netherlands.

Standard and Poor's, 2004. *Research: Bank Industry Risk Analysis*, published 25 November, accessed at www.ratingsdirect.com.

Taylor, A., 2004. 'Global finance: past and present', *Finance and Development*, March, 28-31.

Taylor, A. and Obstfeld, M., 2004. *Global Capital Markets; Integration Crisis and Growth*, Cambridge University Press.

The Economist, 2004s. *A Fair Exchange*, September 30.

The Economist, 2004b. *Time to Hit the Brakes*, May 13.

The Economist, 2005a. *Yuan Step at a Time*, Jan 20.

The Economist, 2005b. *Revaluing China's Currency: What's it Worth*, May 19.

Thorpe, M., 2004. 'Inward foreign investment and the Chinese economy', Ch 3 in Kehal, H. (ed.) *Foreign Investment in Developing Countries*, Palgrave.

Villanueva, D. and Mirakhor, A., 1990. 'Interest Rate Policies, Stabilization and bank Supervision in Developing Countries: Strategies for Financial Reforms', *IMF Working Paper*, February, WP/90/8, IMF.

Wonacott, P. and Wu, J. R., 2004. 'China Orders Commercial Banks to Suspend Lending', *Asian Wall Street Journal*, 28 April.

World Bank, 2005. *World Development Indicator 2005*, Washington DC.

WTO, 2005. World Trade Report, WTO, Geneva.

www.chinaonline, 2004. Retrieved 26 June.

10. The Exchange Rate Debate

James Laurenceson and Fengming Qin

INTRODUCTION

One might imagine that an exchange rate left unchanged for 11 years would not generate much interest. Yet toward the end of 2004 *The Economist* (2004) observed that issues surrounding China's fixed exchange rate, in which the *Renminbi* (RMB) had been pegged to the US dollar at a rate of RMB8.28 against US$1 since 1994, had become amongst the hottest topics in international finance. Since late 2000, much of the interest has been prompted by speculation that China would revalue its currency. The chief impetus for this speculation has been an accusation emanating from US government circles that the dollar peg is a prominent cause of the US trade deficit with China. The contention is that the RMB is pegged at an undervalued rate and is a source of unfair advantage for Chinese exporters. In a report to Congress in May 2005, Secretary of the US Treasury John Snow described China's exchange rate policies as being "highly distortionary" and, if left unaltered, would lead to China being labeled an exchange manipulator under the Omnibus Trade and Competitiveness Act of 1988. Secretary Snow stated in the report that the US government was calling on China to adopt a more flexible exchange rate regime. European Union (EU) officials and the G-7 group have echoed this call as the Euro in particular is seen as having been forced to bear the brunt of the US dollar's depreciation since 2002. Between 2002 and 2004, the EU trade deficit with China more than doubled, compared with the US trade deficit with China which increased by a little over one half (WSJ 2005). In the first half of 2005 trade disputes in textiles became particularly prominent, with both the US and EU erecting punitive measures in May to slow a surge in Chinese imports that resulted from the phasing out of global textiles quotas at the end of 2004.

Outside of government circles, calls for greater exchange rate flexibility also became the norm from economists in international organizations such as the IMF (Rajan and Subramanian 2004; Prasad *et al.* 2005) and the Asian Development Bank (ADB) (IHT 2005), as well as from those based in central banks, research institutes and academia such as Roberts and Tyers (2003), Bergsten (2003), Eichengreen (2004), Goldstein and Lardy (2003), Bernanke

(2005), Roubini and Setser (2005) and Frankel (2005). While most of these authors concur with the US government position that the RMB is undervalued, this is not their primary focus. Rather, the commonality they share is the viewpoint that greater exchange rate flexibility would be in China's own best interests as it would support macroeconomic stability by providing greater monetary independence. This became a topical issue during 2003 and 2004 when inflows of hot money betting on an RMB appreciation correlated with rapid growth in the domestic money supply and in real estate prices in cities such as Shanghai.

In response to accusations of undervaluation, high-level officials in China initially retorted that greater pressure from abroad for more rapid reform would only slow the process down (for example, People's Daily 13 May 2005). July 2005 saw a concession of sorts with the RMB revalued by 2.1 per cent to RMB8.11 against US$1 and the announcement that the currency's value would be linked to an undisclosed basket of currencies. Following this move, officials speaking in the government-run media began referring to the country's new "flexible" or "floating" exchange rate regime (for example, People's Daily 22 September 2005). In reality, however, any newfound flexibility is limited. At the time of writing in September 2005, the most the RMB had been allowed to appreciate was RMB8.08 for US$1, or less than an additional 0.5 per cent over the initial revaluation. Such changes amount to tinkering around the edges and nothing like the degree of flexibility being called for by the consensus position.

This chapter reviews and critically comments on the policy debate surrounding China's exchange rate regime. There are two key issues – firstly, whether the RMB has become significantly undervalued, and secondly, whether China would benefit from adopting a flexible exchange rate regime. The following section finds that the usual justifications given for claims that the RMB is undervalued have a poor basis in evidence. In the third section we offer a critique of the consensus position that China would now be best served by adopting a more flexible exchange rate regime. Our primary purpose here is to present the other side of the flexibility debate, which hitherto has been marginalized in the existing literature. Moving away from a stable exchange rate would be an abandonment of a policy that seemingly has served the country well for more than a decade and in our estimation the case for doing so is far less convincing than the consensus position portrays. The fourth section summarizes the discussion.

THE VALUATION DEBATE

There are four common arguments presented in support of the view that the RMB is significantly undervalued. These are:-

China's Large and Growing Trade Surplus with the US Proves that the RMB is Undervalued and that China is Unfairly Benefiting from Trade.

The problem with this argument is that economic theory does not suggest that any country will or should have balanced trade with each of its trading partners. This will be dynamically determined by many factors, principally comparative advantage considerations. Part of the increase in the US trade deficit with China simply reflects comparative advantage considerations being allowed to run their course after having been suppressed in the past by, for example, barriers to trade such as the Multifibre Agreement. China is also a relatively new member of the global economy and its exports are growing from a very small base. Another part of the rising US trade deficit with China is the result of foreign direct investment emerging as a means of recycling a country's comparative advantage. US firms, as well as those of US trading partners such as Japan and the Asian tigers (Hong Kong, Korea, Singapore, Taiwan), have all been active in relocating labour-intensive manufacturing production to China in a bid to remain competitive. Japan and the tigers have, in effect, transferred part of their trade surplus with respect to the US to China. Quite staggeringly, in 2004 foreign-invested enterprises in China accounted for 57 per cent of the country's total exports, up from just 15 per cent in 1990. As a result, it should come as no surprise that China's rapidly rising share of world merchandise exports is matched almost entirely by a decline in the share of Japan, and to a lesser extent, the tigers. According to World Trade Organization (WTO) statistics, between 1993 and 2003 China's share rose from 2.8 per cent to 5.8 per cent while Japan's share and that of the tigers fell from 9.6 per cent to 6.3 per cent and 10 per cent to 9.5 per cent respectively.

China's export performance over the past couple of decades is far less dramatic than that of Japan's in the post-WW2 period. During 1983-2003, China's share of world exports grew by 3.5 per cent. Yet between 1953 and 1973, Japan's share grew by 4.9 per cent, in spite of having a weaker comparative advantage in labour-intensive manufactured goods and foreign investment contributing virtually nothing to its exports. China's overall trade surplus is also not particularly large at around two per cent of GDP in 2004. This reflects the fact that while China may have a large trade surplus vis-à-vis the US, it has a deficit with respect to other countries. China's trade surplus is routinely less than that recorded by leading OECD trading nations such as Germany and Japan. In 2003, Germany, for example, had a trade surplus equal to 6.3 per cent of GDP. Viewed in this broader perspective, the view that China is pursuing a mercantilist development strategy (for example, Kelly 2005) looks decidedly shaky.

Irrespective of the source of the US trade deficit with China, it is patently clear that a revaluation of the RMB would do little to reduce the US trade deficit overall, which in 2004 was in the order of US$600 billion, or 5.5 per cent of GDP. China accounts for only around 10 per cent of US total trade (and only 3 per cent of EU total trade). As a result, a revaluation of more drastic proportions than even the most ardent China critics are calling for - say to the tune of 50 per cent - would only reduce the dollar's effective (i.e., trade weighted) value by five per cent. Yet between March 2002 and March 2005, the dollar's real effective value fell by 27.6 per cent, a time period during which the US trade deficit only widened. The answer to the problem of the trade deficit lies elsewhere, notably in raising private and public savings rates in the US. McKinnon (2004, p.330) makes the self-evident but important point that as long as the US household savings rate remains unusually low and the US government runs a large budget deficit (3.5 per cent of GDP in 2004), "...the relatively high-savings East Asian countries are virtually forced to run export surpluses in order to lend their 'surplus' savings to the United States - whatever the exchange rate regime".

It is sometimes said that China adopting a more flexible exchange rate would have a broader impact because it would solve a coordination problem faced by other East Asian countries. This line of thinking argues that other East Asian countries are resistant to allowing their currencies to become more flexible (and presumably appreciate) without China doing likewise for fear of their exporters being undercut. There are numerous problems with this argument however. For one, the numbers remain small. WTO statistics show that trade with China plus the six East Asian Traders (Hong Kong, South Korea, Malaysia, Singapore, Taiwan and Thailand) still only amounts to a little over 20 per cent of US total trade. Thus, a general appreciation of these country's currencies to the tune of 25 per cent would only reduce the dollar's effective value by around 5 per cent. Secondly, China's export structure means that it does not heavily compete in third-country markets with many of the East Asian countries that more or less fix their currencies to the dollar anyway. Thirdly, this logic assumes that a coordination failure has been behind the reluctance of East Asian countries to adopt more flexible exchange rate regimes in the past. But the penchant of East Asian countries for maintaining stable exchange rates is more readily explained by the fact that their mutual development has been well-served by them. Since the 1980s Japan has been the exception in East Asia in terms of having a genuinely flexible exchange rate and the performance of its economy since this time has hardly been confidence inspiring for its neighbours.

Another relevant issue here is that the dollar value of overall trade flows is a poor guide to the size and distribution of benefits. US consumers clearly benefit from cheap Chinese imports and Andy Xie from Morgan Stanley has also estimated that for each dollar of China trade the US value-added is six to eight times China's. Thus, while in 2004 the dollar value of US exports to China may only have been 17.7 per cent the dollar value of imports from China, the profits accruing to US firms are likely to have been in excess of those accruing to their Chinese counterparts. It should also not be forgotten that more than half of China's exports originate from foreign-invested companies, including those established with US capital. It is for these reasons that industry bodies in the US have not been particularly vocal in supporting the government's call for an RMB appreciation and they have certainly been much quieter than in the Japan-bashing episodes of the early 1980s.

Finally, it is worthwhile elaborating upon the unusual way in which the statistics collated by the US Department of Commerce deal with Hong Kong's entrepôt trade. The US-China Business Council notes that these statistics count the full value of Chinese re-exports from Hong Kong as being Chinese exports, despite the fact that services (simple processing, packaging, marketing, etc) provided in Hong Kong add roughly 25 per cent to the value of the goods originally exported from China. Meanwhile, all US goods exported to Hong Kong are counted as exports to Hong Kong, even those that are re-exported to China. According to Nicholas Lardy from the Institute of International Economics, after accounting for Hong Kong's entrepôt trade, the actual US trade deficit with China in 2003 was 11.5 per cent less than that recorded by the Department of Commerce.

The Decline in China's Real Effective Exchange Rate Since Late 2001 Means the RMB Must Now be Undervalued.

China's real effective exchange rate fell by 14 per cent between July 2001 and January 2005. A longer-term perspective however shows that this alone does not necessarily imply the RMB is undervalued. The value of the RMB in January 2005 was the same as in early 1996. Moreover, this level was only about eight per cent less than at the height of the Asian financial crisis in the second half of 1997. At this time speculators were betting on an RMB devaluation as the prevailing wisdom was that the Chinese currency had been rendered decidedly overvalued. Debates over China's equilibrium exchange rate over the past decade have amply illustrated the limitations of estimates provided by economists. Estimates of undervaluation currently range between 0-50 per cent. Estimates of overvaluation during the Asian financial crisis were similarly vague.

Productivity Improvements Associated with China's Economic Transformation Mean that the RMB Must Now be Undervalued.

Ceteris paribus, if over the past decade productivity had grown more rapidly in China than in the US, there would be a case for RMB appreciation. The problem though is that it is not at all clear that this happened. It is true that in the late 1970s and 1980s China was able to elicit rapid improvements in total factor productivity by liberalizing its agricultural and non-state sectors. A study by IMF economists (Hu and Khan 1997) estimated that the average annual rate of productivity growth in China over the period 1979-1994 was 3.9 per cent. This compared with around two per cent in other Asian tigers (during 1966-1991) and 0.4 per cent in the US (during 1960-1989). However, Sachs and Woo (1997) warned some time ago that such simple sources of productivity growth associated with China's transitional economy were likely to soon be exhausted and continued gains would be dependent upon reforming the more challenging state-owned sector. Reforming the state sector has been the policy focus since the mid-1990s and while progress has been made, the pace has been more gradual. Anecdotally, the fact that higher economic growth rates over the past decade have required ever-larger shares of GDP be devoted to investment is hardly evocative of an economy experiencing rapid improvements in total factor productivity. Table 10.1 shows that the incremental capital-output ratio in China has remained roughly constant since 1996. US productivity meanwhile picked up during the 1990s. China's experience during the 1980s also shows how the impact of relative productivity movements on the exchange rate can easily be swamped by other factors. By the time a unified exchange rate was adopted in 1994 and the official rate was allowed to converge to the rate in currency swap markets at the time (i.e., the market rate), the RMB had depreciated from RMB1.5 against US$1 at the start of the reform period to RMB8.28 against US$1, in spite of any relative productivity improvements.

The Surge in China's Foreign Exchange Reserves Proves the RMB is Being Held at Below Equilibrium Levels to Boost Exports.

This argument fails to distinguish between the contribution of the trade surplus to foreign exchange accumulation and the contribution of speculative capital inflows betting on an RMB revaluation. Over the period 2001-2004, the current account surplus accounted for just 34 per cent of total reserve accumulation while the dominant source was capital inflows other than FDI (Table 10.2). A study published by economists from the IMF (Prasad and Wei 2005) reported that nearly 75 per cent of the change in capital flows has come from categories of flows sensitive to market expectations on the future trend of the RMB/US$ exchange rate, rather than the underlying fundamentals. Needless to say, speculative sentiments can quickly change.

THE FLEXIBILITY DEBATE

A consensus position has emerged which argues that China would benefit from greater exchange rate flexibility because the increase in monetary independence it entails would be more conducive to maintaining macroeconomic stability. Macroeconomic stability does need to be accorded the utmost importance given that it has underpinned all of China's other successes during the reform period. However, the first point to note in response is simply that international data do not suggest that flexible exchange rate regimes outperform fixed regimes in terms of macroeconomic

Table 10.1 Selected economic data

	1996	1997	1998	1999	2000	2001	2002	2003	2004
Real GDP growth (%)	9.6	8.8	7.8	7.1	8.0	7.5	8.3	9.3	9.5
Gross capital formation (% GDP)	39.3	38.0	37.4	37.1	36.4	38.0	39.2	42.3	
Incremental capital-output ratio	0.24	0.23	0.21	0.19	0.22	0.20	0.21	0.22	
Money supply growth (%)	25.3	20.7	14.9	14.7	12.3	15.0	19.4	19.7	14.8
Domestic credit growth (%)	24.6	19.8	20.0	12.1	11.0	13.6	29.3	19.6	9.2
Fixed investment growth (%)	14.8	8.8	13.9	5.1	10.3	13.0	16.9	27.7	25.8

Source: National Bureau of Statistics and the People's Bank of China.

Table 10.2 China's foreign exchange reserves - sources of accumulation

	1996	1997	1998	1999	2000	2001	2002	2003	2004
Total reserves, inc. gold (US$ billion)	108	143	150	158	169	219	295	457*	619
Total reserve accumulation, inc. gold (RES AC) (US$ billion)	32	36	6	9	11	50	77	162	207
Current account balance (CAS) (US$ billion)	7	37	31	21	21	17	35	46	70
Net FDI (US$ billion)	38	42	41	37	37	37	47	47	61**
Net non-FDI (US$ billion)***	-13	-43	-66	-49	-47	-4	-5	69	77
GDP (US$ billion)	821	903	954	999	1079	1176	1271	1412	1593
CAS (% GDP)	0.8	4.1	3.2	2.1	1.9	1.4	2.8	3.2	3.0
RES AC (% GDP)	3.9	4.0	0.6	0.9	1.0	4.3	6.1	11.5	3.9

Notes: *   In 2003 the Chinese government used US$45 billion from its foreign reserves to recapitalize two state banks. As a result, the 2003 figure for total reserves is the official value plus US$45 billion. The 2004 figure is simply the official estimate. This has been done in keeping with Roubini and Setser (2005).
**   The FDI figure for 2004 it is *not* a net figure. It is simply inward FDI. The source is the National Bureau of Statistics. In previous years, outward FDI recorded in the national accounts has been very small.
***   Net non-FDI is calculated as the residual of the change in total reserve accumulation minus net FDI minus the current account balance.

Source: International Monetary Fund.

stability. In fact, the data speak convincingly to the opposite effect. In a study of this issue, IMF economists, Ghosh *et al.* (1996, p.12), concluded that

> Does the exchange rate regime matter for macroeconomic performance? The experience of IMF member countries since the 1960s suggests that it does. The strongest results concern inflation. Pegged exchange rates are associated with significantly better inflation performance (lower inflation and less variability), and there is at least some evidence of a causal relationship. There is, however, an important caveat. Countries that have frequent parity changes - while notionally maintaining a peg - are unlikely to reap the full anti-inflationary benefits of a fixed exchange rate regime.

Thus, not only does the data point to a better inflationary outcome under a fixed regime, it also appears to lend support to China's reluctance to undertake frequent adjustments at the behest of fluctuations in sentiment regarding the equilibrium value of the RMB.

Much of the recent shift in orthodoxy towards flexible exchange rate regimes appears to have been motivated by the events of the Asian financial crisis. Yet this misses the bigger picture. The same economies that experienced a relatively short period of crisis had earlier experienced long periods of macroeconomic stability and rapid economic growth under a fixed exchange rate regime and returned to a stable exchange rate and strong growth once the crisis had passed (McKinnon and Schnabl 2004). If China was looking for policy inspiration from its neighbours, the Japanese experience would be the one that stands out. A more flexible yen brought on largely by pressure from the US in the early 1980s did nothing to promote macroeconomic stability or steel the Japanese economy against speculative activities and it continues to languish from the bursting of the bubble economy more than a decade ago. It would be a serious misreading of the evidence to claim that the experience of East Asia shows that economic development is best served by flexible exchange rate regimes.

The case for a flexible regime also appears to have been given a popularity boost by increasingly mobile international capital flows. It is often said that given the sheer volume of international capital flows these days if speculators feel a currency is incorrectly valued it would be futile for a central bank to try and defend it. For Mundell (2003), this misses the point. Credibility is the key issue. Mundell points out that we do not see any speculative capital movements within countries as the exchange rate domestically is entirely credible. If a peg is credible, speculation will in fact be discouraged. Juxtaposed against countries such as Thailand during the Asian financial crisis, China has a healthy stockpile of foreign exchange reserves and is running current account surpluses. In the current environment, China's credibility will only be lost if it becomes clear that exchange rate stability is costing the economy excessively in terms of macroeconomic stability.

This leads to our second objection to the consensus position. Despite suggestions to the contrary, it is not at all clear that exchange rate stability has contributed to macroeconomic instability in China in a significant way. According to the consensus view, as hot money has flowed into China the People's Bank of China (PBC) has been forced to buy dollar assets to maintain the exchange rate stability and this has resulted in a rapidly expanding domestic money supply, excessive fixed asset investment and increased inflationary pressure, particularly with respect to asset prices. But as HSBC (2005) has pointed out, total foreign capital inflows in 2004 were only equal to around 20 per cent of the total value of fixed asset investment. If dampening inflationary pressure and slowing the rate of fixed asset investment is the goal, domestic credit is the most obvious place to start. This was precisely the approach taken by the Chinese authorities in 2004 with the growth rate in domestic credit falling from 19.6 per cent in 2003 to 9.2 per cent in 2004 (Table 10.1). Inflation which began rising in 2003 and 2004 began to fall in 2005. World Bank (2005) observes that at the end of the first quarter of 2005, the growth rate in the domestic money supply had slowed to within the target range set by the monetary authorities. Also acting to limit the inflationary pressures wrought by foreign capital inflows has been sterilization activities undertaken by the central bank. Stephen Green from Standard Chartered Bank has estimated that the PBC sterilized 47.5 per cent of foreign exchange inflows during 2004 and around 70 per cent in the first half of 2005. The costs of this sterilization have also been extremely low (see Green 2005).

The fact that exchange rate stability can help to anchor the domestic price level appears to have been forgotten. Xu (2000) showed that a striking long run correlation exists between movements in the domestic price level and the real exchange rate dating back to the start of the reform period. Xu interprets this relationship to be a bi-causal one. Before the adoption of a unified exchange rate in 1994, changes in the official exchange rate followed domestic price level fluctuations (that is, inflationary episodes forced devaluations). Since 1994 when the official rate was allowed to depreciate to the prevailing market rate and by which time China's global trade linkages had strengthened, stability in the exchange rate has helped to secure the domestic price level. Indeed, for all the talk of inflationary pressure in the consensus literature, it is odd that few have sought to explain why actual inflation remains low. For Mundell and McKinnon, the answer is plain enough – the stable exchange rate is doing its job in serving as a price anchor and is doing it very well. The price anchor role of the exchange rate is sometimes dismissed on the basis that bilateral trade with the US represents only a fraction of China's total trade. But this misses the point made repeatedly by McKinnon that the overwhelming majority of trade within East Asia is invoiced in US$ and that other countries in the region (with the notable exception of Japan) also more or less peg to the dollar.

Our third criticism of the consensus view is that it understates the importance of institutions in managing a flexible exchange rate regime. On one hand, in highlighting the dangers posed by hot money inflows, the consensus literature frequently refers to the difficulties faced by the PBC in undertaking effective sterilization when domestic financial markets are underdeveloped. Yet at the same time it calls upon the PBC to use these financial markets to target inflation through open market operations as is done in most OECD economies. Central banks in OECD economies have at their disposal a powerful monetary transmission channel that results from having a complete set of financial markets where interest rates are market determined and where borrowers are sensitive to changes in the cost of borrowing. In contrast, China's financial markets are shallow, incomplete, highly regulated (see Bottelier 2003) and the major borrowers, the state-owned enterprises, in many cases still do not face a hard budget constraint. Thus, the success of inflation targeting in OECD economies over the past couple of decades is of limited relevance to China today. To be sure, as Green (2005) has pointed out, progress in China's domestic financial markets is being made, but for good reason monetary policy in China continues to rely heavily on direct administrative controls such as formal (and informal) limits to credit growth rather than indirect measures such as interest rate adjustments.

In China there is also a distinct absence of financial markets that perform risk management roles such as hedging against exchange rate fluctuations. While bankers and traders in OECD economies have ready access to instruments such as exchange rate futures contracts that can protect them against undesirable exchange rate fluctuations, in developing countries such as China these agents rely on the de-facto hedge of a stable exchange rate. In the aftermath of the Asian financial crisis, using a stable exchange rate to provide a hedge was criticised on the basis that it might worsen the moral hazard in domestic banks and encourage them to over-borrow in foreign currency. McKinnon and Schnabl (2004) have pointed out however that the risk premium in domestic interest rates is dependent upon how stable the domestic currency is relative to the currency of borrowing, that is, the US$. As a result, if the cross rate varies erratically, domestic interest rates will be higher and so too will the margin of temptation to over-borrow in foreign exchange. For this reason they conclude it is not possible to say *a priori* whether a stable exchange rate worsens the moral hazard in poorly regulated banks to over-borrow. In any case, the key issue is the effectiveness of banking sector prudential regulation not the exchange rate regime.

A final concern we have with a flexible exchange rate has to do with the implications increased volatility would have on Hong Kong - the showcase of the one country, two systems approach and an autonomous region that operates a hard peg to the dollar. Hong Kong is the classic textbook example of a small, open country that benefits from a stable exchange rate vis-à-vis its trading partners. Hong Kong's trade is more than two and a half times the size of its GDP. According to Hong Kong trade statistics, total trade (direct and entrepôt) with the mainland in 2004 accounted for 43.7 per cent of its total, followed by trade with the US at 11 per cent. It is often asserted that because China's exports have a high import component, an RMB appreciation would only marginally impact export growth. Yet given the dependence of Hong Kong on trade with the mainland even a modest appreciation would be of concern for the much smaller, more trade dependent economy. Hong Kong has also been by far the largest "foreign" investor in the mainland with the Hong Kong Trade Development Council claiming that at the end of 2004, 47 per cent of overseas registered projects on the mainland had Hong Kong connections. While the consensus literature tends to cite econometric studies which suggest that on average FDI and exchange rate fluctuations are only weakly related, authors such as Mundell (2003) and McKinnon and Schnabl (2003) prefer to point out case studies closer to home that may well be considered more pertinent by China's policy makers. Japanese FDI into many other East Asian countries, for example, has tended to closely follow trend movements in the ¥/US$ exchange rate.

CONCLUSION

The exchange rate debate in China has emerged as one of the most talked about topics in international economics. In our reading of the existing literature, there are numerous myths purporting to be facts and the debate regarding the appropriate degree of exchange rate flexibility is more one-sided than is desirable. There is little solid evidence that China's currency is undervalued and even if it were, given the variation in equilibrium exchange rate estimates offered by economists, reluctance on the part of China's policy-makers to significantly revalue the RMB is unsurprising. Many of the benefits currently accruing to China as a result of a stable exchange rate also appear insufficiently recognized (for example, an anchor for the domestic price level) and similarly many of the costs involved in moving to a flexible regime (for example, institutional constraints). Perhaps the most prominent shortcoming of the consensus position is that it fails to convincingly demonstrate how exchange rate stability is at the root of problems in China's economy today (for example, inflationary pressure). China's economic performance over the past decade suggests that it has not been hopelessly trying to reconcile the "irreconcilable trilemma" from macroeconomic theory, which states that a country cannot simultaneously pursue free capital mobility, a fixed exchange rate and an independent monetary policy. While its capital controls are certainly porous to a degree, when combined with partial sterilization and monetary policy in which administrative tools remain effective, China has been able to maintain both macroeconomic stability and a stable exchange rate.

China is also fortunate in the sense that its high savings rate, cheap labour force and attractive domestic market means that it does not face the same opportunity cost other developing countries might when retaining capital controls (Laurenceson 2005). The usual argument underlying the position that even developing countries are best served by flexible exchange rates is that it will allow them to use an independent monetary policy to maintain macroeconomic stability while removing capital controls, with the assumption being that the benefits of integrating into global financial markets (for example, investment funding, consumption smoothing, and so on) more than outweigh the costs of abandoning a stable exchange rate. But with a savings to GDP ratio consistently around 40 per cent, China already has ample savings to fund investment. The problem for the domestic financial sector has always been one of using existing savings more efficiently rather than the need to mobilize more. Also, it is incorrect to say that China has not liberalized capital controls. Restrictions over FDI have been gradually liberalized to the extent that in 2002 China received more FDI than any other country in the world. Consequently, the opportunity cost to China of maintaining the capital controls that support exchange rate stability is forgoing access to more non-FDI capital (that in aggregate it does not really need anyway) and the chance for domestic savers to earn higher returns abroad. Given that macroeconomic stability, foreign trade and FDI have underpinned the rapid growth in living standards during the reform period, forgoing the opportunities of higher returns abroad is likely to be considered an acceptable sacrifice by the average Chinese saver.

In the longer term, moving to a flexible exchange rate regime may pass the cost-benefit test. Once China's institutional environment has been bolstered, for example, a managed float will become more appealing. Yet based on what we know about the economy at this point in time and the lessons learned from other countries, the area most urgently in need of policy attention is domestic financial reform - strengthening prudential regulation, shoring up the capital base of the banks, resolving ownership ambiguities, instituting effective corporate governance structures and building more complete, unfettered, liquid and transparent direct financial markets.

REFERENCES

Bergsten, F., 2003. 'The correction of the dollar and foreign exchange intervention in the currency markets', *Testimony before the Committee on Small Business*, United States House of Representatives, Washington, D.C., June 25 2005. Available at - http://www.iie.com/publications/papers/bergsten0603-2.htm.

Bernanke, B., 2005. 'Monetary policy in a world of mobile capital', *Cato Journal*, 25(1), 1-12. Available at - http://www.cato.org/pubs/journal/cj25n1/cj25n1-1.pdf.

Bottelier, P., 2003. 'China's emerging debt markets: facts and issues', a paper presented at *China Economic Policy Reform Conference*, Stanford University, 18-

20 September 2003. Available at - http://scid.stanford.edu/events/China2003/Bottelier.pdf.

Eichengreen, B., 2004. 'Chinese currency controversies', *CEPR Discussion Paper No. 4375*. Available at - http://ssrn.com/abstract=549261.

Frankel, J., 2005. 'On the Renminbi: the choice between adjustment under a fixed exchange rate and adjustment under a flexible rate', *NBER Working Paper No. 11274*. Available at - http://www.nber.org/papers/w11274.

Ghosh, A., Gulde, A., Ostry, J., and Wolf, H., 1996. 'Does the exchange rate regime matter for inflation and growth?' *Economic Issues Paper 13*, International Monetary Fund, Washington, D.C. Available at – http://www.imf.org/external/pubs/ft/issues2/.

Goldstein, M. and Lardy, N., 2003. 'Two-stage currency reform for China', *Asian Wall Street Journal*, September 12 2003. Available at - http://www.iie.com/publications/papers/goldstein0903.htm.

Green, S., 2005. 'Get ready for China's greenspan', *Far Eastern Economic Review*, July/August. Available at: http://www.feer.com/articles1/2005/0507/free/p039.html.

Hong Kong and Shanghai Banking Corporation (HSBC), 2005. *China Economic Insight* (April). Available at - http://www.hsbc.com.cn/cn/common/download/aboutus/200504.pdf.

Hu, Z. and Khan, M., 1997. 'Why is China growing so fast?' *Economic Issues Paper 8*, International Monetary Fund, Washington, D.C. Available at - http://www.imf.org/external/pubs/ft/issues8.

International Herald Tribune (IHT) 28 May 2005. *ADB Chief Calls for Letting Yuan Rise*, Available at – http://www.iht.com/articles/2005/05/27/business/yuan.php.

Kelly, P., 28 September 2005. 'Taking a new long view on China policy', *The Australian*. Available at - http://www.theaustralian.news.com.au/common/story_page/0,5744,16742518%255E12250,00.html.

Laurenceson, J., 2005. 'The globalization of China's financial sector: policies, consequences and lessons' in Tisdell, C. (ed), *Globalization and World Economic Policies*, Serials Publications, Delhi, 402-420.

McKinnon, R., 2004. 'The east Asian dollar standard', *China Economic Review*, **15 (3)**, 325-330.

McKinnon, R. and Schnabl, G., 2003. 'Synchronised business cycles in east Asia and fluctuations in the yen / dollar exchange rate', *The World Economy*, **26 (8)**, 1067-1088.

McKinnon, R. and Schnabl, G., 2004. 'The east Asian dollar standard, fear of floating, and original sin', *Review of Development Economics*, **8 (3)**, 331-360.

Mundell, R., 2003. 'Prospects for an Asian Currency Area', *Journal of Asian Economics*, **14 (1)**, 1-10.

People's Daily, 13 May 2005. *China Never Yields to Outside Pressure on RMB Exchange Rate*, by Wen, P. Available at - http://english.people.com.cn/200505/16/eng20050516_185298.html.

People's Daily, 22 September 2005. *RMB Exchange Rate Features "Two Way Fluctuation, More Flexible"*. Available at - http://english.peopledaily.com.cn/200509/22/eng20050922_210064.html.

Prasad, E., and Wei, S., 2005. 'The Chinese approach to capital inflows: patterns and possible explanations', *IMF Working Paper (WP/05/79)*. Available at - http://imf.org/external/pubs/ft/wp/2005/wp0579.pdf.

Prasad, E., Rumbaugh, T. and Wang, Q., 2005. 'Putting the cart before the horse? capital account liberalization and exchange rate flexibility in China', *IMF Policy Discussion Paper (PDP/05/01)*. Available at - www.imf.org/external/pubs/ft/pdp/2005/pdp01.pdf.

Rajan, R. and Subramanian, A., 2004. 'Exchange rate flexibility is in Asia's interest', *Financial Times*, September 26. Available at - http://www.imf.org/external/np/vc/2004/092604.htm.

Roberts, I. and Tyers, R. 2003. 'China's exchange rate policy: the case for greater flexibility', *Asian Economic Journal*, 17 (2), 155-184.

Roubini, N. and Setser, J., 2005. *Will the Bretton Woods 2 Regime Unravel Soon? The risk of a hard landing in 2005-2006*. Available at - http://ideas.repec.org/a/fip/fedfpr/y2005ifebx13.html.

Sachs, J. and Woo, W. T., 1997. 'China's economic growth: explanations and the tasks ahead', in Joint Economic Committee, Congress of the United States, *China's Economic Future*, M. E. Sharpe, New York, 70-100.

The Economist, 2004. 'A fair exchange?' Available at - http://www.economist.com/finance/displayStory.cfm?Story_id=3219515, 1 October.

Wall Street Journal (WSJ) (Eastern Edition), July 5 2005. *Chinese Juggernaut Hits Europe Head On; Strong Euro Fuels Trade Gap, Adds to Continent's Economic Malaise*.

World Bank, 2005. *China Quarterly Update April 2005*. Available at - http://www.worldbank.org.cn/English/Content/cqu04-05-en.pdf.

Xu, Y., 2000. 'China's exchange rate policy', *China Economic Review*, 11 (3), 262-277.

11. Globalization and Economic Development

Abu Siddique

INTRODUCTION

Since the onset of the process of globalization in China in 1978, there has been a genuine interest amongst the practitioners in economic development about its impact on the socio-economic development of that country. In the literature, globalization appears both as a hero and as a villain. The opponents of globalization conjure up a picture of deprivation, disaster and doom, whereas the proponents view it as "a key to future world economic development...inevitable and irreversible".[1] Arguments in favour of the positive impact of globalization on economic development are more or less convincing. The essential ingredients for globalization are: improvement in transport, communication and information technologies; changes in individual tastes and preference; conscious changes in government policy (generally in the direction of reducing or eliminating barriers to cross-border movement of goods, services and capital - though not labour); and changes in corporate strategies (greater emphasis on growing profits through cost reduction rather than price increases). All of these are usually considered pro-growth elements. It is in the social area where the favourable impacts of globalization are questioned. Some even go to the extent of arguing that globalization widens the gap between the rich and the poor; exploits cheap labour and thus compromises labour standards; undermines the sovereignty of the state and pollutes the environment. This chapter is a modest attempt to enhance critical understanding of the complex issues involving the process and progress of globalization and its effects on the economy of China.

The next section examines the concept and measurement of globalization. This is followed by an analysis of the process and progress of globalization in China since 1978. The socio-economic impact of globalization in China is then analyzed. The last section reviews the chapter's finding and draws conclusions.

THE CONCEPT AND MEASUREMENT OF GLOBALIZATION

The Concept of Globalization

The concept encompasses a vast array of notions. The International Monetary Fund (IMF) broadly defines globalization as a historical process resulting from human innovation and technological progress, and the increasing integration of economies around the world particularly through trade and financial flows.[2] The term sometimes also refers to the movement of people (labour) and knowledge (technology) across international borders. Broader cultural, political and environmental dimensions also exist. Scholte (2000) uses five different definitions of globalization. First, globalization means internationalization whereby 'global' describes cross-border relations between countries, and 'globalization' signifies a growth of international exchange and interdependence (for example, flows of capital and trade between countries).[3] Second, globalization implies liberalization which refers to the process of removing government-imposed restrictions on movements between countries in order to create a 'borderless' world economy.[4] Third, globalization is synonymous with westernization or modernization whereby the social structures of modernity (capitalism, rationalism, industrialism and so on) across countries, potentially jeopardise existing cultures in the process. Fourth, globalization as universalization refers to a fusion of cultures through the dispersion of experiences and ideas to people throughout the world.[5] Finally, globalization is deterritorialization, which refers to a far-reaching change in the nature of social space. Although territory still matters, it no longer constitutes the whole of our geography.[6]

It appears from the analysis above that the exact definition of globalization is debatable as it is perceived in different ways by different people. Globalization in this chapter is defined as a process whereby a country's peoples are integrated more closely with the global economy through 'free' and increased movement of goods and services, capital, finance, technology and knowledge.

The Measurement of Globalization

A number of varying methods exist in literature to measure the progress of globalization in a country. The Globalization Index created by A.T. Kearney (which comprises 62 countries) considers the following indicators to ascertain the degree to which a country has experienced globalization.[7]

- Economic integration: trade, foreign direct investment, portfolio capital flows and investment income.
- Technological connectivity: Internet users, Internet hosts and secure servers.

- Personal connectivity: international travel and tourism, international telephone traffic, and remittances and personal transfers (including worker remittances, compensation to employees and other person-to-person and non-governmental transfers).
- Political engagement: memberships in international organizations, personnel and financial contributions to UN Security Council missions, international treaties ratified and governmental transfers.

The IMF's approach includes indicators such as trade, capital movements, movement of people and spread of knowledge (and technology) within a given country.[8] For the purposes of this analysis however, due to lack of data on all the indicators of globalization with regard to China, a greater emphasis will be placed on economic integration of China in terms of expansion of trade accompanied by trade reforms, attraction of foreign investment through appropriate policy reforms and expansion of the private sector.

GLOBALIZATION IN CHINA

When Did It Begin?

Identifying when the process of globalization 'begins' in a country is a most difficult task. It depends on the timing of steps taken by a country to remove various barriers that are considered major obstacles to the free movement of goods, services and factors of production. Unfortunately, "there is little consensus about identifying dates when countries may be said to have 'globalized' or 'liberalized'" (Round and Whalley 2003, p.4). Dollar and Kraay (2001) identify the timing of globalization of a number of countries with the following trade related measures:

- growth in trade relative to GDP; and
- decline in average tariff rates.

Although these measures are not free from shortcomings, they can roughly measure the onset and subsequent progress of globalization in a country that was previously 'non-globalized'. For the purpose of analysis, the year 1978 will be used for the onset of globalization in China on the grounds that it was in 1978 that China first opened its door to the global community through the introduction of a set of policies that Howell (1993) describes as the 'Open Policy'.[9] It "refers to the set of policies adopted by the reformist leadership since the Third Plenum of the Eleventh Central Committee in December 1978 to promote the expansion of economic relations with the capitalist world economy. It consists of a set of subpolicies in the spheres of foreign trade, foreign direct investment and foreign borrowing" (Howell 1993, p.3).

Thus the 'Open Policy' was introduced by the government to achieve three broad objectives: to integrate China with the wider global community; to make China attractive to overseas investors; and to increase China's share to global trade. Obviously these are three basic ingredients of the process of globalization as defined in this chapter.[10]

What Prompted the Communist Government to Embrace Globalization?

Globalization essentially contains the elements of a capitalist economy, such as right to private property, free flow of goods and services, determination of prices of goods and services and factors of production by the forces of demand and supply and so on. But all these were unpalatable to the communist regime of China. Since the establishment of the People's Republic of China in 1949, the entire propaganda machinery of China was directed towards the evils of capitalism such as exploitation of labour by the capitalists and the emergence of global imperialism. However, China's policy of international isolation in the name of protecting the interests of the people of China was increasingly becoming unsustainable. A number of domestic and international developments prompted the Chinese government to give up the policy of international isolation in favour of globalization, three of which are considered critical and are discussed below.

Decline in standard of living under the communist regime

The standard of living of the vast majority of the people of China did not improve noticeably in spite of three decades of rule by the communist government. Between 1950 and 1978, real per capita income of the Chinese people merely doubled from a relatively low base of US$439 to US$895.[11] The average wage of state employees in 1978 was 5.5 per cent lower than it had been in 1957. Similarly, the average wage of industrial workers was 84 per cent lower.

Economic prosperity in the neighbouring countries through economic integration

During the same period the per capita income of Hong Kong increased from US$2,218 to US$9,377 (a remarkable fourfold increase from a much higher base level).[12] Hong Kong is one of the four countries which Gustav Ranis once described as the Gang of Four (the other three members of the "gang" being: South Korea, Taiwan and Singapore). In addition to Hong Kong, these three countries also noticed remarkable increases in real per capita income during this period. For example, Singapore's real per capita income increased from US$497 in 1950 to US$1,215 in 1978, South Korea's from US$6,829 to US$15,505 and Taiwan's from US$3361 to US$7,733.[13] In addition to China, North Korea and Myanmar - the other two countries dominated by the planned economy and driven by the principles of socialism - also remained economically backward in the region.

Thus, measured in terms of real per capita income, China showed poor economic performance when compared to its best performing neighbours where economic activities were largely dictated by market forces. These economies were also integrated into the global economy.

Political will of the government of China

Ironically, the major players in the economic transformation of Hong Kong, Singapore and Taiwan were of Chinese origin and many of them maintained close contact with their friends and relatives in the Republic of China ruled by the communist regime. The affluence of the people in these countries was not unknown to the people of China and to Chinese officials.

It was obvious that something was wrong with the system in place and that it was not working for the improvement of the standard of living of the people in spite of all the rhetoric made by the leaders of the country regarding public consumption. All China needed was a bold leadership which was prepared to swallow its pride and admit publicly that economic liberalization and embracing the principles of a market economy was inevitable in order to achieve the national goal of material progress in the future. It happened when Deng Xiaoping took control of the Communist party in 1978. He went ahead with the introduction of a set of reforms that opened China's door to the process of globalization.

Saich (2004, pp.241-42) argues that the failure of the ambitious post-Mao strategy to improve economic performance significantly influenced the Central Committee of the Chinese Communist Party (CC CCP) to "focus more sharply on the need for fundamental economic reform". He is also of the view that due to failure in delivering the promised material progress and subsequently improving the standard of living of the vast majority of people, the CC CCP had been gradually losing its legitimacy. Thus introduction of economic reforms through gradual reduction in the restrictions on the flow of goods, services, technology and capital was the only option left to the CC CCP to reassert its legitimacy.[14] Thus, Saich (2004, p.242) rightly observes, "More than any other post-1949 leadership, Deng Xiaoping and his supporters tied their legitimacy to their ability to deliver the economic goods."

Deng Xiaoping's main aim was to build a *xiaokang* (moderately well-off) society by the end of the 20th century (Huang 2004, p.94). He was hoping to attain a per capita gross domestic output of US$800 by the end of the 20th century (Lu 2002, quoted in Huang 2004, p.94).

Policy Reforms in Trade and Investment

Trade reforms

Prior to 1978, China was more or less a closed economy. Foreign trade was under the iron grip of the central planning authority and "foreign trade plans were parts of China's economic plans" (Chow 2002, p.293). Before 1979, the central government controlled more than 90 per cent of trade and enjoyed monopoly over 3000 types of commodities (Wan *et al.* 2004, p.2). The commodities traded by China are classified into two categories - plan-commanded goods (both value and volume of trade are strictly controlled) and plan-guided goods (only the value of trade is controlled).

Although a number of economic reforms were commenced in China with the introduction of its 'Open Policy' in 1978, no substantial reform took place in the trade sector until China applied for membership of the World Trade Organization (WTO) in July 1986. China's aspiration to become a member of the WTO acted as a catalyst for implementing reforms in the trade sector. In 1985, the number of goods that were plan-commanded or plan-guided was cut to about 100 and by 1991 almost all exports were deregulated, with only 15 per cent controlled by specially appointed trading companies. Similarly, the proportion of plan-commanded imports in total import volume was reduced from 40 per cent in 1985 to 18.5 per cent in 1991, and by 1994 almost all planning on imports and exports was abolished except the extremely important goods (Wan *et al.* 2004, p.2). A number of export processing zones (EPZs) were also established and special loans were approved to targeted companies for promoting exports (Chow 2002, p.295). In the EPZs, foreign enterprises were allowed to operate either independently or jointly with the Chinese. This was a very significant step on the part of a communist government and proved to be extremely successful in terms of attracting foreign direct investment and expanding export trade (this will be discussed later). The provision of export subsidies was abolished in 1991 and in 1996 the RMB became convertible for the current account. Finally, the Foreign Trade Law, passed in May 1994, was another significant step taken by Chinese government towards the liberalization of the trading sector of the country (Zhang 2000, pp.3-4).

At the beginning of the economic reform, the tariff level was very high in China. However, the average rate of tariff was gradually reduced.[15] While the unweighted average rate of tariff in China was as high as 55.6 per cent in 1982, by 2003 it fell to 11 per cent (Lardy 2002; p.34, Ito 2003, p.7). China also made numerous efforts to reduce its qualitative restrictions on imports. In 1992 as many as 1,247 commodities were subject to qualitative restrictions and accounted for 20 per cent of total import commodity tariff items. By 1996, qualitative restrictions were imposed on only five per cent of total imported commodities (Zhang 2000, p.5). These reforms in import trade significantly reduced the importance of the tariff as a source of government revenue (Table 11.1). During 1985-89, the average ratio of duties collected on imports in China was 10.3 per cent, a figure that came down to 4.7 per cent during 1990-94 which fell to a minimum of 3.2 per cent by 1995-2000. In that period it was lower compared to that of India (24.5 per cent), Brazil (8.0 per cent per cent) and Thailand (5.0 per cent).

Table 11.1 Import duties in selected developing countries

Country	Ratio of duties collected to imports (means, %)		
	1985-89	1990-94	1995-2000
China	10.3	4.7	3.2
Mexico	5.2	5.7	2.0
Korea, Rep. of	8.0	5.3	3.6
Chinese Taipei	7.1	4.9	3.5
Malaysia	6.4	4.0	2.3
Thailand	11.3	9.0	5.0
Brazil	8.2	8.1	8.0
India*	54.8	38.4	24.5
Indonesia*	5.2	5.0	2.4
South Africa*	6.6	4.4	3.8

Note	* Data are on a fiscal year basis.
Source:	World Trade Organization, World Trade Report 2003.

Trade reform in China is very much linked to a number of other reforms in China such as foreign exchange reform, state-owned enterprises (SOEs) reform, financial market reform and maroeconomic reform (Drysdale 2000, p.21). These reforms have important implications for future socio-economic development in China. For example, with the introduction of non-state-owned enterprises, the SOEs have been facing tough competition in the input and output markets due to their inefficiency. SOEs are also undergoing thorough reforms. The overall size and relative importance of the state-owned sector in China has been declining rapidly. Consequently, a large number of workers in this sector have been laid off, a situation that is regarded as a potential threat to social stability in China (Sun 2000, p.112).

Foreign direct investment reforms

Attracting foreign direct investment is a very challenging task on the part of a national government. In the case of China, the most serious impediment to attracting direct foreign investment is the presence of a huge state sector which owns and runs the SOEs. These SOEs directly compete with the foreign investors in attracting resources for production and in marketing the products under the direct patronage of the government. Hence foreign investors compete on an uneven footing with the SOEs. However, the presence of the overseas investors is forcing SOEs to become efficient or to get out of business. The government is gradually allowing more power to regional SOEs, where in turn, senior management is forced to gradually apply the market principles for the sake of survival.

In spite of the existence of the SOEs, China has a number of attractions for foreign investors. The supply of labour for producing labour intensive goods is almost unlimited, although there exist shortages of skilled labour for certain hi-tech industries. The rate of economic growth has been very high since the 1980s, with some minor fluctuations, which has resulted in the expansion of demand for goods and services in the domestic market. The presence of overseas Chinese entrepreneurs in the neighbouring region is also a plus for China as these people are more familiar with business culture in China and are also able to take advantage of the "open policy" of China.

The first step toward opening up the economy of China to overseas investors was taken in 1979 with announcement of the Law on Chinese-Foreign Equity Joint Ventures. However, China was not yet an attractive destination for overseas investors. It was still a highly regulated economy and the availability of quality infrastructure was very limited. Moreover, there were not enough safeguards to protect the interest of the overseas investors. In addition, the attitude of many top communist party leaders was quite hostile towards the overseas investors. They feared that foreign investors were there to exploit the cheap labour and to reap the benefit to their advantage (Chow 2002, p.306).

To overcome the above problems, the government of China initially established four special economic zones (SEZs) – three in the Guangdong province bordering Hong Kong and the fourth in the Fujian province which is also along the sea coast northeast of Guandong and across the strait from Taiwan. These were experimental zones where the government introduced a number of incentives such as provision on infrastructure, special business laws and favourable tax conditions in order to attract direct foreign investment. Initially, only joint ventures with Chinese nationals were permitted to operate but by 1986, solely-owned foreign enterprises were also allowed (Chow 2002, p.306). The SEZs became extremely successful. Their number and relative importance as sources of export earnings gradually increased over the years.

Progress of Globalization in China

Trade relative to GDP

The removal of tariff barriers usually enhances economic growth through reduction in costs of production. Goods and services become cheaper for both producers and consumers. Firms are also forced to become more efficient in order to make profits. Globalization also leads to increased specialization through competitive advantage, which results in greater production capacity and therefore increased output and consumption. The findings of an empirical study by Frankel and Romer (1999) suggest that an increase in the ratio of trade to GDP by one per cent raises the level of income by between 0.5 per cent and 2 per cent. As mentioned in earlier, one way of measuring the progress in achieving globalization in a country is to estimate the trend in the ratio of total trade over GDP. This ratio is also considered an indicator of openness to trade. Openness to trade is a vital element of the process of globalization. It "creates new investment opportunities and strengthens and deepens the financial sector, which in turn plays a crucial role for the mobilization and efficient allocation of resources for investment" (World Trade Organization 2003, p.89).

In the years leading up to globalization, China experienced fairly minimal growth in its trade to GDP ratio, averaging a ratio of about 16.7 per cent. However, after the onset of globalization in 1978, China experienced a marked increase in this ratio. Between 1978 and 2002, its trade to GDP ratio increased by 200 per cent, reaching a high of 49.0 per cent in 2002 (Table 11.2). The average annual rate of growth of this ratio was over 8 per cent during 1978-2002. In 1978, China ranked 32nd in the world in terms of international trade. It ranked 15th in 1989, 10th in 1997 and 6th in 2001 (Wan *et al.* 2004, p.3).

Trends in foreign direct investment

The first step taken to encourage foreign direct investment was the establishment of three special economic zones (SEZs) in Guangdong. However, the flows of FDI to China remained negligible until 1984.[16] In that year, 24 additional SEZs were opened. Rapid expansion of FDI began from 1992 when Deng Xiaoping made his famous tour of South China (Wan *et al.* 2004, p.3). In the same year, the establishment of a 'socialist market economy' was also declared as the ultimate goal of economic reform by the central committee of the CCP.

Subsequently, the state monopoly over the distribution of inputs and output was abolished and foreign and domestic trade sectors were opened to non-state owned and foreign-funded enterprises (Wan 2004, pp.118-19). All these steps made China an attractive destination for foreign direct investment. Actual investment jumped from US$4,366 million in 1991 to US$11,007 million in 1992 (Table 11.2). In 2002 China overtook the United States to become the world's top recipient of foreign direct investment by attracting FDI of almost 53 billion US dollars. The ratio of FDI to GDP also increased from a mere 0.4 per cent in 1984 to 4.4 per cent in 2002 (Table 11.2). China has also made significant progress in outflow of investment in recent years. China's investment abroad nearly tripled from US$2,562.49 million in 1997 to US$6,885.398 million in 2001 (Wan *et al.* 2004, p.3).

Zhou (2000, pp.225-7) observes that since 1979, FDI in China has gone through four distinct stages: the initial stage (1979-87); the development stage (1988-91); the period of rapid growth (1992-95); and the adjustment period (1996 onwards). Zhou also notes that during the period of rapid growth, utilization of foreign direct investment in China displayed several important features including the expansion of foreign investment projects, a strong growth in solely foreign-owned enterprises (FOEs), emergence of competition between FOEs and SOEs and dominance of FDI as a source of overseas capital.

Progress in information and communication technology

The government of China also made significant effort to promote the telecom sector in China. However, the growth of telecom infrastructure was not great until the beginning of the 1990s. Between 1978 and 1985, the capacity of the switchboard ranged between four and six million lines. By 1990 it shot up to 12.3 million lines and then to a staggering 350.8 million in 2003 (Table 11.3). Similarly, the number of fixed line subscribers grew from 1.8 million in 1978 to 196 million in 2003. Most remarkable increases were noticed in the mobile telephone subscribers - from 0.01 million in 1990 to 270 million in 2003 (Table 11.3). Side by side, the capacity of mobile telephone exchanges also witnessed significant progress. The country had only 0.05 million mobile telephone exchanges in 1990. By 2003, the number increased to 336.9 million. Similar increases are also noted in the capacity of long distance telephone exchanges and long distance optical cable and microwave lines. The rapid increases in the IT infrastructure in China significantly boosted the capacity of technological and personal connectivity in China which are two important indictors of progress of globalization in a country.

By the end of 2002, China's efforts to globalize the economy brought expected results. Average annual rates of growth of the principal indicators of GDP are shown in Table 11.4 with growth in each of the indicators during the three sub-periods being quite spectacular.

Table 11.2 Main globalization indicators of China: 1978-2003

Year	Exports (X) US$m	Imports (M) US$m	X+M	FDI US$m	X/GDP	(X+M)/GDP (%)	FDI/GDP (%)
1978	9,955	11,131	21,086		6.8	14.3	
1979	13,614	15,621	29,235		7.8	16.7	
1980	18,189	20,049	38,238		9.7	20.3	
1981	22,007	22,014	44,021		11.4	22.8	
1982	21,913	18,939	40,852		10.8	20.2	
1983	22,151	21,323	43,474	916	9.7	19.1	0.4
1984	24,871	26,185	51,056	1,258	9.7	19.9	0.5
1985	27,343	42,491	69,834	1,661	9.0	22.9	0.6
1986	31,060	43,164	74,224	1,874	10.5	25.1	0.6
1987	39,487	43,216	82,703	2,314	14.7	30.8	0.7
1988	47,540	55,251	102,791	3,194	15.5	33.5	0.9
1989	52,538	59,142	111,680	3,392	15.3	32.6	0.9
1990	62,091	53,345	115,436	3,487	17.5	32.5	0.9
1991	71,910	63,791	135,701	4,366	19.1	36.0	1.0
1992	84,940	80,585	165,525	11,007	20.3	39.6	2.2
1993	91,744	103,959	195,703	27,515	21.2	45.3	4.9
1994	121,006	115,615	236,621	33,767	22.3	43.6	5.3
1995	148,780	132,084	280,864	37,521	21.2	40.1	5.4
1996	151,048	138,833	289,881	41,725	18.5	35.5	5.4
1997	182,792	142,370	325,162	45,257	20.3	36.2	5.4
1998	183,712	140,237	323,949	45,463	19.4	34.2	5.1
1999	194,931	165,699	360,630	40,319	19.7	36.4	4.2
2000	249,203	225,094	474,297	40,715	23.1	43.9	3.9
2001	266,098	243,553	509,651	46,878	22.6	43.3	4.2
2002	325,565	295,203	620,768	52,743	25.7	49.0	4.4

Sources: Unless stated, the statistics are calculated by the author. Trade statistics are drawn from the World Bank, World Tables (DX for Windows). FDI statistics are from China Statistical Year Book, various issues.

Table 11.3 Progress in information and communication technology: 1978-2003

Year	No of fixed-line phone subscribers (million)	Number of subscribers of pagering services (million)	Number of mobile telephone subscribers (million)	Capacity of long-distance telephone exchanges (circuit)	Local switchboard capacity million lines	Capacity of mobile telephone exchanges (millions)	Length of long-distance optical cable lines (km)	Length of long-distance microwave lines (km)
1978	1.8574				1,863	4.059		13,958
1980	2.1404				1,969	4.432		13,958
1985	3.8254				11,522	6.134		17,275
1990	11.6292	0.437	0.018	161,370	12.318	0.051	3,334	33,626
1995	101.3966	17.392	3.629	3,518,781	72.036	7.967	106,882	79,634
2000	210.7542	48.843	84.533	5,635,498	178.256	139.586	286,642	129,147
2001	219.9823	36.064	145.222	7,035,769	255.663	219.263	399,082	164,052
2002	192.7910	18.721	206.005	7,730,133	286.568	274.003	487,684	193,636
2003	196.0283	10.576	269.953	8,693,998	350.825	336.984	594,303	119,886

Source: China Statistical Yearbook 2004.

Table 11.4 Growth rates of principal driving forces of globalization: 1981-2002

Year	RGDP	Exports	Imports	Total Trade	FDI
1981-90	9.4	13.4	12.1	12.3	21.8*
1991-00	10.1	15.3	16.0	15.5	37.1
2001-02	7.8	14.6	14.7	14.6	13.8

Note: * For the period 1984-90.

Source: Estimated from China Statistical Year Book – various issues.

ECONOMIC IMPACT OF GLOBALIZATION

The process of globalization leaves both favourable and unfavourable impacts on an economy. In the case of China, the favourable impact centres on its excellent macroeconomic performance during the period of globalization. Globalization has provided the nation with unprecedented opportunities for achieving economic prosperity. China has also witnessed significant structural changes in its economy during the period 1978-2002. From a negative perspective, globalization may widen the gap between the rich and poor and between the rural and urban areas, reduce the labour standards and lead to environmental degradation. This section will deal with the impact of globalization on China.[17]

Macroeconomic Performance

Data in Table 11.5 demonstrate that since the onset of the process of globalization in 1978, the country has achieved remarkable progress in key macroeconomic areas. Its real GDP increased by 857 per cent between 1978 and 2002. China also had the fastest economic growth in the world, with an average annual increase of 9.5 per cent. Per capita income of the Chinese people nationwide increased by 638 per cent over 25 years and real per capita household consumption increased from a mere US$58.00 in 1978 to US$403 in 2002. Gross domestic savings and gross capital formation were already high in the late 1970s and these were even higher by the end 2002. Similarly, real per capita gross capital formation increased from US$59 to US$388 (a 6.6 fold increase).

China's remarkable growth rates are consistent with experiences of other countries which are 'late comers' in the race of economic development. According to the Relative Backwardness Hypothesis developed by Gerschenkron, "the lower a country's economic level (measured by GNP per capita) at its modern economic growth starting point, the higher its economic growth rate is thereafter" (Minami 1994, p.38). According to this hypothesis, latecomers are able to adopt the advanced technology which has already been developed by the advanced countries and can achieve higher rates of economic growth in a relatively shorter period of time than that of the countries which are already developed. Gerschenkron used this hypothesis to explain the history of industrialization in France, Germany and Russia. These countries were 'late comers' in European development.[18]

China also achieved remarkable progress in the areas of trade, investment, transport, communication and human resource development which have already been discussed in the preceding section.

Structural Changes

Globalization in China led to significant structural changes in the economy. Three indicators of structural changes are used in this study: changes in the composition of output by industry (Table 11.6); changes in the composition of employment by industry (Table 11.7); and changes in composition of merchandise trade (Table 11.8).

Data in Table 11.6 exhibits the changes in the composition of output by the three broad sectors in China since 1978. It is not surprising to notice that with the modernization of the economy, the primary industry lost its importance in terms of its contribution to national wealth. Its overall contribution decreased by almost half (from 28.1 per cent in 1978 to 14.6 per cent in 2003). The contribution of the secondary industry experienced a modest increase of 4 per cent during this period while that of the tertiary industry increased by approximately 10 per cent.

Although primary industry's contribution to national output was less than one third in 1978, it was the largest employer in that year, employing 70.5 per cent of total employed persons. However, the relative importance of the industry as an employer gradually decreased over the years and by 2003 the industry was responsible for employment of about 50 per cent of the working population in China (Table 11.7). The secondary industry's employment contribution increased from 17.3 per cent in 1978 to 21.6 per cent in 2003. The contribution of tertiary industry increased by almost two and half times from 12.2 per cent in 1978 to 29.3 per cent in 2003 (Table 11.7). The structural changes that took place in industrial employment have significant implications for long-term socio-economic development in China. Usually, with the modernization of agriculture, it uses more capital-intensive technology and therefore needs less labour. Thus it releases more labour which Lewis (1954) describes as "the unlimited supply of labour". The success of a development strategy depends on the ability of the industrial/urban sectors to absorb the surplus labour released by the rural/agricultural sector. If the rate of absorption of surplus by the industrial sector is less than the rate at which it is released by the agricultural sector, it leads to higher rate of unemployment.

The most noticeable structural change took place in the composition of trade during the years of globalization (Table 11.8). At the beginning of the 1980s the contribution of primary goods and manufactured goods to total export earnings was almost equal. However, since the mid-1980s the manufacturing sector has overtaken the primary sector. The contribution of primary goods to China's total export earnings significantly decreased from 1985 and by 2003 it came down to only eight per cent. Thus 92 per cent of China's export earnings came from the exports of manufactured goods. Within the manufacturing sector, the relative importance of light and textile industries as sources of export income has gradually decreased since the

Table 11.5 Basic macroeconomic indicators of China: 1978-2002

Year	Real GDP (US$ in 1995 prices)	Per capita real GDP (US$ in 1995 prices)	GDP growth rates (%)	Inflation rates (%)	Per capita gross capital formation (US$ in 1995 prices)	Per capita household consumption (US$ in 1995 prices)	Gross domestic savings (% of GDP)	Gross capital formation (% of GDP)
1978	141	148	11.7	1.3	59	58	37.7	38.0
1979	151	157	7.6	3.6	60	62	35.8	36.5
1980	163	167	7.8	3.8	63	66	34.9	35.2
1981	172	173	5.2	2.3	60	70	32.9	32.5
1982	187	186	9.1	-0.2	64	73	34.8	33.2
1983	208	204	10.9	1.1	70	85	34.5	33.8
1984	239	231	15.2	4.9	82	98	34.4	34.4
1985	272	259	13.5	10.1	104	116	33.6	37.8
1986	296	278	8.8	4.6	110	124	34.8	37.7
1987	330	305	11.6	5.1	115	135	36.1	36.1
1988	367	334	11.3	12.1	126	157	35.7	36.8
1989	383	342	4.1	8.8	126	164	35.3	36.0
1990	397	350	3.8	5.7	124	159	37.9	34.7

Year								
1991	434	377	9.2	6.7	132	170	38.1	34.8
1992	495	426	14.2	7.9	147	204	37.7	36.2
1993	562	478	13.5	14.6	182	234	41.8	43.3
1994	633	532	12.6	19.9	208	247	43.1	41.2
1995	700	581	10.5	13.2	237	264	43.1	40.8
1996	767	630	9.6	5.9	253	295	41.7	39.6
1997	835	679	8.8	0.8	264	315	43.0	38.2
1998	900	725	7.8	-2.4	278	334	42.3	37.7
1999	964	769	7.1	-2.2	292	362	40.5	37.4
2000	1041	825	8.0	0.9	304	386	39.0	36.3
2001	1119	880	7.5	1.2	344	394	40.9	38.5
2002	1208	944	8.0	-0.3	388	403	43.4	40.4
Average			9.5	5.18				

Source: Compiled from: World Bank, *World Tables* (DX for Windows)

Table 11.6 Change in composition of industrial output (%)

Year	Primary industry	Secondary industry	Tertiary industry	Total
1978	28.1	48.2	23.7	100.0
1980	30.1	48.5	21.4	100.0
1985	28.4	43.1	28.5	100.0
1990	27.1	41.6	31.3	100.0
1995	20.5	48.8	30.7	100.0
2000	16.4	50.2	33.4	100.0
2001	15.8	50.1	34.1	100.0
2002	15.3	50.4	34.3	100.0
2003	14.6	52.2	33.2	100.0

Source: Estimated from China Statistical Yearbook 2004.

Table 11.7 Change in composition of employment by industries: 1978-2003 (%)

Year	Primary industry	Secondary industry	Tertiary industry	Total
1978	70.5	17.3	12.2	100.0
1980	68.7	18.2	13.1	100.0
1985	62.4	20.8	16.8	100.0
1990	60.1	21.4	18.5	100.0
1995	52.2	23.0	24.8	100.0
2000	50.0	22.5	27.5	100.0
2001	50.0	22.3	27.7	100.0
2002	50.0	21.4	28.6	100.0
2003	49.1	21.6	29.3	100.0

Source: China Statistical Yearbook 2004

Table 11.8 Changes in composition of merchandise exports from China (1980-2003, percentage share)

Category of products/year	1980	1985	1990	1995	2000	2003
Primary goods	50.3	50.6	25.6	14.4	10.2	7.9
Manufactured goods, of which	49.7	49.4	74.4	85.6	85.0	92.1
Chemicals and related products	6.2	5.0	6.0	6.1	4.9	4.5
Light and textile industrial Products, rubber products, Minerals metallurgical products	22.1	16.4	20.3	21.8	17.1	15.8
Machinery and transport equipment	4.7	2.8	9.0	21.1	33.1	42.8
Products not otherwise classified	1.1	12.5	18.7	0.0	0.1	0.2
Total	100	100	100	100	100	100

Source: Estimated from China Statistical Yearbook 2004.

1980s. The share of these industries of total export earnings decreased from 22 per cent in 1980 to 16 per cent in 2003. On the contrary, the share of heavy industries such as machinery and transport equipment increased from a meagre 4.7 per cent in 1978 to 42.8 per cent in 2003. Similarly, the share of miscellaneous industrial products increased from 15.7 per cent in 1980 to 28.8 per cent in 2003. Together, the contribution of machinery and transport equipment and the miscellaneous industrial products to the total export earnings from the manufactured goods of China amounted to 77 per cent in 2003.

The Rise of the Private Sector

Although the process of globalization commenced in 1978, tension emerged among the leadership as China embraced the principles of a market economy. Up until the early 1990s, the process of globalization (including foreign-owned enterprises operating in the SEZs) was "tightly controlled and managed by the state" (Zheng 2004, p.3), but this control was relaxed in 1992 when capitalism was "legitimized as a way of globalizing the country and integrating it with the international community" (Zheng 2004, p.3). From that time the private sector in China expanded gradually and gained importance in terms of employment and production of industrial output. The total number of persons employed by private enterprises (employing more than eight persons) increased from 2.3 million in 1992 to 20.2 million in 1999. Similarly the total number of persons employed by the smaller enterprises (employing less than eight persons) increased from 2.5 million in 1992 to 5.4 million in 1997. In terms of production of industrial output, the contribution of state-owned enterprises declined from 51.5 per cent in 1992 to 26.5 per cent in 1999. On the contrary the contribution of privately-owned enterprises of various categories, being 48.5 per cent in 1992, rose to 73.5 per cent in 1999 (Zheng 2004, pp.66-7).

Globalization and Inequality in China

It is often argued that globalization leads to increases in inequality, that is, it widens the gap between the rich and the poor. Literature on inequality in post-globalization China more or less confirms that inequality has increased since the process of globalization began in China in 1978. Four types of inequality can be identified: inequality at the national level, inequality in the urban area, inequality between rural and urban areas and inequality between regions. Zheng (2004, p.144) estimated inequality in China at the national level with the aid of the Gini coefficient in the 1980s and 1990s. The Gini co-efficient in China increased from 0.299 in the 1980s to 0.388 in the 1980s. The World Bank (1997) also estimated that the Gini coefficient in China increased from 28.8 in 1981 to 38.8 in 1995.[19] Between 1986 and 2000, the Gini coefficient of urban China increased from 0.20 to 0.32 (Meng *et al.* 2004, p.200). Again, the size distribution of income in urban areas in China between 1990 and 1998 demonstrates that while the share of the bottom 20 per cent of the population rapidly declined from 9.0 per cent in 1990 to 5.5

per cent in 1998, that of the top 10 per cent increased from 23.6 per cent in 1990 to 38.4 per cent in 1998 (Table 11.9)

Table 11.9 Growing inequality in the size distribution of income in urban China 1990-1998

Year	Income of top 20% relative to Income of bottom 20%	Bottom 20%'s share of total income	Top 20%'s share of total income	Top 10%'s share of total income
1990	4.2 times	9.0%	38.1%	23.6%
1993	6.9 times	6.3%	46.5%	29.3%
1998	9.6 times	5.5%	52.3%	38.4%

Source: Zheng (2004, p.145)

Rural-urban inequality in China also increased during the period of globalization. Khan (1996, p.33) uses two measures to capture the inequality between urban and rural areas - the ratio between manufacturing wages and agricultural wages and the ratio of per capita disposable income of the urban households to per capita net income of the farmers. The first ratio increased from 1.22 in 1980 to 1.52 in 1994 and the second ratio initially declined from 2.37 in 1978 to 1.72 in 1985 and then rose steadily to reach 2.6 in 1994. However, using openness as a proxy for globalization and applying a different methodology, Wei and Wu (2001) observe that openness and urban-rural inequality are negatively associated in China. Those cities that have had a greater increase in trade-to-GDP ratio have also tended to witness a reduction, rather than increase, in the urban-rural inequality (Wei and Wu 2001, p.7).

Regional inequality also worsened during the period of globalization. This becomes clear when China is divided into three regions: the east, central and west (Table 11.10). As shown in Table 11.11, the eastern coast attracts a much higher proportion of FDI and trade than the central and western regions. Wan *et al.* (2004) conducted a very comprehensive study to examine the relationship between regional inequality and globalization in China. Their findings suggest that globalization adds cumulatively to regional inequality in China (Wan *et al.* 2004, p.1). Details of regional inequality in China are exhibited in Table 11.11. China's development policies since 1978 are mainly responsible for the emergence of regional inequality. The central and western areas were in a relatively disadvantageous position compared to the coastal provinces at the beginning of globalization in China. The globalization policy of the government was very much biased towards the coastal provinces as will be seen from per capita fiscal spending by region between 1980 and 1998 (Table 11.12).

Table 11.10 The three regions of China

Region	Provinces	Number of provinces (2002)	% of China's population (1995)	% of China's area
Coastal (Eastern)	Liaoning, Hebei, Beijing, Tianjin, Shandong, Jiangsu, Shanghai, Zhejiang, Fujian, Guangdong, Hainan, Guangxi	12	41	15
Central	Jilin, Heilongjiang, Shanxi, Inner Mongolia, Anhui, Jiangxi, Henan, Hubei, Hunan	9	36	29
Western	Shaanxi, Gansu, Qinghai, Ningxia, Xinjiang, Sichuan, Chongqing, Guizhou, Yunnan, Tibet	10	23	56

Source: Lai (2002, p.434).

Table 11.11 Regional disparities in China (2001)

		Coastal	of which		Central	Western	National
			South	East			
Basic indicators	Population distribution (%)	41.6	13.3	10.7	35.3	23.1	100.0
	GDP distribution (%)	59.6	16.6	19.9	26.9	13.6	100.0
	Per capita GDP (national = 100)	143.3	124.9	185.4	76.0	58.7	100.0
Industrial structure	Weight of agricultural sector (%)	11.4	13.7	8.8	18.7	20.1	15.2
Ratio of state-owned cos.	Weight of state-owned cos. in urban employment (%)	45.8	42.3	39.4	55.7	59.3	51.5
	Weight of state-owned cos. in fixed investment (%)	40.6	37.8	39.3	53.0	55.1	47.3
	Distribution of FDI by region (%)	84.7	35.5	25.4	10.5	4.8	100.0
Progress in marketing opening	Distribution of exports by region (%)	91.2	42.3	30.3	5.9	2.9	100.0
	Ratio of foreign companies in exports (%)	53.6	56.1	49.3	16.1	10.0	50.1

Source: Ito (2003, p.9).

Table 11.12 Per capita fiscal spending by region

Region	Level (in yuan)			Ratio to national level		
	1980	1993	1998	1980	1993	1998
Coastal	61	339	811	1.07	1.20	1.30
Central	54	223	472	0.94	0.79	0.76
Western	56	276	519	0.97	0.98	0.83
Nation	57	283	622	1.00	1.00	1.00

Source: Lai (2002, p.440).

CONCLUSION

Since the late 1970s, the government of China has achieved considerable progress in globalizing the economy. Indicators of economic integration such as foreign direct investment, imports and exports as a percentage of GDP have all climbed during the decades of globalization relative to the non-globalization period. Globalization brought fundamental changes to the economic management of China. The monopolistic position of the State-owned Enterprises (SOEs) as the producers and distributors of consumer goods and industrial inputs has significantly declined. The SOEs are now facing fierce competition with the private owned enterprises in both the factor and product markets. Over 90 per cent of industrial products are now produced according to signals given by the market and their prices are also determined by the market (Huang 2004, p.57).

With gradual decline in the importance of the SOEs, the privately owned enterprises are becoming more dominant in the economy in terms of generating income, creating employment opportunities and earning foreign exchange through exports of goods and services. The performance of foreign-owned enterprises operating in the special economic zones has been especially outstanding. China has been the most attractive destination for foreign direct investment in recent years. All this has resulted in remarkable growth in the real GDP of China since the process of globalization began in 1978. The country has also achieved significant progress in the areas of information and communication technology.

However, in relation to inequality and development it has been observed that inequality over this period (based on Gini coefficient data) has increased and the evidence of a widening between the urban and rural sectors has also been noticed. However, when analyzing the implications of globalization for China in relation to inequality and development, the impact of other relevant variables on inequality and development must also be taken into consideration. Furthermore, China is not yet fully globalized. It is relatively unglobalized in comparison to the rest of the world. Referring to the CSGR Globalization Index published in 2005, of the 185 countries studied, China was ranked 160, Singapore 2, Hong Kong 10, Taiwan 31 and South Korea 50. [20]

Despite its very low 'globalized status' in the region and globally, China has achieved remarkable economic progress and structural changes in the economy which will lay the foundation for further economic progress in China in the coming years. However, future progress in the process of globalization will depend on China's ability to maintain its international competitiveness in the globalized world economy as well as to minimise the adverse effect of globalization on inequality and poverty.

NOTES

1. IMF Staff, 2000. 'Globalization: threat or opportunity', International Monetary Fund, 2000, www.imf.org/external/np/exr/ib/2000/041200.htm, 27 September 2004.
2. Ibid.
3. Scholte, J., 2000. Globalization: A Critical Introduction, Macmillan Press Ltd, London, p.15.
4. Ibid.
5. Ibid., p.16.
6. Ibid.
7. A.T. Kearney, 2005. 'Measuring Globalization: The Global Top 20', Foreign Policy, May/June, p52, http://www.atkearney.com/, 15 June 2005.
8. IMF Staff (2001), op. cit., pp.3-4.
9. It is popularly referred to as 'Open Door Policy' in contemporary literature on China's economic development (see Howell 1993, p.3).
10. 1978 is also considered by many as the year when the process of economic transition (from centrally planned to market economy) began in China. For example, according to Khan (1996, p.3), "the liberalization of the Chinese economy and the currently ongoing process of globalization of the world economy have approximately the same date of origin. Indeed the simultaneous occurrence of the two phenomena is far more than a coincidence. They are causally related." What happened in China was that it was simultaneously going through the processes of globalization and economic transition from 1978.
11. Groningen Growth and Development Centre and The Conference Board, Total Economy Data Base, January, 2005, www.ggdc.net, 01 July 2005.
12. *Ibid.*
13. *Ibid.*
14. Two approaches are considered while facing economic transition from a planned economy to a market economy: the big bang or shock therapy or the incrementalist or gradual approach. China opted for the second approach. See Saich (2004, p.237).
15. China has a discriminatory system of tariffs - it imposes a lower rate of tariff (preferential) on the goods from its trading partners with which it has established free trade agreements and a relatively higher rate of tariff (general) on the goods imported from the rest of its trading partners (see Zhang 2000, pp.5-6) .
16. Total FDI during 1979-1984 was US$3060 million.
17. The impact of globalization on labour standards and environment has been omitted due to limited space.
18. For a summary of Gerschenkron's Model, see Rosovsky, H. 1961, *Capital Formation in Japan 1868-1940*, New York: Free Press of Glencoe, pp.91-104.
19. Cited in Wei and Wu (2001, p.7).

20. The CSGR globalization Index measures the economic, social and political dimensions of globalization for 185 countries on an annual basis over the period 1982 to 2001, and combines these into an overall globalization index, or score, for each of these countries during this time period. For details, see Lockwood and Redoano (2005).

REFERENCES

Chow, G. C., 2002. *China's Economic Transformation, Massachusetts*, USA and Oxford, UK, Blackwell Publishers Limited.

Dollar, D. and Kraay, A., 2001. 'Trade, growth and poverty', paper presented to the WIDER Conference on *Growth and Poverty*, http://www.wider.unu.edu/conference-2001-1/dollar%20kraay.pdf, 22 April 2004.

Drysdale, P., 2000. 'Open regionalism, APEC and China's international trade strategies', in Drysdale, P., Zhang, Y. and Song, L. (eds), *APEC and the Liberalization of the Chinese Economy*, 15-30, Asia Pacific Press at the Australian National University.

Frankel, J. and Romer, D., 1999. 'Does trade cause growth?' *The American Economic Review*, **89/3**, 379-399.

Garnaut, R. and Song, L. (eds), 2004. *China: Is Rapid Growth Sustainable?* Canberra: Asia Pacific Press.

Groningen Growth and Development Centre and The Conference Board, 2005. *Total Economy Data Base*, January, www.ggdc.net, 01 July 2005.

Howell, J., 1993. *China Opens Its Doors: The Politics of Economic Transition*, Hemel Hempstead: Harvester Wheatsheaf; Boulder, Colo.: Lynne Rienner.

Huang, J., 2004. *The Dynamics of China's Rejuvenation*, Hampshire and New York, Palgrave Macmillan.

IMF Staff, 2000. 'Globalization: threat or opportunity', *International Monetary Fund*, http://www.imf.org/external/np/exr/ib/2000/041200.htm, 27 September 2004.

Ito, S., 2003. 'Does China's globalization and structural reform pose a threat to Japan?' *NLI Research*, 5 September 2003.

Kearney, A. T., 2005. 'Measuring globalization: The global top 20', *Foreign Policy*, May/June, 2005, http://www.atkearney.com, 15 June 2005.

Khan, A. R., 1996. *Globalization, Employment and Equity*, ILO, Regional Office for Asia and the Pacific, Bangkok, April.

Lai, H. H., 2002. 'China's western development program: Its rationale, implementation, and prospects', *Modern China, 28/4*, 432-466.

Lardy, N. R., 2002. *Integrating China into the Global Economy*, Washington, D. C.: Brookings Institution Press.

Lewis, W. A., 1954. 'Economic development with unlimited supply of labour', *Manchester School*, 22, 139-191.

Lockwood, B. and Redoano, M., 2005. 'The CSGR globalization index: an introductory guide', *Centre for the Study of Globalization and Regionalisation Working Paper 155/04*, www2.warwick.ac.uk/fac/soc/csgr/index/citation/, 23 May 2005.

Lu, X., 2002. 'Blueprint for xiakang society in China', *China Daily*, 3 December.

Meng, X., Gregory, R. and Wang, Y., 2004. 'Poverty and inequality in urban China in the 1990s', in Garnaut, R. and Song, L. (2004) (eds), *China: Is Rapid Growth Sustainable?* Canberra: Asia Pacific Press.

Minami, R., 1994. *The Economic Development of Japan: A Quantitative Study*, New York: St. Martin Press.

Rosovsky, H., 1961. *Capital Formation in Japan: 1868-1940*, New York: Free Press of Glencoe.

Round, J. and Whalley, J., 2003. 'Globalization and poverty: implications of South Asian experience for the wider debate', http://www.gapresearch.org/production/JJoverview.pdf, 18 April 2004.

Saich, T., 2004. *Governance and Politics of China*, Hampshire and New York: Palgrave Macmillan.

Scholte, J., 2000. *Globalization: A Critical Introduction*, Macmillan Press Ltd, London.

Sun, X., 2000. 'APEC investment, trade liberalization and China's economic adjustment', in Drysdale, P., Zhang, Y. and Song, L. (eds), *APEC, and the Liberalization of the Chinese Economy*, Asia Pacific Press at the Australian National University, 109-118.

Wan, G., Lu, M. and Chen, Z., 2004. 'Globalization and regional income inequality: evidence from China', *UNO-WIDER*, November 2004.

Wang, X., 2004. 'Marketisation in China: progress and prospects', in Garnaut, R. and Song, L. (eds), 2004. *China: Is Rapid Growth Sustainable?* Canberra: Asia Pacific Press, 118-136.

Wei, S. J. and Wu, Y., 2001. 'Globalization and inequality: evidence from within China', *National Bureau of Economic Research*, Working Paper 8611.

World Bank, *World Tables* (dx for windows).

World Bank, 1997. *Sharing Rising Incomes - Disparities in China*, Washington D. C.

World Trade Organization, 2003. *World Trade Report 2003*, http://www.wto.org/english/res_e/booksp_e/anrep_e/world_trade_report_2003_e.pdf, 1 August 2005.

Zhang, Y., 2000. 'Liberalization of the Chinese economy: APEC, WTO and tariff reduction', in Drysdale, P., Zhang, Y. and Song, L. (eds), *APEC and the Liberalization of the Chinese Economy*, Asia Pacific Press at the Australian National University, 3-14.

Zheng, Y., 2004. *Globalization and State Transformation in China*, Cambridge University Press.

Zhongguo tong ji nian jian / Guo jia tong ji ju bian, Zhongguo tong ji nian jian (Peking, China). *China Statistical Yearbook 2004*, Beijing: Zhongguo tong ji chu ban she.

Zhou, X., 2000. 'Impact of capital inflows and technology transfer on the Chinese economy', in Drysdale, P., Zhang, Y. and Song, L. (eds), *APEC and the Liberalization of the Chinese Economy*, Asia Pacific Press at the Australian National University, 225-242.

Index